JN101337

# 目次

Table of Contents



## 算数 Mathematics

subject 1

### 第一章 計算



### 第二章 図形

## 国語 Kokugo(Japanese)
subject 2



## 理科 Science
subject 3

## 教職英語検定とは

教職英語検定は、日本のグローバル化に対応し、小学校から高校までの学校教育を担う教職員や教職員を目指す学生が、英語による授業・教科指導を行う力(教職英語と定義)を習得し、その習得した英語力を知ることを目的としています。

## 教職英語検定の特色

教職英語検定は、文部科学省の学習指導要領を基本として、日本の公立学校教育の現場に即した教職英語を習得でき、また習得した力を知ることができることが大きな特色です。
本検定は、小学校教諭用・中学校教諭(理数)・高校教諭(理数)別に、レベルは、基礎、標準、実践の三つに分けて実施します。
検定は、基礎はリスニングと筆記、標準はリスニングと筆記と英作文、実践はリスニングと筆記と英作文を一次試験、グループ討議を二次試験とする構成です。
出題の範囲は、小学校教諭用については、基礎、標準レベルは、低学年から高学年までの算数・国語・理科・社会・図工・体育・音楽・家庭科の科目及び対応する学習指導要領、実践レベルは、総合学習、児童教育に関する研究。論文が加わります。
中学校教諭用並びに高校教諭用については、基礎、標準レベルは１年生から３年生までの数学、理科の科目及び対応する学習指導要領、実践レベルは、総合学習、中等教育または高等教育に関する研究、論文が加わります。
高校教諭用の理科は、物理、化学からの2教科選択です。

# 本書について

This book

本書は、小学校教諭向けのテキスト第１巻で、算数、国語、理科の科目が収録され、
指導計画参考例がついています。
社会、図工、体育、音楽、家庭科は、小学校教諭向けのテキスト第２巻に掲載されています。
各教科の内容は、学習指導要領を踏まえて、日本の教育方法に沿っています

01 各教科の単元ごとに分かれており、学年をまたぐ単元については、低学年、中学年、高学年の順に配置し、取り上げた学年を参考表記しています。

02 全て授業として構成されています。文中に使用している「」、『』は、伝聞あるいは区別・強調が必要な場合につけており、本来の使用方法とは異なりますが、誤用ではありません。

03 人物の呼称については、英語圏では、Mr. Mrs. Ms. を名前の前につけたり、ファーストネームを使うことが多くありますが、日本の生活慣習から違和感を生じないよう、本テキストでは、児童は「○○ - san」、先生は「○○ sensei」を使用しています。

04 ローマ字は学校教育の指導に則り、原則、訓令式で記載しています。英語での表記ができない日本語（例えば本は２冊、傘なら２本等の助数詞）は、英語のページであっても、英語もしくはローマ字をつけて日本語を記載しています。この場合のローマ字は、英語を母国語とするネイティブスピーカーが、訓令式では発音に支障が生じるため、ヘボン式で記載しています。

05 各シーンは、左のページに日本語、右のページに英語が記載されています。
記載されている英語は、日本語授業を直訳するのではなく、内容を基本として、英会話らしい表現で記載しています。
本書が学校教育を担う教職員の皆様の英語力向上の一助になることを願っております。

教材制作部一同

# 年間カレンダー例

Sample Annual Calendar

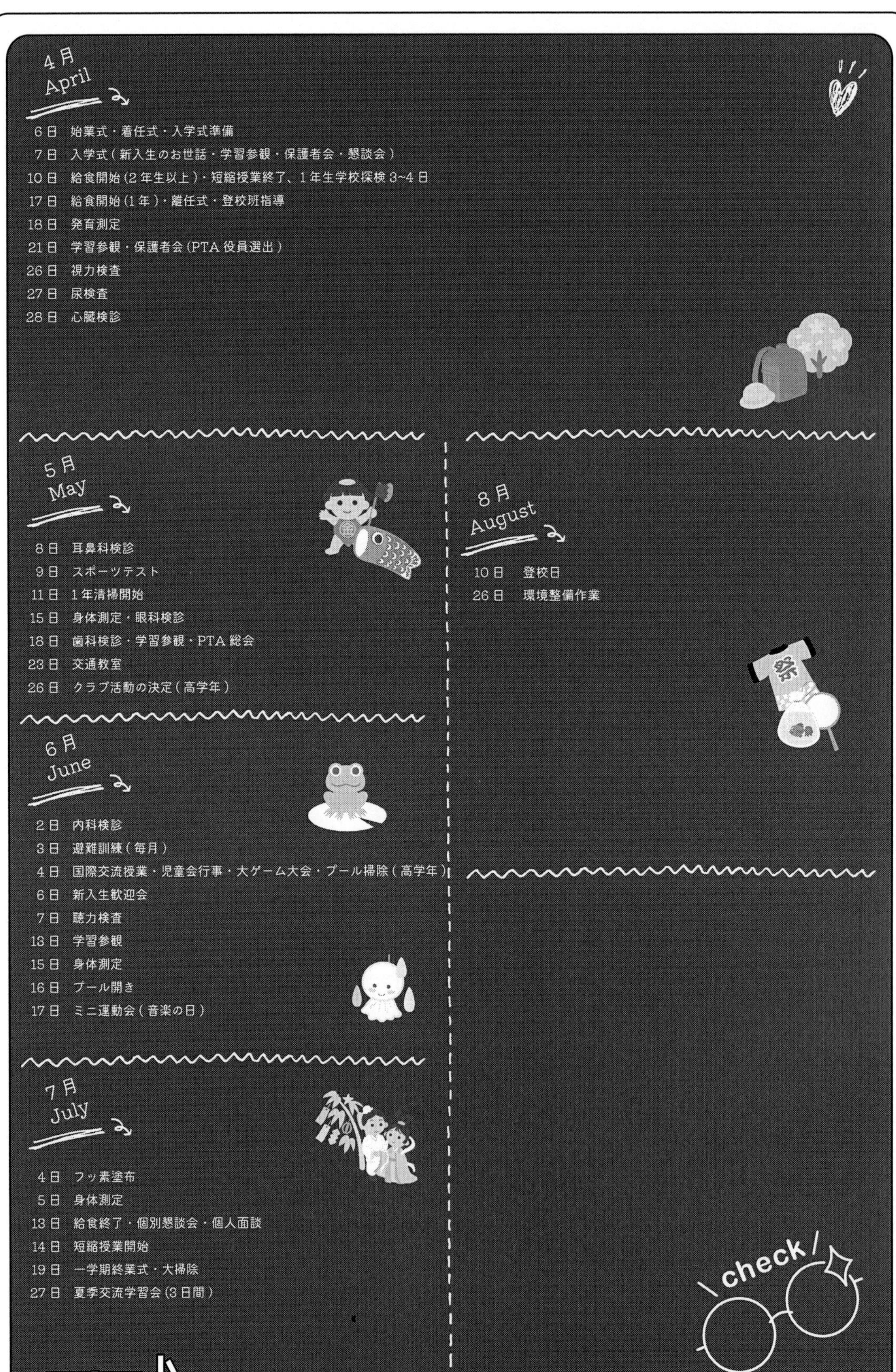

4月
April

6日 始業式・着任式・入学式準備
7日 入学式（新入生のお世話・学習参観・保護者会・懇談会）
10日 給食開始（2年生以上）・短縮授業終了、1年生学校探検 3~4日
17日 給食開始（1年）・離任式・登校班指導
18日 発育測定
21日 学習参観・保護者会（PTA役員選出）
26日 視力検査
27日 尿検査
28日 心臓検診

5月
May

8日 耳鼻科検診
9日 スポーツテスト
11日 1年清掃開始
15日 身体測定・眼科検診
18日 歯科検診・学習参観・PTA総会
23日 交通教室
26日 クラブ活動の決定（高学年）

6月
June

2日 内科検診
3日 避難訓練（毎月）
4日 国際交流授業・児童会行事・大ゲーム大会・プール掃除（高学年）
6日 新入生歓迎会
7日 聴力検査
13日 学習参観
15日 身体測定
16日 プール開き
17日 ミニ運動会（音楽の日）

7月
July

4日 フッ素塗布
5日 身体測定
13日 給食終了・個別懇談会・個人面談
14日 短縮授業開始
19日 一学期終業式・大掃除
27日 夏季交流学習会（3日間）

8月
August

10日 登校日
26日 環境整備作業

## 4月 April

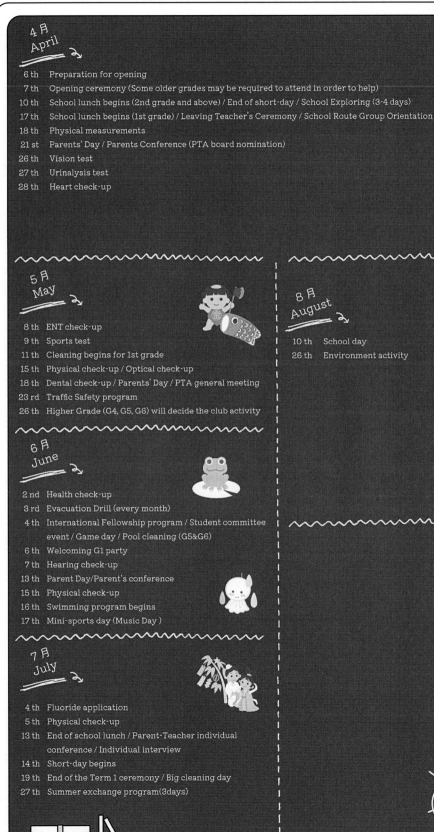

6 th Preparation for opening
7 th Opening ceremony (Some older grades may be required to attend in order to help)
10 th School lunch begins (2nd grade and above) / End of short-day / School Exploring (3-4 days)
17 th School lunch begins (1st grade) / Leaving Teacher's Ceremony / School Route Group Orientation
18 th Physical measurements
21 st Parents' Day / Parents Conference (PTA board nomination)
26 th Vision test
27 th Urinalysis test
28 th Heart check-up

## 5月 May

8 th ENT check-up
9 th Sports test
11 th Cleaning begins for 1st grade
15 th Physical check-up / Optical check-up
18 th Dental check-up / Parents' Day / PTA general meeting
23 rd Traffic Safety program
26 th Higher Grade (G4, G5, G6) will decide the club activity

## 6月 June

2 nd Health check-up
3 rd Evacuation Drill (every month)
4 th International Fellowship program / Student committee event / Game day / Pool cleaning (G5&G6)
6 th Welcoming G1 party
7 th Hearing check-up
13 th Parent Day/Parent's conference
15 th Physical check-up
16 th Swimming program begins
17 th Mini-sports day (Music Day )

## 7月 July

4 th Fluoride application
5 th Physical check-up
13 th End of school lunch / Parent-Teacher individual conference / Individual interview
14 th Short-day begins
19 th End of the Term 1 ceremony / Big cleaning day
27 th Summer exchange program(3days)

## 8月 August

10 th School day
26 th Environment activity

check

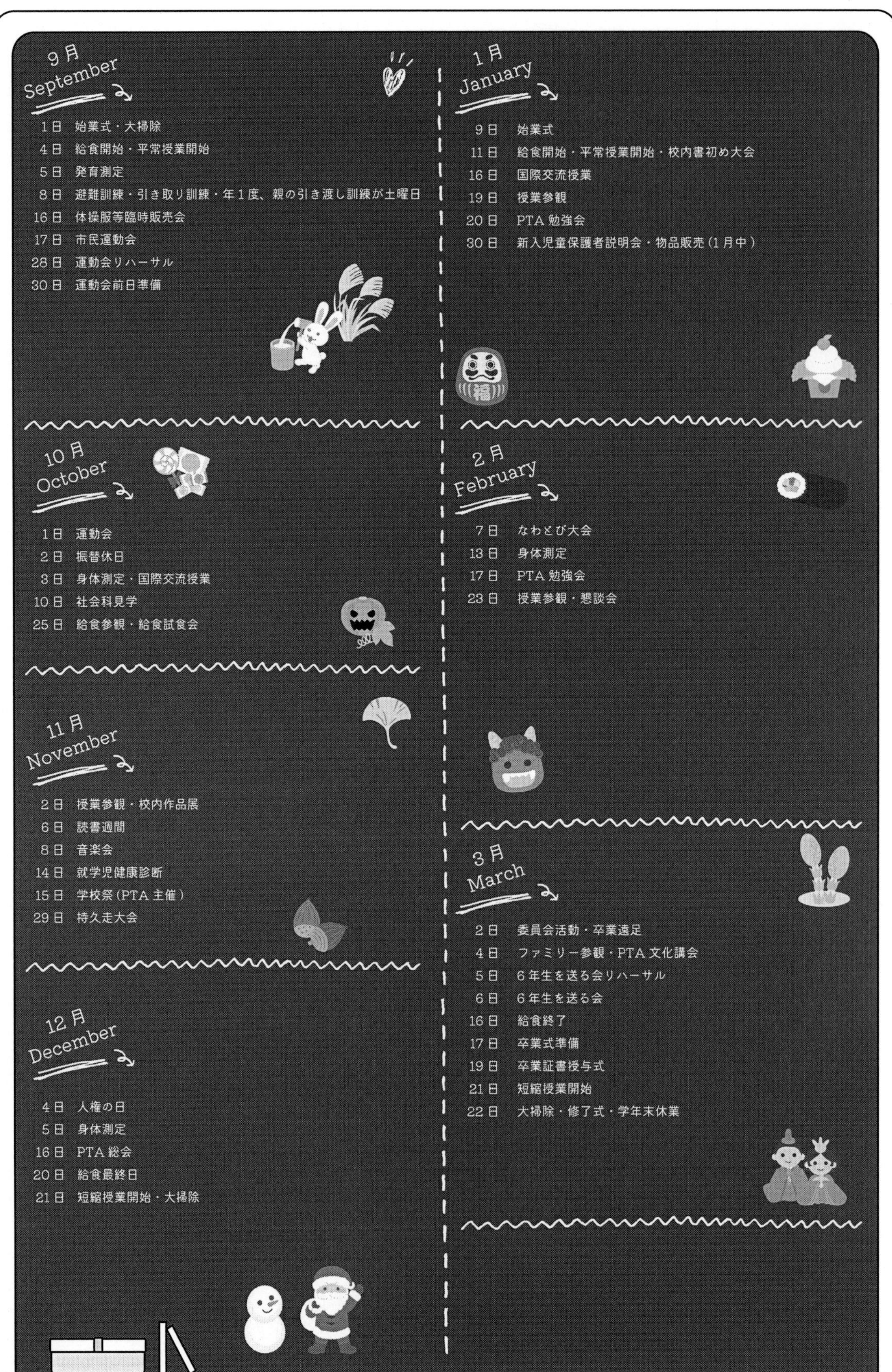
9月
September
1日　始業式・大掃除
4日　給食開始・平常授業開始
5日　発育測定
8日　避難訓練・引き取り訓練・年1度、親の引き渡し訓練が土曜日
16日　体操服等臨時販売会
17日　市民運動会
28日　運動会リハーサル
30日　運動会前日準備
10月
October
1日　運動会
2日　振替休日
3日　身体測定・国際交流授業
10日　社会科見学
25日　給食参観・給食試食会
11月
November
2日　授業参観・校内作品展
6日　読書週間
8日　音楽会
14日　就学児健康診断
15日　学校祭（PTA 主催）
29日　持久走大会
12月
December
4日　人権の日
5日　身体測定
16日　PTA 総会
20日　給食最終日
21日　短縮授業開始・大掃除
1月
January
9日　始業式
11日　給食開始・平常授業開始・校内書初め大会
16日　国際交流授業
19日　授業参観
20日　PTA 勉強会
30日　新入児童保護者説明会・物品販売（1月中）
福
2月
February
7日　なわとび大会
13日　身体測定
17日　PTA 勉強会
23日　授業参観・懇談会
3月
March
2日　委員会活動・卒業遠足
4日　ファミリー参観・PTA 文化講会
5日　6年生を送る会リハーサル
6日　6年生を送る会
16日　給食終了
17日　卒業式準備
19日　卒業証書授与式
21日　短縮授業開始
22日　大掃除・修了式・学年末休業

# 年間カレンダー例

Sample Annual Calendar

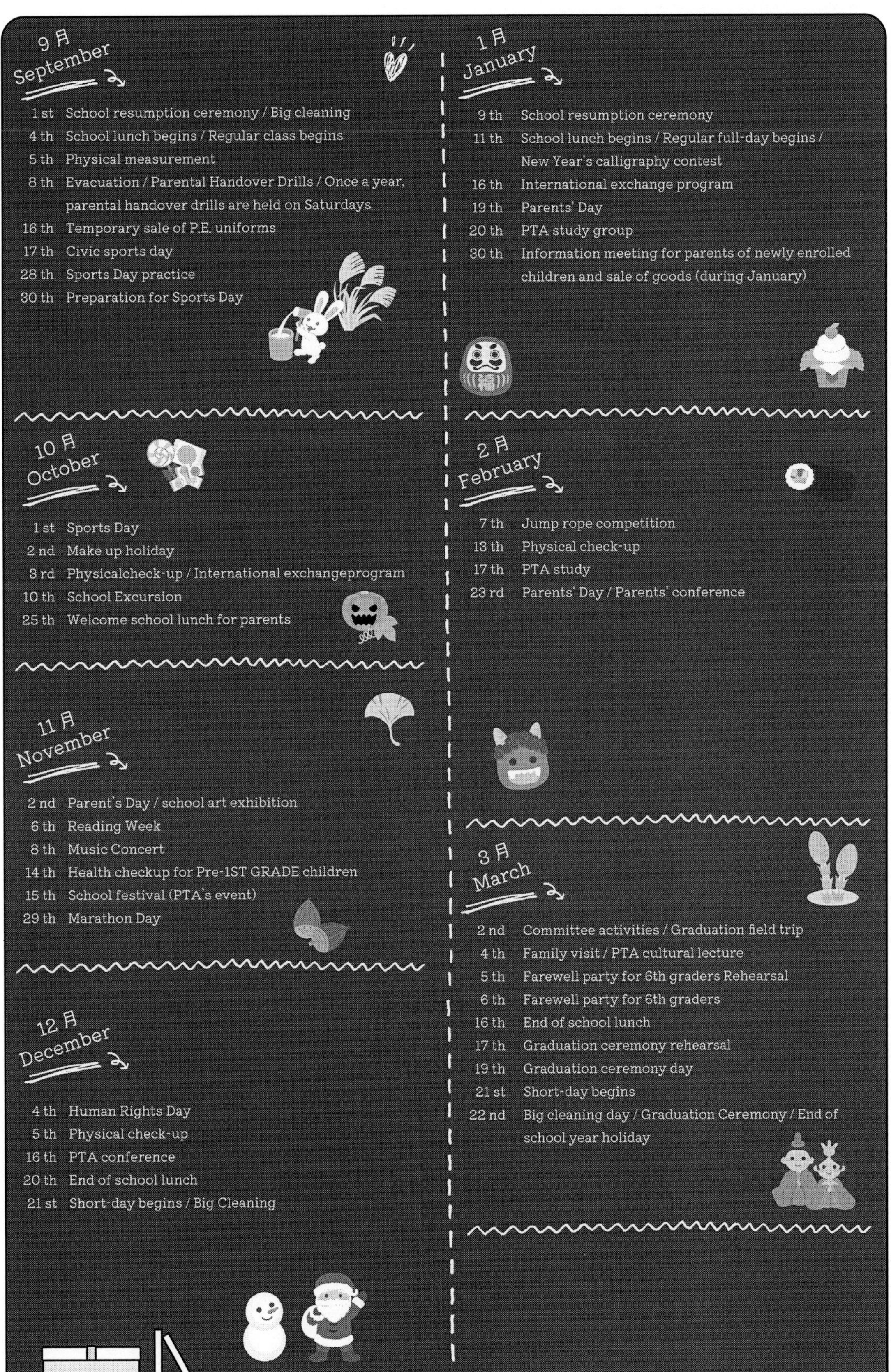

9月
September

1 st School resumption ceremony / Big cleaning
4 th School lunch begins / Regular class begins
5 th Physical measurement
8 th Evacuation / Parental Handover Drills / Once a year, parental handover drills are held on Saturdays
16 th Temporary sale of P.E. uniforms
17 th Civic sports day
28 th Sports Day practice
30 th Preparation for Sports Day

10月
October

1 st Sports Day
2 nd Make up holiday
3 rd Physicalcheck-up / International exchangeprogram
10 th School Excursion
25 th Welcome school lunch for parents

11月
November

2 nd Parent's Day / school art exhibition
6 th Reading Week
8 th Music Concert
14 th Health checkup for Pre-1ST GRADE children
15 th School festival (PTA's event)
29 th Marathon Day

12月
December

4 th Human Rights Day
5 th Physical check-up
16 th PTA conference
20 th End of school lunch
21 st Short-day begins / Big Cleaning

1月
January

9 th School resumption ceremony
11 th School lunch begins / Regular full-day begins / New Year's calligraphy contest
16 th International exchange program
19 th Parents' Day
20 th PTA study group
30 th Information meeting for parents of newly enrolled children and sale of goods (during January)

2月
February

7 th Jump rope competition
13 th Physical check-up
17 th PTA study
23 rd Parents' Day / Parents' conference

3月
March

2 nd Committee activities / Graduation field trip
4 th Family visit / PTA cultural lecture
5 th Farewell party for 6th graders Rehearsal
6 th Farewell party for 6th graders
16 th End of school lunch
17 th Graduation ceremony rehearsal
19 th Graduation ceremony day
21 st Short-day begins
22 nd Big cleaning day / Graduation Ceremony / End of school year holiday

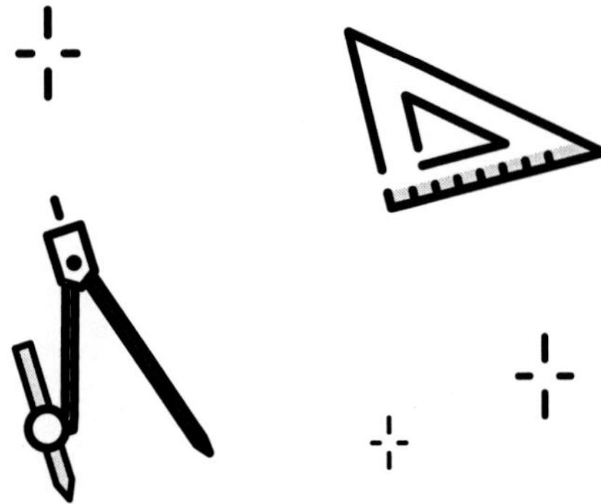

# 算数

subject 1

## Mathematics

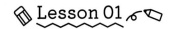

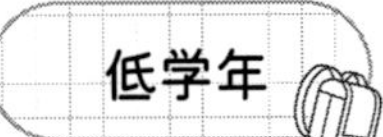


## 数の基本

なかまづくりとかず

**先生**

1 今日は、仲間つくりを勉強します。仲間ってわかりますか。

2 こちらのカードにはいろんな花が描いてありますね。これは花という仲間なんですね。

では、教科書の２ページ目を開いてください。ここには、いろんな生き物が描いて
3 あります。じゃあ、鉛筆で、それぞれのなかまを囲んでください。

4 終わった人は、鉛筆を机の上において他の人が終わるまで静かに待っていてください。

5 では、教科書を閉じて、みんな、先生の方を見てください。

6 今度は、どちらが多いかを考える勉強です。

7 こちらのカードに描いてあるリンゴとミカンは、同じ数です。

8 では、次のカードを見て下さい。リンゴとミカンは同じ数ではないですね。

9 リンゴとミカンを一つずつ、線で結んでみましょうね。

はい、ミカンがひとつ、線を結べませんでしたね。だから、リンゴより一つ、ミカンが
10 多いことがわかります。

このように、どちらが多いかなと思ったら、線で結んだり、同じ数だけ、色を塗ったり
11 すると、わかりやすいですね。

低学年

## 数の基本

数

**先生**

1 はい、こちらを見てください。カードにクレヨンの絵が一本ずつ描いてあります。

2 このカードにはクレヨンが１本、このカードには２本、このカードには３本描かれています。

3 では、こちらのカードには、何本描いてありますか？

4 何もありません。これを、「れい」とか「ゼロ」と言います。

5 だから、数えるときには、0, 1, 2, 3… となります。

6 なぜ？ないなら、数えないでいいじゃないの？

このカードを見てください。「れい」「0」と言う数字がないと、このお皿にバナナがない
7 ということが言えません。だから、「れい」、「ゼロ」という数字が必要です。

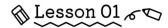

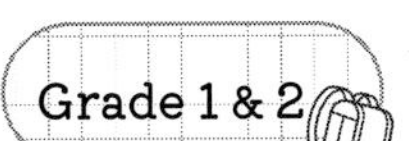


## Basics of Numbers

### Grouping and Numbers

Teacher

1 Today, we are going to study grouping. Do you know what grouping means in Math?
Here's an example. You can see many flowers on this card, so we can say that it is part of
2 the flower group, right?

Now, please open to page two of the textbook. There are many different types of animals.
3 I want you to circle the animals which you think belong to the same group.
For those who are finished, please put down your pencils and sit quietly until the others
4 have finished.
5 Now, close your textbook and everyone, please look at me.
6 Next, we'll think about which is greater.
7 On this card the number of apples and oranges are the same.
8 Now, please look at the next card. The numbers of apples and oranges are not the same, right?
9 So, let's draw a line to connect the apples to the oranges one by one.
There's one orange without a line connected to an apple. Therefore, we can see that there are
10 more oranges than apples.
Like we just did, if you are wondering which has more or less, drawing a line or coloring them
11 are easy ways to figure it out.

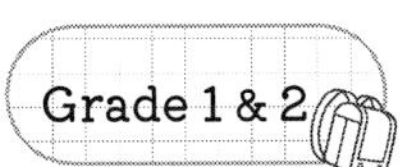


## Basics of Numbers

### Numbers

Teacher

1 OK, please look here. I'm going to show you some cards with crayons drawn on them.
2 This card has one crayon, this next card has two crayons, and then this card has three crayons.
3 OK, now, how many crayons do you see on this next card?
4 There's nothing. So, we call this 'zero'.
5 This means that when we count, we should actually count 0, 1, 2, 3, 4 …
6 But why? If there's nothing, we don't have to count it, right?
Well, please look at this card. If we don't have this expression 'zero' we wouldn't be able to
7 say that there are no bananas on this plate.

低学年

## 数の基本 3

どちらがおおきい

先生

1 簡単な式を書きますね。2+3=5、5-3=2。

2 この式は、どちらも、「=」の右と左が同じ数字ですね。

3 つまり、右と左が同じ出ないと、=を使った式をつくれません。
たとえば、7と5では、7が大きいですね。だから、式で表しても、3+4は、
2+3より大きい。右と左の大きさの大小を表す記号が、「不等号記号」と言って、
4 「>」という記号で表します。

大きく開いている方が、大きな数であることを表します。
5 逆に言えば、とがっている方は小さい数です。

低学年

## 数の基本 4

何番目

先生

1 数え方を学習しましょう。
みんな、このカード①を見てください。見てわかるように、7人のお友達が、
2 並んでいます。みんな、同じ方を向いています。
3 真ん中のお友達は、わかりますか。黄色い服を着ている人です。
4 お友達の名前を、太郎君としましょう。
5 太郎君は前から4番目、後ろから4番目にいると数えます。このように。
6 数える時、数字の後に「番目」をつけます。

このカードを見ると、正しい数え方がわかります。顔が向いている方が前ですから、
7 その先頭から1,2,3と数えて4だから4番目となります。
だから、例えば先頭から4人は座ってくださいと言われたら、先頭から太郎君までが
8 座ります。
9 わかったかどうか知りたいので、もう一回質問しますね。
10 太郎君の次のお友達までだと、何番目で何人が座ることになりますか。

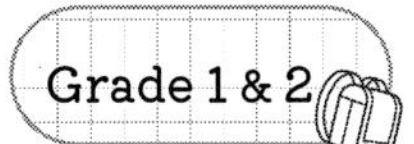


## Basics of Numbers

Which one is bigger?

Teacher

1 Let me write a simple equation. 2+3=5 5-3=2
You can see that for both equations, the right side and the left side of the equal sign have
2 the same number.
3 Meaning, we only use the equal sign when both sides have the same value.
Now, for example, if we have seven and five, seven is obviously larger than five. In other words,
three plus four is larger than two plus three. When we want to express the condition that one
4 value is larger than another, we use the “greater-than” sign, like this >.

So, the “greater-than” sign is used when one number is larger than the other and when one
5 value is smaller than another, we use a “less-than” sign, like this <.

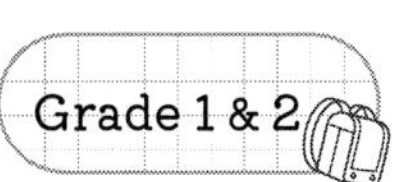


## Basics of Numbers

Orders

Teacher

1 We will learn more about how to count.
Everyone, please look at the card① here. As you can see, there are seven friends lined up.
2 All of them are facing the same direction.
3 Can you see the one in the middle? The one wearing a yellow shirt?
4 Let’s call him Taro-kun.
5 In this case, we can say that Taro is fourth from the front or fourth from the back.
When counting the order of things, you don’t say just 1, 2, 3, 4 but you say, first, second, third,
6 fourth and so on.

This card here shows you how to count correctly. On this card all the friends are facing forward
7 so we should start counting from the first person. 1, 2 ,3, and so 4 becomes fourth.
Therefore, for example, if I ask you to sit down in the fourth chair from the front, that means
8 you would sit where Taro-kun is.
9 Just to make sure you have a clear understanding, let me ask you one more question.
10 If I ask you to sit down behind Taro-kun, what position would that be?

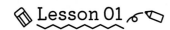

## 数の基本 4

何番目

先生

1 では、今日学習した何番目という学習をもっと広げてみましょう。

2 カードを見てください。

食べ物が、たくさん並んでいます。さっきのカードのお友達とは,並び方が違います。

3 さっきのカードの並び方は、横に並んでいるといいます。

4 右と左、上と下は皆さん分かりますか。

お友達の顔が左を向いていて、左が前ですから、お友達は、左から右に横に並んでいる

5 といいます。

このカードでは、食べ物が、上から下に並んでいます。このような並び方を、

6 上から下に縦に並んでいるといいます。

7 この言い方を使って、先ほどのカードとこのカードで、数え方を練習しましょう。

このカードでミカンは、上から3番目にあって、ミカンまでは3つあり、

8 下から4番目でみかんまで4つあります。

説明するときは、上からと下からしてみましょう。

9 そうすると、全体がわかりますよね。

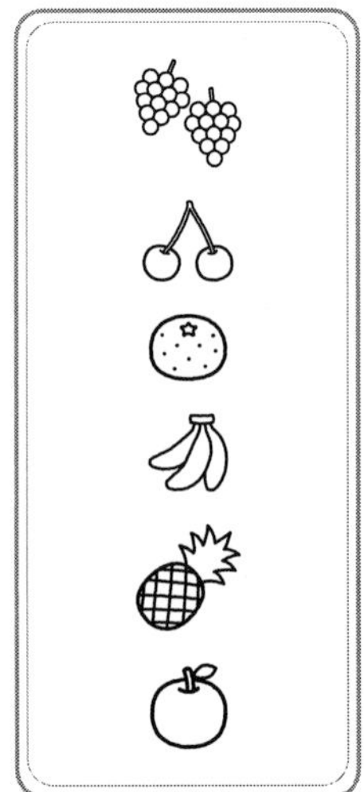

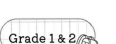

Grade 1 & 2

# Basics of Numbers

## Orders

**Teacher**

1 Now, let's study even more about counting like we did today.

2 Please look at these cards.

3 As you can see, there are a lot of foods lined up. But do you see a difference in how they are lined up compared to the card with friends that I just showed you before?

4 We can say that the friends in the last card were lined up from left to right. Everyone understands right and left, top and bottom, right?

5 The children's faces are facing left, so you can see the first person is at the very left. So, we say they are lining up from left to right.

6 On this card, the food is arranged from top to bottom. So, in this case we say they are lined up vertically from top to bottom.

7 Let's now practice counting with the previous card and this card using the same expressions.

8 On this card, the orange is the third position from the top and there are three items before the orange, and from the bottom, it's in the fourth position and there are four foods before the orange.

9 When explaining, let's do it from the top and from the bottom. That way you can see the whole picture.

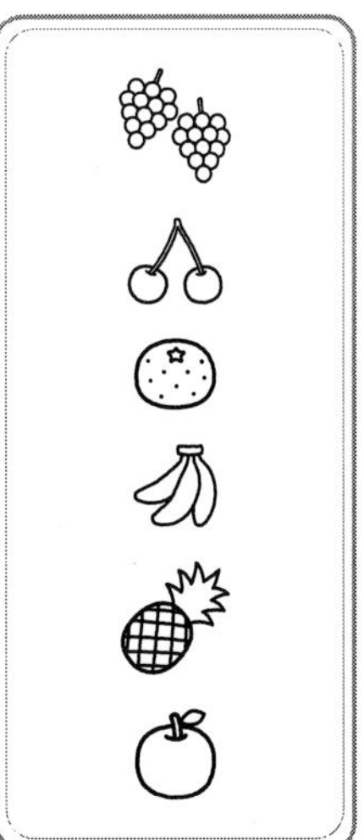

低学年

## 足し算

先生

1 これまで数の勉強をしてきましたね。
2 数は、0, 1, 2, 3, 4, 5, 6, 7, 8, 9, 10 でしたね。
3 1の次は 2、2 の次は 3 ですね。1 の次は 2 で、3 ではありません。

今日は、この意味について、学習していきます。これは、数は前の数に 1 を足してい
4 るからです。これを数の足し算といいます。
5 1に 1 を足したら 2、2 に 1 を足したら 3 ですね。

6 逆にいえば、1 に 2 を足したら 3、1 に 3 を足したら 4 となります。
つまり、2 に 1 を足しても、1 に 2 を足しても、3 になりますし、3 に 1 を足しても、
7 1に 3 を足しても、4 になるわけです。さらに、2 に 2 を足しても、4 になります。
8 つまり、足し方はいくつか方法があって、同じ答えを導くことができます。

先生

1 この足すということを、算数では「+」と書きます。
2 そして、その結果を書くときに「=」と書きます。
3 「+」は、縦に上から下に、そのあとに左から右に横に線をひきます。

4 線の長さは同じにします。
5 「=」は、先に上の線を左から右に、次に下の線を左から右に同じ長さで引きます。

6 二本の線は、同じ長さです。
7 5に 3 を足したら 8 で、5+3=8 と書くことを学習しました。
この 5+3=8 という表し方を「式」といい、何かと何かを足すことを「計算する」といい、
8 計算したら、こうなりましたということを「答え」といいます。
9 5+3 という計算をしたら、8 という答えになりました、ということですね。
10 そして、決まりがあって、計算は = の左側でやって、その答えを = の右側に書きます。
11 この決まりは、皆さんが何年生になっても変わりません。

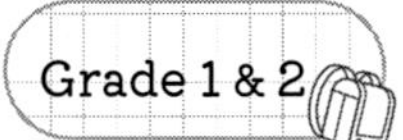

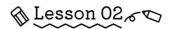

# Addition

Teacher

1 We have learned numbers so far.

2 Now, we can count 0, 1, 2, 3, 4, 5, 6, 7, 8, 9 and 10, right?

3 The number next to one is two, and after two is three. The number after one is two and not three.

Today, we will learn about what this means. This is because we added 1 to the previous number.

4 It's called addition.

5 Essentially, we learned that adding one to one you get two. Then adding one to two you get three.

6 Using the same idea, adding two to one you get three, and adding three to one you get four.

Meaning, adding one and two, and adding two and one both become three. Adding one and

7 three and adding three and one both become four. Adding two and two is four.

8 So, in other words, there are several ways to add and get the same answer.

Teacher

1 In Math, we write a plus like this "+" for addition.

2 And, we write equal as "=".

To write the plus sign "+"start with a vertical stroke from top to bottom, and then write

3 a horizontal line from left to right.

4 The length of the lines should be the same.

For the "=", the top line is drawn first from left to right, then the bottom line is drawn from

5 left to right.

6 The two lines must be the same length.

7 So far, we learned that adding three to five becomes eight and we write it as 5+3=8.

This way of expressing 5+3=8 is called a " formula," and adding something to something else

8 is called "calculating," and when you calculate, what you get is called an "answer.

9 When doing the addition of 5+3, we get 8. This 8 is called the answer.

10 The answer must always be written on the right-hand side of the equal sign, meaning 5+3=8.

11 This rule will never change no matter what grade you are in.

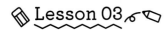

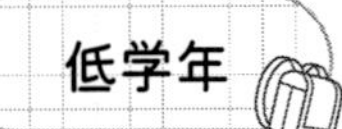


## 引き算

先生

では、カードを見てください。4 個のリンゴがあります。そこに、2 個のリンゴを足すと、
1 6 個ですね。では、4 個のリンゴから 1 個食べていたら、何個残りますか。

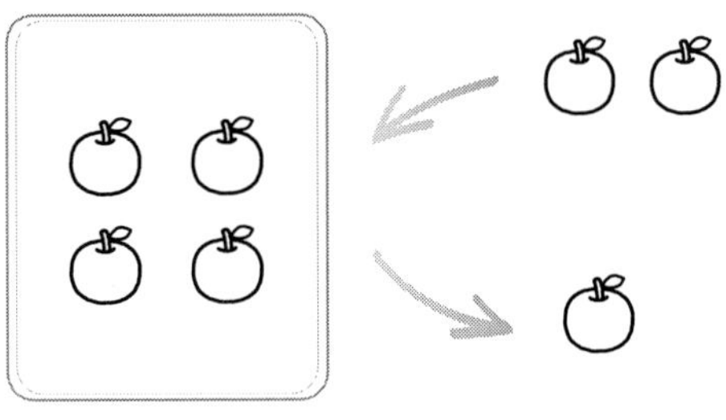

クラス

2 3 個!

先生

1 4 個のリンゴから 1 個食べたら、お皿の上のリンゴは 3 個になりました。
2 2 個食べたら・・・・みんなわかりますね。そう、2 個になります。
これを 4 から 1 を引いて、3 になりました、4 から 2 を引いて、2 になりました、
3 と言います。式にすると、4-1=3、4-2=2 と書きます。
4 今度は、「引く」という計算の勉強をして、これを引き算といいます。
足し算は、足す数字を前と後ろをひっくり返しても、同じ答えになりますが、引き算は、
気を付けなければいけないことがあります。それは、小さな数字から大きな数字は、
引けないということです。つまりね、「－」の前は、大きい方の数字か同じ数字で、
5 「－」の後ろは、同じ数字か小さい数字ということです。
6 9 から 3 を引く場合、9-3=6 という式になります。
7 では、3-3 は?
8 同じ数字から同じ数字を引くと、0 になります。
足し算の時を思い出してね。何かの数字に 1 を足すと、一つ大きな数字になりますが、
9 0 を足しても、同じ数字のままでしたね。
10 引き算でも、どんな数字から 0 を引いても、同じ数字のままです。

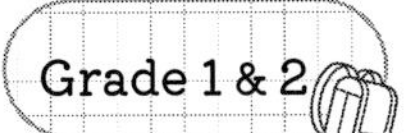


# Subtraction

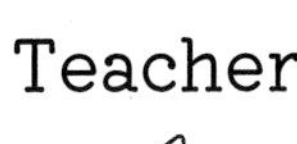

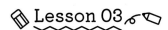

OK, please look at this card here. There are four apples. Now, if we add two apples to it,
1 then it becomes six. But what if I eat one apple from this card? Now how many apples are left?

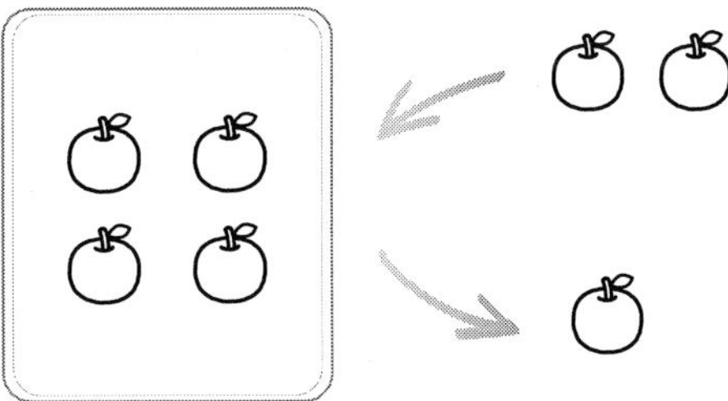

2 3 apples !

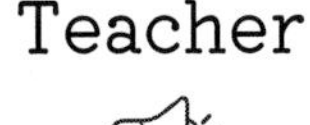

1 f you eat one apple from four, then the number of apples left on the plate would be 3.
2 What if we ate two apples? You know how many we have then, right? Yes, two apples remains.
Four minus one is three, and four minus two is two. If you put this into a formula, it's 4-1=3
3 and 4-2=2.
4 This time we are going to study minus and this is called subtraction.
When adding, you can get the same answer in any order, but in subtraction, you must be careful.
You must not subtract a bigger number from a smaller number. In other words, the number
5 before the minus sign must be bigger or the same as the number after the minus sign.

6 So, subtracting three from nine equals six, which is written as 9-3=6.
7 Now, what about three minus three?
8 Subtracting same number from the same number equals zero.
Remember when we were doing addition? Remember when we were adding. If you add 1 to
9 any number, you would get a larger number, but if you add 0, you still get the same number.
10 It's the same in subtraction, if you subtract 0 from any number, it remains the same number.

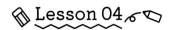

低学年

## 大きな数

先生

1 数字は、どんどん広がっていけます。

2 今日は、10 より大きな数の書き方と、どう読むのかを学習しましょう。

3 すべての数字は、0 から 9 の数字で表します。

黒板に書いてある、12, 24, 25, 11, 19、30、100、500、1000、どれも、
4 0 から 9 の数字が使われていますね。

5 10 や 99 は二つの数字が並んでいますね。

6 これを二桁と言います。

7 100 や 500 は、3 つの数字だから三桁、1000 は、4 つの数字だから四桁といいます。

8 0 から 9 までは、数字が 1 つだから一桁です。

9 今日は、9+5 はいくらだろうという問題を学習しましょう。

10 9 の次は 10 で、9 に 1 を足すと 10 になることは学習しました。

9 に 1 を足すためには、5 を、その前の数である 4 と 1 に分けて、9 と 1 を足して 10 にて、
11 残り 4 ですから、14 という答えになります。

12 つまり、9+5 を 9+1+4 の 3 つの足し算に変えるとよいですね。

13 では、二桁からの引き算の学習をしましょう。

14 12-2 は 10 と 2 から 2 を引くので、答えが 10 となることは学習しましたね。

10 より大きな数は、10 と一桁の数字に分けて、10 から引く数字を引いて、その答えに、
15 分けた一桁の数字を足します。

13-6 を計算してみます。13 を 10 と 3 に分けます。10 から 6 を引くと、答えは 4 だと
16 わかります。そして、その 4 に 3 を足すと 7 とわかります。これで、13-6=7 です。

17 これを計算式にすると、13 を 10 と 3 に分けて、10-6=4、4+3=7、答え 7 となります。

12.24.25.11.19.30.100.500.1000

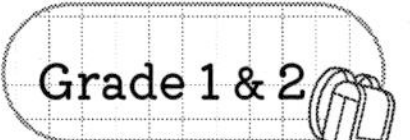


# Big Numbers

Teacher

1 Numbers get larger and larger as we count.
Today, we will learn how write numbers larger than 10 and how to read those bigger
2 numbers.

3 All the numbers in the world contain the numbers 0 to 9.
For example, 12, 24, 25, 11, 19, 30, 100, 500, 1000. All of these are expressed by usings
4 the numbers 0 to 9.
5 We can see that there are two numbers next to each other for numbers 10 through 99.
6 These are called two-digit numbers.

7 Numbers like 100 and 500 are called 3-digit numbers and 1000 is a 4-digit number.
8 Numbers 0 to 9 are called 1-digit numbers, as they are only one number.

9 Today, we are going to learn about adding problems like nine plus five.
10 The number next to nine is ten, so if you add one to nine, then that would be ten.
To add 1 to 9, we need to divide 5 into its preceding numbers, 4 and 1, and then add 9 and 1 to
11 get 10, which leaves 4, so the answer is 14.
12 In other words, we can change 9+5 to 3 additions of 9+1+4.

13 Next, let's do subtraction of 2-digit numbers.
14 We learned that 12 subtracts 2 from 10 and 2, so the answer is 10, right?
For subtracting numbers bigger than 10, you can change it to 10 and a single-digit number
15 then subtract the number from 10 and add the single-digit number to the answer.

Let's do 13-6. Firstly, we can change 13 to 10 and 3. Now, we know that 10-6 would be 4.
16 So now add 4 to the 3 and that would be 7. That's how we know 13-6 is 7.
17 To put this into a formula, we divide 13 into 10 and 3. 10-6=4, 4+3=7, and the answer is 7.

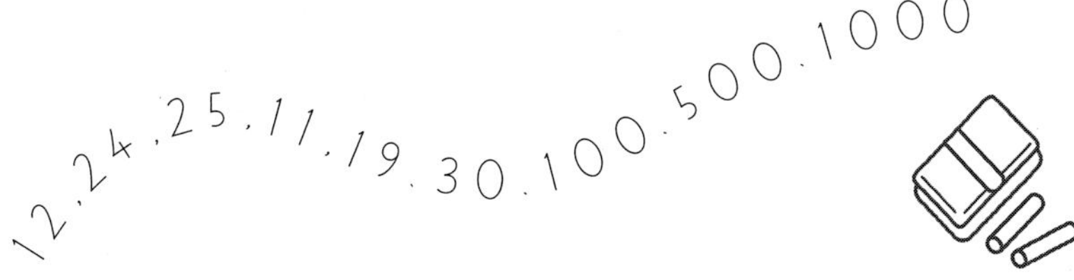

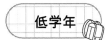

低学年

# 時刻と時計 1

時計

先生

1 では、こちらを見てください。これは、時計です。
2 時計は、時間を知るために使います。
時間は、何時何分と表します。この、何時何分というのを、時計では、短い針と長い針
3 の二つの針で表し、短い針が何時、長い針が何分を表します。

そして、時計をみてください。一番上に 12、それから、グルッと右回りに
4 1、2、3 ･･･11 と、数字が書いてありますね。この数字は、短い針のための数字です。
5 長い針のための数字は、数字と数字の間に、細い線が 4 本ずつ書いてありますね。
6 これで表します。
長い針のスタートラインは、時計の一番上の 12 という数字で、ここから細い線を 1,2,3
7 と数えていきます。さあ、細い線が、時計の中に何本あるか、数えてみましょうね。
8 1,2,3…60 ありますね。
短い針は、1 から 12 までの数で、何時と教えてくれます。長い針は、0 から 60 までの
9 数字で、何分と教えてくれます。
時計の針は、長い方も短い方も、一番上の 12 の数字からスタートして、1,2,3 という数字
10 の方から、グルーと回って 12 のところに戻っています。
11 それと、短い針は、今、どこにいますか？
12 8 時なのに、8 の数字のところではなくて、8 と 9 の真ん中にありますね？
長い針が、グルーと 1 回まわっている間に、短い針は少しずつ進んで、長い針が 30 の
ところまで来たら、次の数字との間の半分、長い針が 1 回まわったら、次の数字に進ん
13 でいます。

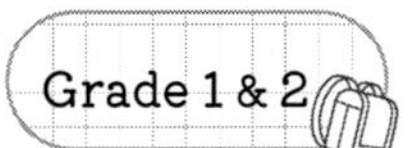


## Time and Clocks

Time

Teacher

1 OK, please look up here. This is a clock.
2 A clock is used to tell you the time.
The time is expressed in minutes and hours. In a clock, the hour and minute are represented
by two hands, a short hand and a long hand. The long hand shows hours and the shorthand
3 shows minutes.

Look at the clock now. You can see the number 12 on the top and also the numbers
4 1 to 11 around the clock. These numbers are used for the short hand.
5 The numbers for the long hand are written with four thin lines between each number.
6 This is how it is represented.
The long hand starts at the top where it says 12, then counts 1, 2, 3 from there. Now, let's see
7 count how many thin lines there are on a clock. 1, 2, 3…60.
8 There are 60 lines, right?
The short hand tells us the hour between 1-12, and the long hand tells us the minutes
9 between 0-60.
The hands of the clock, both long and short, start with the number 12 at the top, move towards
10 1, 2, 3 until they come back around to 12 again.
11 And where is the shorter hand now?
12 Why is it not exactly at number 8 although it's 8 o'clock? Instead, it is between 8 and 9, right?
This is because while the long hand moves around once, the short hand also moves bit by bit.
And when the long hand reaches 30, the short hand is right in the middle of the current number
and the next number. When the long hand goes all the way around once, then the short hand
13 will be right on the next number.

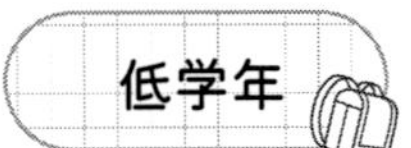


## 時刻と時計 1

時計

先生

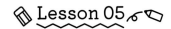

1 1日は、24時間です。時計は、12時間しかありません。
2 これは、1日の時間を2つに分けているからです。
短い針と長い針が、12の文字盤で一緒になっているところからの12時間を午前といい、
3 昼に、もう一度、12の文字盤で一緒になったところからの12時間を午後といいます。
4 今は、午前10時23分といいます。
12時になると、午後に切り替わって、給食が始まる時間は、12時15分と言わず、
5 午後12時15分といいます。
6 12ですが、午前12時とは言いません。午前0時といいます。
7 午後は12時です。

## 時刻と時計 2

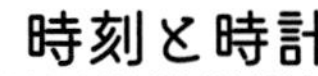

カレンダー

先生

1 時計を使って、1日は24時間、1時間は60分を勉強しました。
カレンダーを見てください。大きく、月と書いてあって、1月、2月 ･･･
2 12月と書いてあります。
3 12か月でこれで1年です。
4 4月は30日、5月は31日、6月は30日となっていますね。
5 2月なんか28日しかないですね。
6 月ごとに、その月の日数が決まっています。月ごとに、日数がデコボコで覚えられませんね。

7 秘密の覚え方を、先生が教えますね。
皆さん、左手を出して、げんこつを作ってください。そうしたら、手の甲に指の骨が
8 でた山のところと、へこんだ谷の部分ができますね。
9 人差し指の山に右手の人差し指をのせて、こんな感じに。
そこが、1月、指を隣の谷に動かしてそこが2月、中指の山に動かして3月、
次の谷が4月、次の山が5月、次の谷が6月、最後の小指の山が7月、
10 指を人差し指の山にもどして、そこが8月です。

11 わかりましたか？
12 山のところは31日、谷のところは30日です。2月だけは28日です。

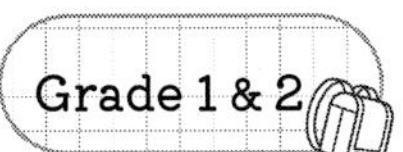

## Time and Clocks 1

Grade 1 & 2

### Time

Teacher

1 One day is 24 hours. But the clock only shows 12 hours, right?

2 This is because we divide a day into halves.
From the point where the short hand and long hand cross at number 12, we call it a.m.

3 And then, once the clock reaches 12 again at noon, we call it p.m.

4 Right now, it is 10:23 a.m.

5 At 12:00, we switch to the afternoon, and the time when school lunch begins is 12:15 p.m.

6 When we want to describe 12:00, we actually don't say 12:00 a.m. We usually say 0:00 a.m.

7 It is called midnight.

## Time and Clocks 2

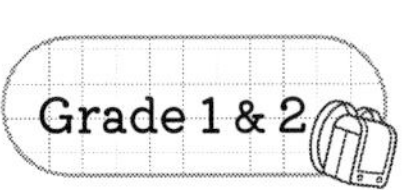

Grade 1 & 2

### Calendar

Teacher

1 We used a clock to learn that a day has 24 hours and 60 minutes equals an hour.
Please look at the calendar. You can see the months written in a big letters; January, February
2 …December.

3 There are 12 months in a year.

4 April has 30 days, but May has 31 and June also has 30 days.

5 And February only has 28 days.
So, we can see from here that there is a set number of days for each month. But, because each
6 month is different, it's difficult to memorize, isn't it?

7 But let me show you a secret.
Everyone, hold out your left hand and make a fist. Do you see the bumps from your knuckles,
8 like mountains and valleys?

9 Now, put your right hand index finger on top of your left index finger knuckle, like this.
That is January. Move your finger to the valley next to it. That's February. And then move it to the second mountain, which is your middle finger knuckle; this is March. Next, that valley is April, then the next mountain is May, then June is a valley, and then July. Your left index finger should
10 now be on the last mountain. For August, we count this mountain one more time for August.

11 What do you think this means?
OK, the mountains are for the months with 31 days, and the valleys are for the months with 30 days.
12 Except February, which only has 28 days.

低学年

# 単位

先生

時計を使って、60分が1時間、反対に言うと、1時間は60分ともいえること、
1 24時間が1日、1日は24時間ともいえることを学習しました。
2 これを単位といい、時計で習ったのは、時間の単位です。
3 他に、長さや重さにも単位があります。
定規を出してください。定規に、短い線が書いてあって、長い線に1、
4 次の長い線に2と書いてありますね。
5 1と2の数字の間の短い線はいくつあるか、誰か教えてくれますか。
6 短い線が9本あります。そして、長い線のところに、1と書いてあります。
7 短い線は、mmという長さを表す単位です。10mmで、1cmという単位に変わります。

8 つまり、長い線に書いてある1,2,3という数字はcmの長さの単位です。

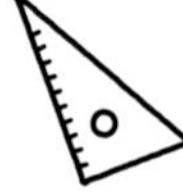

先生

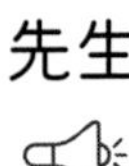

1 黒板に書いた表を、ノートに、同じように書いてください。
上から3つ目の左端のマスからスタートして、横に10マス目まで、定規を使って、
2 真っすぐ線を引きます。
次に、左端の3つ目のマスから下に4つ、つまり、7つ目のマスに、同じように
3 線を引きます。
4 定規を使わないと、曲がって、まっすぐに引けません。
定規は、横に線を引くときは、引く線の下に添えて、縦に線を引くときは、
5 左側に添えますよ。上や右側だと、線が引きづらいですね。

そこまでいいですか。線が曲がったり、マスからはみ出したりして、書き直すときは、
6 消しゴムできれいに消してください。
7 消しゴムで消すときは、ページを反対の手でしっかり押さえてくださいね。
8 押さえないと、ページがずれて破れたり、グシャグシャになったりします。

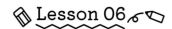

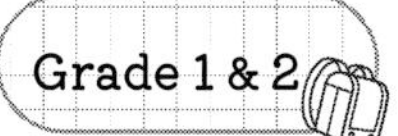
Grade 1 & 2

# Units of Measurement

**Teacher**

Using a clock, we learned that 60 minutes can be called an hour, and conversely, an hour can be
1 called 60 minutes; 24 hours can be called a day, and a day can be called 24 hours.
2 This is called a unit of measure, and what we learned with clocks is a unit of time.
3 There are also units of length, weight and so on.
Take out your rulers, please. There are short lines. The first long line says one
4 and the next long line says 2, right?
5 Can anyone tell me how many short lines are in between one and two?
6 There are 9 short lines. Then the first long line says one.
The short lines are called millimeters, they're a unit of length. 10mm can be called one
7 centimeter, which is the same length.
8 So, the numbers 1, 2, 3 written on the long lines indicate centimeters.

**Teacher**

1 Please copy down in your notes what I write on the blackboard.
Using a ruler, draw a straight line from the third square on the left to the tenth square
2 on the side, starting from the third square from the top.
Next, draw a line in the same way from the third square on the left to the four squares
3 below, in other words, to the seventh square.
4 If you don't use a ruler, the line will bend and cannot be drawn straight.
The correct way to use a ruler is to place the ruler just underneath where you want to draw a line,
when you want to make a straight line going down, then place it on the left side. It maybe a little
5 challenging to draw a line from above or right side.

Is everyone okay so far? If you have curvy lines, or the line got out of the space,
6 then please use an eraser to erase the lines.
7 When erasing with the eraser, please hold the page firmly with your other hand.
8 If you do not hold the page firmly, the page may shift, tear, or become crumpled.

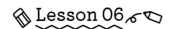

低学年

# 単位

先生

1 時間が分と時、長さがcmとmmという単位で表すことが分かりました。

2 それ以外に、様々な単位があります。

3 みなさん、鉛筆を右手にもって、消しゴムを左手に持ってください。

4 どちらが重いですか。

5 そうですね、消しゴムの方が重いですね。これが重さという単位です。

6 重さという単位は、kg、g で表します。

7 どれくらい入るかというのが、「かさ」という単位です。

8 「かさ」の単位は 「ℓ」、「dℓ」で表します。

9 生活の中でも、重さやかさをよく使っています。

10 kgとｇ、ℓとdℓは、時間が60分で1時間と表すのと同じ関係にあります。

1 kgは1000g、1 ℓは10 dℓです。ちなみに、1 cmは10 mmでしたね。100 cmは
11 1mといいます。

12 だから、1mは1000 mmとなります。

1 dℓは100m ℓ という単位になっていて、1 ℓは10 dℓ、1,000m ℓ とあらわすことが
13 できます。

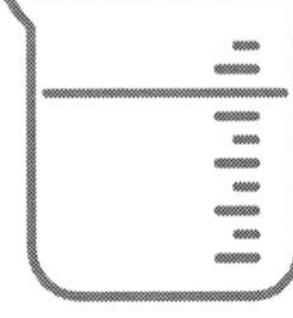

Grade 1 & 2

# Units of Measurement

Teacher

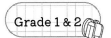

We learned that time can be expressed by hours and minutes, and length can be expressed by
1 centimeters and millimeters.
2 There are, of course, many other different types of units.
3 Hold a pencil in your right hand and an eraser in your left hand.
4 Which one do you think is heavier?
5 We can feel that the eraser is heavier, right? This is because the weight of each object is different.
6 To express weight, we use units called kilograms (kg) and grams (g).
7 And the correct expression for measuring amounts of water is called volume.

8 The units for volume are liter and deciliter.
9 In our daily lives, we use these measurements pretty often.
And just like telling time, kilograms and grams as well as liters and deciliters have a defined
10 relationship.
11 1kg equals 1,000g; 1 ℓ is equal to 10 dℓ. By the way, 1 cm is 10mm right?

12 If it is 100cm, this is equal to 1m.
This also means that 1m is 1,000mm. Similarly, 1dl is equal to 100ml and 1 ℓ is 10 dℓand
13 that is also 1,000ml.

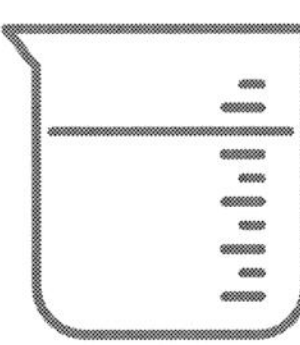

中学年

## 掛け算 1

基本

先生

1 算数で習う大切なことは、数の計算です。
2 計算ができないと、普段の生活で困ることだらけです。
今、先生は「生活に困ることがある」というのではなく、「生活に困ることだらけです」
3 と言いましたね。要するに、たくさん困る場面がある、ということです。
4 だから、計算ができるようになるというのは、大変、重要です。
5 これが、算数の一番の目的です。
これまで、足し算と引き算を学習してきました。5+5＝10 ですね。この足し算が、
もっとたくさんになったら、例えば、5 を 10 回、5+5+5+5+5+5+5+5+5+5. 足し算する
6 となると、繰り返し、同じ数を足し続けないといけなくなって、不便ですね。
7 そこで、使う計算が掛け算といいます。
8 今日は、掛け算の学習をします。
9 掛け算とは、同じ数を何回加えたかの回数を数えて、同じ数に加えた回数を掛けたら
10 足し算と同じ結果になるという計算です。
11 4の足し算が、書いてありますね。4＋4＋4＋4＋4 です。
12 掛け算では、4×5 として、20 になります。
13 掛け算は、九九といって、暗記してしまう事が必要です。

14 暗記しないと使えませんから、絶対暗記します。

15 では、九九の表を見てください。
九九の表は1の段から９の段まであって、格段に１から９までを掛けた数字が並んでいて、
16 その答えが＝で結ばれています。
読み方は、覚えやすいように５句のリズムを取って、且つ数字のみを発音して
17 覚えていきます。『いちかけるいちはいち』と言わず、『いちいちがいち』と発音します。

| 1の段 | | | | |
|---|---|---|---|---|
| いち | | いち | が | いち |
| 1 | × | 1 | = | 1 |
| いち | | に | が | に |
| 1 | × | 2 | = | 2 |

| 2の段 | | | | |
|---|---|---|---|---|
| に | | いち | が | に |
| 2 | × | 1 | = | 2 |
| に | | に | が | し |
| 2 | × | 2 | = | 4 |

| 3の段 | | | | |
|---|---|---|---|---|
| さん | | いち | が | さん |
| 3 | × | 1 | = | 3 |
| さん | | に | が | ろく |
| 3 | × | 2 | = | 6 |

| 4の段 | | | | |
|---|---|---|---|---|
| し | | いち | が | し |
| 4 | × | 1 | = | 4 |
| し | | に | が | はち |
| 4 | × | 2 | = | 8 |

| 5の段 | | | | |
|---|---|---|---|---|
| ご | | いち | が | ご |
| 5 | × | 1 | = | 5 |
| ご | | に | | じゅう |
| 5 | × | 2 | = | 10 |

| 6の段 | | | | |
|---|---|---|---|---|
| ろく | | いち | が | ろく |
| 6 | × | 1 | = | 6 |
| ろく | | に | | じゅうに |
| 6 | × | 2 | = | 12 |

| 7の段 | | | | |
|---|---|---|---|---|
| しち | | いち | が | しち |
| 7 | × | 1 | = | 7 |
| しち | | に | | じゅうし |
| 7 | × | 2 | = | 14 |

| 8の段 | | | | |
|---|---|---|---|---|
| はち | | いち | が | はち |
| 8 | × | 1 | = | 8 |
| はち | | に | | じゅうろく |
| 8 | × | 2 | = | 16 |

| 9の段 | | | | |
|---|---|---|---|---|
| く | | いち | が | く |
| 9 | × | 1 | = | 9 |
| く | | に | | じゅうはち |
| 9 | × | 2 | = | 18 |

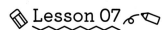

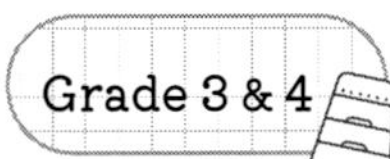


# Multiplication

## Basics

Teacher

1 The most important thing we will learn from arithmetic is how to calculate numbers.
2 If you can't calculate, you will have a lot of trouble in your daily life.
Notice I said that 'it WILL be very difficult' instead of 'it COULD be very difficult'. Being able to
3 calculate is an important part of our daily lives.
4 These are reasons why it is really important to learn how to calculate.
5 That's the greatest purpose of math.

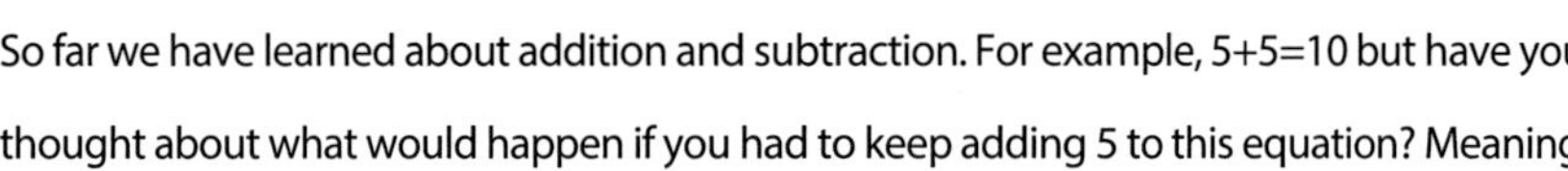

So far we have learned about addition and subtraction. For example, 5+5=10 but have you ever
thought about what would happen if you had to keep adding 5 to this equation? Meaning, if
6 you have to add 5 (5+5+5+5+5+5+5+5+5+5) 10 times. That's going to be a hassle to write, isn't it?
7 This is where the concept of multiplication comes in.
8 Today, we are going to learn about multiplication.
9 So, say, if we multiply a number, that means you add a certain number many times to the
10 original number. The number of times you add is determined by the multiplier.
11 Here, you see an addition problem that consists of many 4s, right? 4+4+4+4+4.
12 In that case, we can actually express this as 4×5, which equals 20.
To do multiplication, it is actually easier if we memorize all the combinations of most frequently
13 used ones.
If you don't memorize them, the calculation won't be any quicker than just adding the numbers
14 together. Therefore, it's a must to memorize certain combinations.
15 Please look at this multiplication chart.
The multiplication diagram consists of rows and columns from 1 to 9. The numbers you see inside
16 the grid represent the product of the number of the row times the number of the column.
Usually, we read the equation like this: 1 times 1 equals 1. But, to help us memorize the chart easier,
17 we can instead use a simplified expression: 『いちいちがいち』

(※米国では、"one times one is one"と発音していますが、「日本の九九のリズム」にあいませんので、本書では、「日本の九九のリズム」に合わせて発音します)

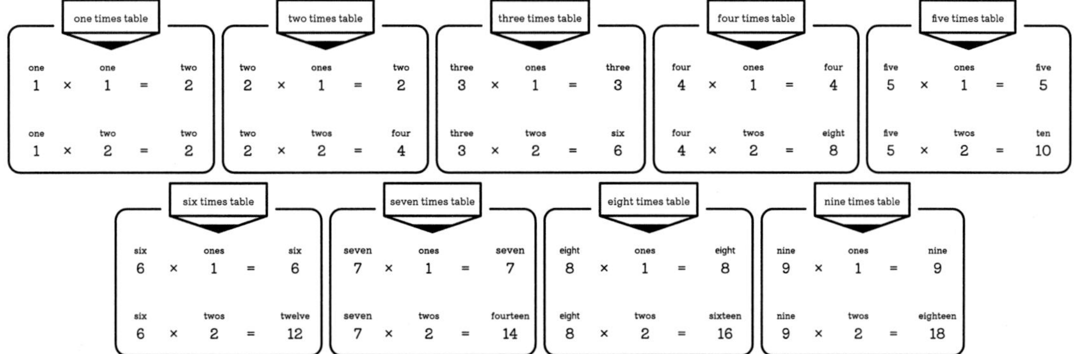

one times table
one 1 × one 1 = two 2
one 1 × two 2 = two 2
two times table
two 2 × ones 1 = two 2
two 2 × twos 2 = four 4
three times table
three 3 × ones 1 = three 3
three 3 × twos 2 = six 6
four times table
four 4 × ones 1 = four 4
four 4 × twos 2 = eight 8
five times table
five 5 × ones 1 = five 5
five 5 × twos 2 = ten 10
six times table
six 6 × ones 1 = six 6
six 6 × twos 2 = twelve 12
seven times table
seven 7 × ones 1 = seven 7
seven 7 × twos 2 = fourteen 14
eight times table
eight 8 × ones 1 = eight 8
eight 8 × twos 2 = sixteen 16
nine times table
nine 9 × ones 1 = nine 9
nine 9 × twos 2 = eighteen 18

中学年

# 掛け算 1

基本

先生

1 掛けるマーク「×」の前の数字を「掛けられる数」、後ろの数字を「掛ける数」と言います。

2 九九を覚えているとて、下記計算が簡単に理解できます。

3×5＝15、5×3＝15　だから、「掛けられる数」と「掛ける数」を逆にしても同じ答えの

3 数字になります。

3×4+3＝15、3×6－3＝15　だから、3×5＝3×4+3=3×6－3　つまり、「掛けられる数」である× マークの前の数字に、「掛ける数」である× マークの後の数字が、減ったりした場合、掛けられる数にその増えたり、減ったりした数の差を掛けた数を「足し算」したり、

4 「引き算」すると同じ数になります。

5 でも、さっきは「掛ける数」を分けて足しても同じ数になることを学習しました。

6 「掛けられる数」を分けて足しても同じです。

7 12×5 でやってみますよ。

8 12 は分けると、9 と 3なりますね。だから、12×5 は、9×5 と 3×5 を足してもよいのです。

掛けられる数」、「掛ける数」いずれも、2 桁の場合は、それぞれを 1 桁の数字に分けて、

9 その答えを足し算すればよいことを学習しました。

10 それと、2 桁の数字を分ける場合、10 と 1 桁の数字にすれば、簡単です。

11 つまり、12×3 の場合、10×3 と 2×3 に分けられると、分かりやすいです。

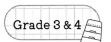

Grade 3 & 4

# Multiplication

## Basics

Teacher

The number in front of the multiplication mark “x” is called the “ multiplicand “ and the number
behind is called the “multiplier”. Remembering the multiplication, the following calculations
2 can be easily understood.
3 x 5 = 15 and 5 x 3 = 15. So, if you reverse the “multiplier” and the “multiplicand”, you will get
3 the same answer number.

3×4+3=15, 3×6-3=15 So, 3×5=3×4+3=3×6-3 In other words, if the number before the x mark,
which is the “ multiplicand,” is less than or equal to the number after the x mark, which is
4 the “multiplier” the number to be multiplied is increased or decreased.

5 We learned earlier that dividing and adding “multipliable numbers” results in the same number.
6 The same is true if you separate and add the “multipliable numbers.”
7 Let’s try 12 x 5.
8 If we divide 12, it becomes 9 and 3. So 12 x 5 can be added to 9 x 5 and 3 x 5.
We have learned that for both “multiplier “ and “multiplicand “ numbers, in the case of
two-digit numbers, we can divide each into one-digit numbers and add the answers to the
9 two-digit numbers.
And, if you want to separate a two-digit number, it’s easier if you make it a ten and a one-digit
10 number.
In other words, in the case of 12 x 3, it is easier to understand if you can divide it into 10 x 3
11 and 2 x 3.

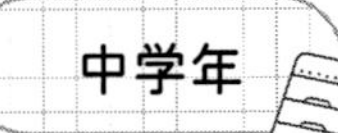


中学年

# 掛け算 2

## 筆算

先生

1 掛け算を計算するときの筆算の方法を書きます。

2 「掛けられる数」、「掛ける数」の順で、一の位を縦に揃えて書きます。
「掛ける数」の横に少し離して、これは掛算をする計算式ですということが分かるように、

3 「×」マークを書きます。

4 書き終わったら、定規を使って線を引きます。

```
   1 2
×    4
```

5 「掛けられる数」の一の位の 2 に掛ける数 4 を掛けてその答えを一の位に書きます。

```
     1 2
×      4
①→     8
```

次に「掛けられる数」の十の位の 10 にかける数 4 を掛けて、
その答えを十の位に書きます。この時、一の位が何もありませんから、

6 何もない時は 0 ですね。0 と付け加えます。

```
     1 2
×      4
②→   4 0
```

7 ②の 10×4 と①の 2×4 の答えを足して、48 となります。
大切なのは、十の位を計算するときに一の位には必ず 0 を書いて

8 おくことです。これは、二桁同士の数の掛け算をするときも同じです。

先生

1 12×31 の計算をしてみましょう。

2 まず、掛けられる数の一の位に掛ける数の一の位を掛けた計算をします。これが①です。

3 次に、掛けられる数の十の位に掛ける数の一の位を掛けた計算をして、これが②です。
それから、掛けられる数の一の位に掛ける数の十の位の数字を掛けます。答えを書くときに先ほども言いましたが、十の位の計算ですよ。一桁の位に必ず 0 を書き加えます。

4 これが③です。

最後に、掛けられる数の十の位に掛ける数の十の位の数字を掛けます。

5 十の位と十の位の掛け算ですから、一の位と十の位に 0 を書き加えないといけません。

6 これを間違えてると答えがおかしくなります。これが④です。

7 全部を足すと、①+②+③+④の答えを足して、372 となります。

```
                   1 2
×                  3 1
(2 × 1)              2  --> ①
(10 × 1)           1 0  --> ②
(2 × 30)           6 0  --> ③
(10 × 30)        3 0 0  --> ④
```

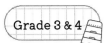

# Multiplication 2

## How to do multiplication

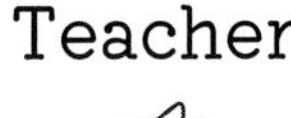


1 This is the writing method used to do the multiplication.

2 First write the multiplicand ", then "multiplier ", with the first place aligned vertically.

3 Next to the multiplier write an "X" mark to indicate that it is a formula for multiplication.

4 When you have finished writing, use a ruler to draw a line.

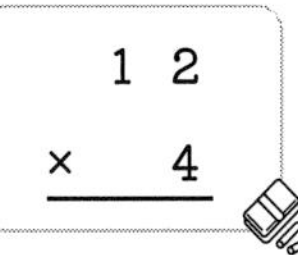


5 Multiply the first place the number 2 multiplied by the number 4 to get the answer. Write in the first place.

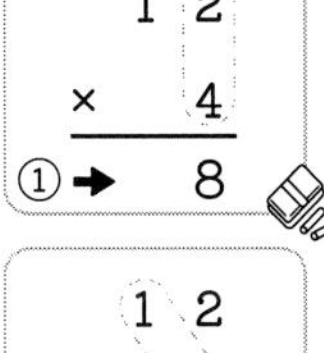


6 Then multiply the number 4 by the number 10 to the tens place of the "multiplicand", Write the answer to the tenth place. At this time, the first place has nothing, so when there is nothing, it is 0. 0 is added.

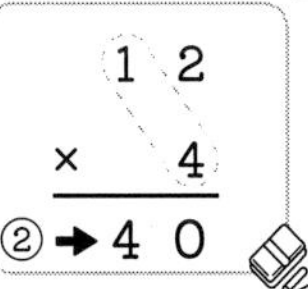


7 Adding the answers of 10 x 4 in ② and 2 x 4 in ①, we get 48.

8 The important thing is that when calculating the tenths, always write a zero in the first place. The same is true when multiplying two-digit numbers.

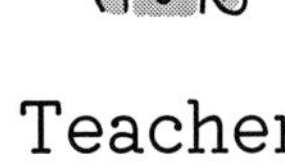

1 Let's calculate 12 x 31.

2 First, multiply the number in the ones place of the multiplicand by the number in the ones place of the multiplier. This is ①.

3 Next, we move to the tens place and multiply the tens place of the multiplicand by the ones place of the multiplier. which is ②

4 Then multiply the ones place of the multiplicand by the tenth place of the multiplier. As I said earlier when writing the answer, it's the calculation to the tenths place. Always add a zero to the first digit. This is ③.

5 Finally, multiply the tenth places of the multiplicand by the tenth places of the multiplier Since the tens place is multiplied by the tens place, we must add zeros to the ones and tens places.

6 If you get this wrong, the answer will be wrong. This is ④.

7 Adding them all together, the answer to ① + ② + ③+ ④ = 372.

```
                  1 2
×                 3 1
( 2 × 1 )           2 --> ①
(10 × 1 )         1 0 --> ②
( 2 × 30)         6 0 --> ③
(10 × 30)       3 0 0 --> ④
```

低学年

# 分数

先生

1 リンゴが３個あって、それを３人で分けるなら、一人１個ずつでよいですね。

2 でも、リンゴが１個しかなかったら、どうやって、３人で分けますか。

3 この計算を分数といいます。

4 １個を３人で分けるので、一人ずつ３分の１となるといい、1/3 と書きます。

5 １個を４人で分けるなら、4 分の１ずつになるといい、1/4 と書きます。

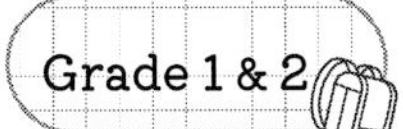


# Fractions

Teacher

If there are three apples and we need to distribute them between three people, then
1 the answer is simple: the three of them get one apple each.
2 However, if there's only one apple, what would you do?
3 We have a math term to describe this. We call them 'fractions'.
If we have to express a situation where we need to cut one apple into three pieces equally,
4 we say that each person gets one-third of the apple: 1/3.
Similarly, if we have to share it between four people, then we say that each person gets
5 one-fourth of the apple: 1/4. This symbol can also be expressed as "one over four".

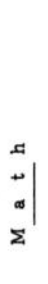

中学年

## 割り算

基本

先生

1 今日は、新しい計算方法を学習します。割り算という計算方法です。

2 3×2＝6 を掛け算と学習しました。

3 そうすると　3×□＝6の問題では、□に 2 が入ることがすぐわかりますね。

4 6を□で割ると3になる□に入る数字は何ですかというのが割り算という計算です。

5 式で表すと、6÷□＝3と書き表します。

÷マークより前の数字を「割られる数」、マークより後ろの数字を「割る数」といい、

6 この式では、割る数が□で、そして□が 2 と分かります。

7 □の場所が変わると、6÷2＝□の□が3となりますね。

この計算が合っているかは、「割る数」と答えを掛けると「割られる数」になりますから、

8 これで確かめます。

9 □の場所を移動して、□の数字を確認してみます。

10 6÷□＝3、だから□は 2、6÷2＝□、だから□は 3、2×3＝□、だから□は 6 ですね。

□が割られる数だと、□÷2=3 の□は6で正しいかどうかを確認したい場合、割る数×答え、

11 つまり、2×3 の掛け算をすると確認できます。

12 この確認方法を検算といいます。

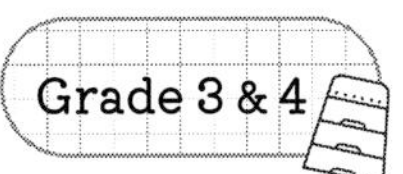


# Division

## Basics

**Teacher**

1 Today you will learn a new method of calculation. It is a calculation method called division.

2 We learned that 3 x 2 = 6 is multiplication.

3 Then, in the problem 3 x □ = 6, you can easily see that 2 should be placed in the □.

4 The calculation method called division is to find what number goes into □ so dividing 6 by □ gives 3.

5 When I write it as a formula, it is written as 6 ÷ □ = 3.

6 The number before the ÷ mark is called the dividend, and the number after the mark is called the divisor. In this formula, the divisor is □, and □ is 2.

7 If the location of □ changes, then 6 ÷ 2 = □ and □ is 3, right?

8 To check if this calculation is correct, multiply the "divisor" by the answer to get the "dividend".

9 Let's move the location of the □ and check the □ numbers.

10 If 6 divided by □ = 3, then □ is 2; If 6 divided by 2 = □, then □ is 3; If 2 x 3 = □, then □ is 6.

11 If □ is the dividend, and you want to check whether the □ in □ ÷ 2 = 3 is correct at 6, you can check by multiplying the divisor x the answer, in other words, 2 x 3.

12 This method of confirmation is called verification.

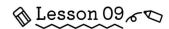

中学年

# 割り算 2

## あまりのある計算

先生

1 割り算の基本を学習しました。

2 では、割り切れないという学習をします。

3 例えば、6÷3＝2 です。では、7÷3 はいくらでしょうという問題です。

4 6 は 3×2 と掛け算で検算できますから割り切れます。

5 3 に何も掛けても 7 にはなりませんね。こういう場合、どういう風に書いたらいいという学習です。

6 7÷3=2 あまり 1 と書きます。

7 あまりの 1 というのは、7 を 3 で割れませんので、3 で割れる数字で 7 に近いのは 6 なので、6 を 3 で割ります。割らない 1 を余りとして書きますということです。

8 3×2=6、3×3＝9 ですね。

9 だから、6 と 9 の間の 7 と 8 は割り切れません。

10 こういう割り切れない数を余りとして書くというルールです。

11 練習してみましょう。

12 55÷6、47÷6、33÷6 をやってみましょう。

13 55÷6＝9 あまり 1、47÷6＝7 あまり 5、33÷6=5 あまり 3 となりましたか。

14 この答えがあっているか、検算をします。

15 検算の方法は、割る数×答えでしたね。ですから、これに余りを足すと、割られる数にあっているかを確認します。

Grade 3 & 4

# Division

## Calculating with Remainders

**Teacher**

1 We have learned the basics of division.

2 Now, we will learn about what we call indivisible numbers.

3 For example, 6÷3 = 2. Then the question is how much is 7÷3?

4 6 is divisible because it can be verified by multiplication with 3 x 2.

However, multiplying 3 by anything does not equal 7, does it? In this case, let's learn how to
5 write this problem.

6 Write 7÷3 = 2 remainder 1.

The remainder 1 means that 7 cannot be divided by 3, so the number divisible by 3 that is
closest to 7 is 6, therefore 6 is divided by 3. As the 1 is not divisible by 3 it is written as the
7 remainder.

8 3 x 2 = 6 and 3 x 3 = 9.

9 So, 7 and 8 which is between 6 and 9 are not divisible (indivisible).

10 The rule is to write these indivisible numbers as remainders.

11 Let's practice together.

12 Let's try 55÷6, 47÷6, and 33÷6.

13 55÷6 = 9 remainder 1, 47÷6 = 7 remainder 5, 33÷6 = 5 remainder 3?

14 We can check this answer to see if it is correct.

15 To verify we multiply the divisor x the answer then add the remainder.

中学年

# 割り算 3

## 筆算

先生

1 掛け算と同じように、割り算にも筆算があります。
計算式だけ見ると、6×2＝12、6÷2＝3、掛算マーク、割り算マークが違うだけですが、
2 筆算になると書き方がかなり違います。

```
   1
3)48
  3↓
  18
```

3 では、黒板を使って筆算の説明をしていきます。
4 48÷3 の場合です。
「割る数」を書き、その横に「)」のマークを付け、「割られる数」をその横に書いて、
5 「割られる数」の上に定規で線を引きます。
8 「割られる数」の上の線の上に答えを書きますから、線の上は必ず一行あけて、つまり、
割り算の筆算は一行を空けてから書き出します。

掛算は一の位から計算しましたが、割り算では、「割られる数」の一番大きい位から、
9 今回の計算だと、十の位が大きいですから、十の位から計算していきます。

10 「割られる数」の 10 の位の数字、この式では 4 ですが、この数字に「割る数」の数字、
この式では 3 という数字がいくつ入るかを線の上の 4 の上に一つしか入りませんから
11 1 と書いて、4 の数字の下に 3 と書きます。

この 3 という数字は、「割る数」の 3 に、4 の上に書いた数を掛けた数、つまり、3×1 の
12 答えです。
3 の下に定規で線を引き、4 から 3 を引いた差を十の位の下に書いて、その横に
13 「割られる数」の一の位の数、この式では 8 ですから、8 を下ろして書きます。
14 つまり今度は 18 という数字を「割られる数」として計算しますということになります。
18 を 3 で割ると答えは 6 ですから、その 6 を 1 の位に書いて、
15 「割る数」の 3 に、8 の上に書いた 6 を掛けた 18 を書きます。
上の 18 から下の 18 を引いた答えを書きます。18-18＝0
16 ですから、0 と書きます。
17 線を引いて 0 と書くことで、割り切れたことを示します。
18 余りの計算では、線の下に余る数字を書きます。

```
  16
3)48
  3↓
  18
  18
   0
```

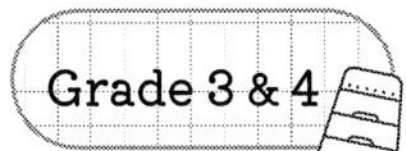


# Division

## How to do Division

**Teacher**

1 Similarly to long multiplication, we will learn long division.

2 Looking at just the formulas, 6 x 2 = 12, 6 ÷ 2 = 3, only the multiplication and division marks are different, but when we do long division the writing style is quite different.

```
   1
3) 48
   3↓
   18
```

3 Now, let me explain using the blackboard.

4 Let's use 48 ÷ 3 as an example.

5 Write the "divisor," 3 then a) mark. Next to it, write the "dividend", and draw a line with a ruler over the "dividend.

6 Since the answer is written on the line above the "dividend," be sure to leave the space.

9 In multiplication, we calculated from the ones place, but in division, we start from the highest place of the "dividend," and in this calculation, the tenth place is the largest, so we start from the tenth place.

10 Above the number in the tens place of the "dividend" which in this formula is 4, we write 1.

11 You can fit 3 into 4 only 1 time, right? Next, we write the number 3 under the number 4.

12 This 3 is the answer when you multiply the divisor 3 x the quotient 1 which is written above the number 4.

13 Draw a line with a ruler under 3, write the difference of 4 minus 3 under the tens place, and next to it, write down the number of the first place of the dividend which in this formula is 8, so 8 is written down. In other words, the number 18 is now the "dividend".

14 So, we will repeat this calculation using the new dividend.

15 When we divide 18 by 3 the answer is 6, so write that 6 in the first place, write 18, which is thedivisor, the number 3 , multiplied by 6 written above the 8 in 48.

16 Subtract the lower 18 from the upper 18 and write the answer : 18-18 = 0 Therefore, it is written as 0.

17 Draw a line and write 0 to indicate that it is divisible.

18 If there was a remainder, we would write the number below the line.

```
   16
3) 48
   3↓
   18
   18
    0
```

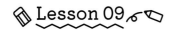

中学年

## 割り算 3

### あまりのある筆算

先生

48÷3＝16 の筆算は分かりましたね。あまりのある筆算の場合の書き方を学習して
1 おきましょう。
2 分かりやすいように 49÷3 を見ましょう。
「割られる数」の十の位の数字 4 に「割る数」の数字 3 がいくつ入るかを、線の上の 4 の
上に書いて、4 の数字の下に 3、その下に差し引いた 1、これに一桁の数字の 9 を下ろ
3 してきて、19 と書き、19 の上に定規を使って線を引きます。

19 を 3 で割ると、3 に何も掛けても 19 にはなりませんから、答えが 19 に近くて 3 で
割り切れる数字は 18 で、割ると答えは 6 ですから、その 6 を一の位に書いて、
「割る数」の 3 に 9 の上に書いた 6 を掛けた 18 と書き、19 から 18 を引いた余りの 1 を
4 線を引いて書きます。

これで、この計算は、答えが 16 あまり 1 とできたら、16 の横に点を 3 つ打って 1 と
書きます。
5 筆算が終わったら、問題の計算式 49÷3 に、49÷3＝16 あまり 1 と書きます。

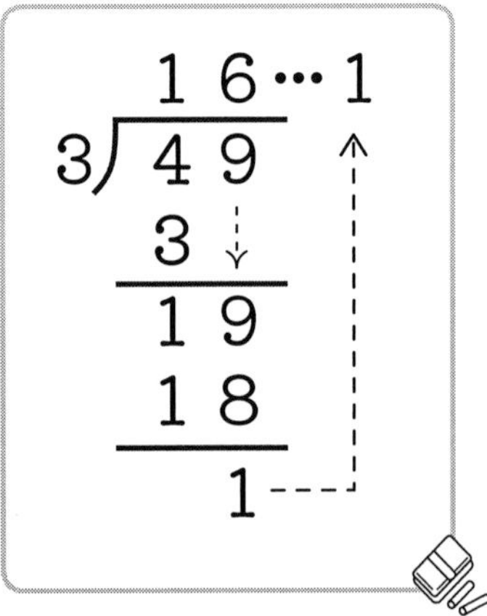

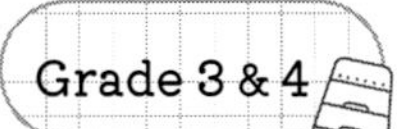

Grade 3 & 4

# Division

## How to do Division with Remainders

Teacher

So we have gone through how to do long division using the formula 48 ÷ 3 = 16.
1 Next, we will practice long divisions with a remainder.
2 To make it easier for you to understand, let's look at 49 divided by 3.
First think about how many of the divisor which is 3 would fit into the number 4 in the tens
3 place of the dividend and write the answer above the 4. The answer is 1, right?

Now let's divide 19 by 3. We can see that multiplying 3 by anything does not equal 19, so
the number whose answer is close to 19 and divisible by 3 is 18, and when divided, the answer
is 6, so we write that 6 in the first place. Next write 18 under the 19, which is the "divisor,"
4 3 multiplied by 6 written above the 9, and draw a line under the 18. 19 minus the 18 =1.

Now, for this calculation, to show the remainder, we write the answer as 16, write three dots
5 next to the 16 and then write 1.

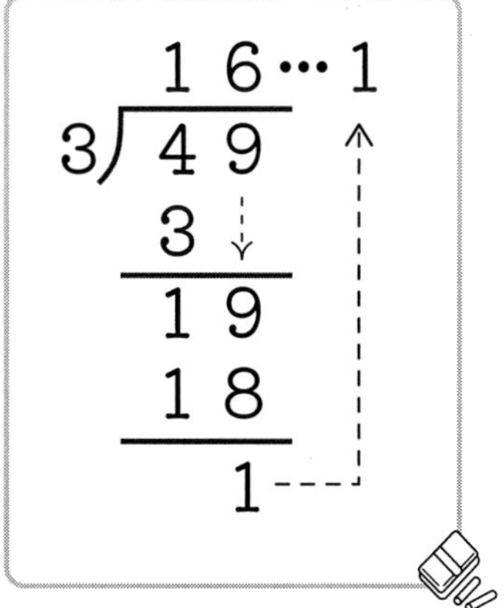

中学年

## 小数点

たし算/引き算

先生

0, 1, 2, 3 などの数字を整数といい、その中で、1、2、3 等の数字を自然数といいます。

整数とか、自然数という呼び方をしているのは、それ以外の呼び方の数字があるからです。例えば、1 ㎝は 10 ㎜ですね。ということは、1 ㎜は分数で表すと 1 ㎝の 1/10 ということです。これを 0.1 ㎝とも表すことができ、この表し方を少数、0 の後の点を小数点といいます。

1/10 が 0.1、1/100 が 0.01 と表し、小数点以降の 0 の数が多いほど小さくなっていきます。0 の数が多いほど大きな数字となる自然数とは逆になりますから、覚えておきましょう。

1 ㎝は 10mm、1 ㎝の半分は 5mm です。半分を分数で表すと 1/2 ですね。ですから、1/2 は少数でいうと 0.5 となり、5 ㎜は 0.5 ㎝と表します。
また、この数の表し方を使うと、1m は 100 ㎝という表し方を 1 ㎝は 0.01m と逆を言うことができます。同様に、1mm は、0.001m となります。
少数点を使った数の表し方は分かりましたね。

先生

少数のある足し算、引き算を勉強します。
2.3+1.2 の足し算をしてみましょう。筆算です。
「足される数」を上にその下に「足す数」を書きます。

```
   2.3
+  1.2
------
   3.5
```

「足す数」の横にこの計算が足し算であることを表すため、+ マークを書き、定規で下線を引きます。
数字は小数点で揃えます。小数点のある数の計算をするときはいつも一緒です。
小数点のある数と小数点のない数を足し算、あるいは引き算するときは、小数点のない数に小数点以下の数字を「.0」で加えると、計算ミスを防ぐことができます。
「足さたれる数」の小数点以下と「足す数」の小数点以下を足します。
ここでは、0.3 + 0.2 で 0.5 です。
これに、整数の 2 と 1 を足して、3 ですから答えは 3.5 です。
5.6 + 2.7 の足し算の筆算をしてみましょう。
小数点以下の 0.6 と 0.7 を足すと 1.3 になりますから、1.3 と書き、その下に整数の 5 と 2 を書き揃えます。
1 と 5 と 2 がそろっていて、0.3 の下は何も書かないか、0 を加えます。

```
   5.6
+  1.2
------
   1.3
   5(.0)
   2(.0)
------
   8.3
```

1 + 5 + 2 で 8 ですから、答えは 8.3 となります。

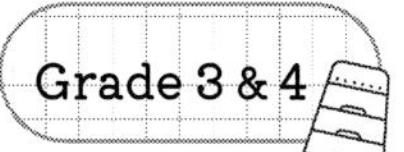


# Decimals

## Addition / Subtraction

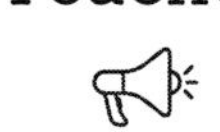


1 Numbers such as 0, 1, 2, 3, etc. are called integers, and numbers such as 1, 2, 3, etc. are called
natural numbers.
2 We call them integers or natural numbers to differentiate them from other numbers.
For example, 1cm is 10mm. This means that 1mm is 1/10 of 1cm when expressed as a fraction.
This can also be expressed as 0.1cm. This expression is called a decimal number and the point
3 after 0 is called a decimal point.

Remember that 1/10 is represented as 0.1 and 1/100 as 0.01, and the more zeros after the
4 decimal point, the smaller the number. This is the opposite of natural numbers where the
more zeros, the larger the number.
1cm is 10mm and half of 1cm is 5mm. If we express half in fractions, it is 1/2.
5 Therefore, 1/2 is 0.5 and 5mm can be expressed as 0.5 cm.
Also, using this way of expressing numbers, we can reverse the expressions. For example, to say
6 that 1 meter is 100 cm is to say 1cm is 0.01 m. Similarly, 1mm is 0.001m.
7 Now we know how to express numbers using the decimal point.

```
  2.3
+ 1.2
-----
  3.5
```

Teacher

1 Now, we are going to study addition and subtraction with decimals.
2 Let's add 2.3 + 1.2.
The first number should be written on top of the and the second number should be written
3 below it.
Next to the second number write a + symbol to show that this calculation is an addition,
4 and underline it with a ruler.
The Numbers should be aligned with the decimal point. It is always the same when calculating
5 a number with a decimal point.
When adding or subtracting numbers with a decimal point to a number without a decimal point,
6 ".0" prevents calculation errors. First calculate the numbers after the decimal point.
7 In this equation it is 0.3 + 0.2 equals 0.5.
6 Add this to the integers 2 and 1, and the answer is 3, so the answer is 3.5.
7 Now let's try to write the addition of 5.6 + 2.7.
Add 0.6 and 0.7 to the decimal point to get 1.3, so write 1.3, Below that,
7 write the integers 5 and 2 together.
Also are all your numbers aligned vertically? 1 + 5, + 2 should be written
6 under each other. It is optional to add .0 under .3
7 Since 1 + 5 + 2 is 8, the answer is 8.3.

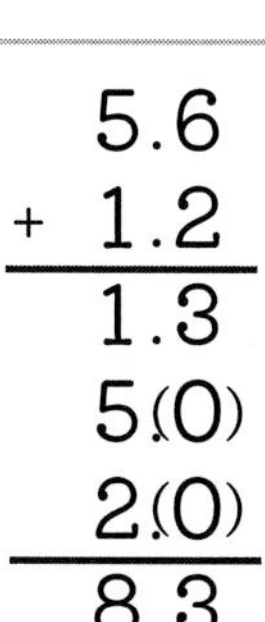

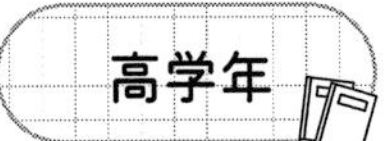


## 小数点

### 掛け算/割り算

先生

1 1は0.1の10倍、0, 01の100倍なんだとわかります。

2 では、3.6は0.1の何倍ですか。22は0. 1の何倍ですか。

3 3.6は0.1の36倍、22には0.1の220倍です。

4 06は01×6、3は0.1×30ですから、3.6は36倍となります。

5 30×0.1＝3、6×0.1＝0.6だから、36×0. 1 ＝3.6です。

6 小数点以下の数字を掛けると、小数点以下の桁数分、掛けられた数が小さくなります。

7 では、3.6÷0.1はいくらになりますか。

8 3.6÷1 ＝3.6。これは分かりますね。3.6÷10は?

9 10で割ると割われる数字が一桁小さくなりますね。

10 10倍で割ると1桁小さくなるので、逆に10分の1で割ると1桁大きくなります。

11 だから、0, 01で割ると2桁大きくなります。

12 つまり、小数以下の数字が付いている数で割る場合は、割る数の一番小さい桁数と同じ桁数分、割られる数の小数点を右にずらします。

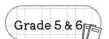

Grade 5 & 6

# Decimals

## Multiplication / Division

Teacher

1 We can see that 1 is 10 times 0.1 and 100 times 0.01.

2 So, what is 0.1 times 3.6? and 0.1 times 22?

3 3.6 is 36 times 0,1 and 22 is 220 times 0.1.

4 0.6 is 0.1 × 6 and 3 is 0.1 × 30, so 3.6 is 36 times.

5 3.0 × 0.1 = 3 and 6 × 0.1 = 0.6, so 36 × 0.1 = 3.6.

6 Multiplying by the decimal point reduces the multiplied number by the number of decimal places.

7 So how much is 3.6 ÷ 0.1?

8 3.6 ÷ 1 = 3.6. You understand this, right? 3.6 divided by 10 is how much?

9 If you divide by 10, the decimal place will move one space to the left and the number you are dividing will be one digit smaller.

10 Dividing by 10 makes it one digit smaller, and conversely, dividing by one-tenth the decimal place will move one space to the right and makes the result one digit larger.

11 So, dividing by 0.01 makes the results two digits larger.

12 In other words, when dividing by a number with a decimal point, we move the decimal place by the same number of digits as in the divisor.

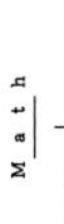

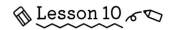

## 小数点 2

掛け算/割り算

先生

1 つまり、小数点のある掛け算は、掛けられる数に、掛ける数の小数点分左にずらします。

2 小数点のある割り算の場合は右にずらします。

計算中は小数点のことは気にしないで、答えが出た時に、小数点を掛ける数分左にずら
3 したり、右にずらしたりします。

3.00 1×0.01 なら、掛けられる数である 3.001 に、かける数が小数点 2 桁ですから、小数点の位置を左に二つずらし、0.03001、3.001÷0.01 なら、割られる数である 3.001
4 の小数点の位置を右に二つずらし、300.1 になるわけです。

5 3.11×2.1 のひっ算をしてみましょう。

```
     3.1 1
×      2.1
----------
     3 1 1
   6 2 2 0
----------
   6 5 3 1

A  6.5 3 1
```

掛ける数の小数点以下の桁数は 2 ですが 掛ける数の小数点以下に 1 桁ありますから、
6 小数点以下の桁数は 3 桁です。

7 だから、6531 の右から 3 つ目の 6 と 5 の間に小数点が来ます。

後で小数点以下の桁数を数えますから、ひっ算の時は桁数を合わせて行う必要は
8 ありません。

9 4.55÷3.5 のひっ算をしてみましょう。

```
         1
3.5)4.5 5
    3.5
    1.0 5
```

```
        1 3
3.5)4.5 5
    3.5
    1.0 5
    1.0 5
        0

A  1.3
```

10 割る数の小数点が 1 桁なので、割られる数の小数点右に一つ ずれます。

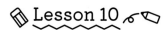

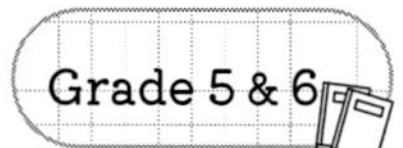


## Decimals

### Multiplication / Division

Teacher

That is, when we multiply, we must move the decimal point to the left by the number of
1 decimal digits in the numbers being multiplied.
2 For division with a decimal point, shift the decimal point to the right.
During the calculation, do not worry about the decimal point; when you get the answer,
3 shift the decimal point to the left or to the right depending on the situation.
Let's look at 3.001 × 0.01, the number to be multiplied, 3.001, has two decimal places,
so the decimal point is shifted two places to the left, 0.03001, and if 3.001 divided by 0.01,
4 the number to be divided, 3.001, is shifted two places to the right, 300.1.
5 Let's write out the calculation of 3.11 × 2.1.

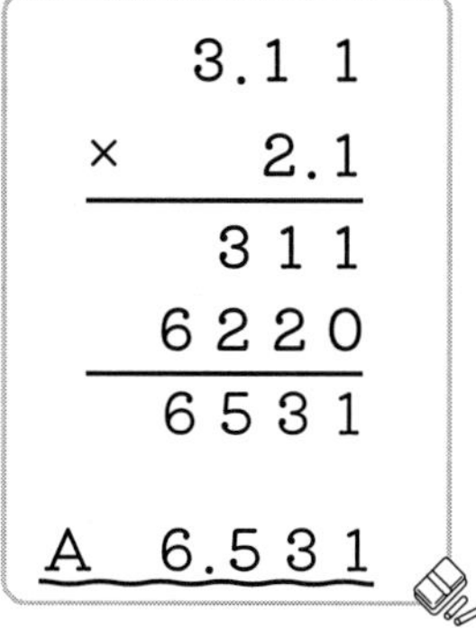


The number of decimal places of the number to be multiplied and the multiplier has one
6 decimal point. the number of decimal places in the final answer is 3.
7 So, the decimal point comes in between the 6 and 5 from the right of 6531.
We will count the number of decimal places later, so there is no need to align the number of
8 digits calculating on paper.

9 Let's do the calculation on paper 4.55 ÷ 3.5

```
        1
3.5) 4.5 5
     3.5
     1.0 5
```

```
       1 3
3.5) 4.5 5
     3.5
     1.0 5
     1.0 5
         0

A  1.3
```

Since the decimal point of the number to be divided has one decimal place, the answer is
10 shifted one place to the right of the decimal point of the number to be divided.

Math

高学年

# 整数の性質

## 公倍数

先生

少数、分数といった数の計算を少しお休みして、数字の性質を学習しましょう。

1 数字には偶数と奇数があります。

2 整数の中で、2で割り切れる数を偶数、割り切れない数を奇数といいます。

3 数の大きさは関係ありません。4でも2732でも2で割り切れれば偶数です。

4 次に、公倍数という数字です。

5 公倍数とは、二つの数字のどちらの倍数でもあるという数字です。

6 例えば、5の倍数は5、10、15, 20となります。

7 九九ですぐにわかりますね。

8 4の倍数は、4、8、16、20ですね。5と4で共通する倍数は20です。

9 この20が5と4の公倍数となるわけです。

10 次の公倍数は40、60、80ですね。その中で一番小さい公倍数を最小公倍数といい、4と5の場合は、20となるわけです。

11 これは2つの数字の公倍数でしたが、3つでも4つでも同じです。

12 では、4、5、6の公倍数を考えてみましょう。

13 6の倍数は6,12, 18,24, 30, 36, 42, 48, 54, 60です。

14 そのうち5との公倍数は、5の倍数は一桁が5か0なので、30と60です。そしてこれに4の倍数がないかをみると60が4×15で倍数と分かるので、4、5、6の最小公倍数は60と分かります。

15 最小公倍数が60、では次の公倍数はいくつですか。

16 120で、次は180です。60が公倍数なので、その2倍、3倍も公倍数です。

17 素数という数字があります。

18 これ以上割り切れないという数字です。

19 例えば1, 2, 3はもう割り切れませんね。4は2で割れますね。5は割り切れない。6は3と2で割れます。7は割り切れません。8は2で割れ、9は3で割れ、10は2と5で割れます。

20 この割れない数字、1, 2, 3, 5, 7などが素数です。

21 素数はたくさんあります。他にありますか。

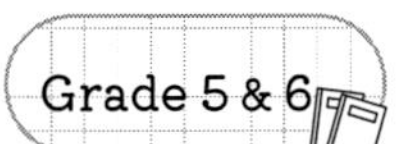

# Lesson 11

算数

Mathematics

Grade 5 & 6

## Properties of Integers Commutative 1

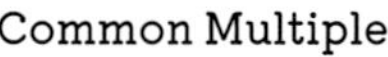

### Common Multiple

Teacher

Let's take a short break from calculating numbers such as decimals and fractions to study
1 the properties of numbers.

Among integers, numbers that are divisible by 2 are called even numbers, and numbers
2 that are not divisible by 2 are called odd numbers.

3 The size of the number does not matter; whether it is 4 or 2732, if it is divisible by 2, it is even.

4 Next, there is a number called a common multiple.

5 A common multiple is a number that is a multiple of either of two numbers.

6 For example, multiples of 5 are 5, 10, 15, and 20.

7 You can easily see this with 99 from the <u>multiplication table</u>.

8 The multiples of 4 are 4, 8, 16, and 20. the common multiples for 5 and 4 is 20.

9 So, this 20 is the common multiple of 5 and 4.

The next common multiples are 40, 60, and 80. The smallest common multiple is called
10 the least common multiple, and in the case of 4 and 5, it is 20.

11 This was the common multiple of two numbers, but it is the same for three or four.

12 Now let's consider the common multiples of 4, 5, and 6.

13 The multiples of 6 are 6, 12, 18, 24, 30, 36, 42, 48, 54, and 60.

Of these, the common multiples of 5 are 30 and 60, since the first digit of a multiple of 5 is
either 5 or 0. And if we look for a multiple of 4 in this, we find that 60 is a multiple of $4 \times 15$,
14 so we know that the least common multiple of 4, 5, and 6 is 60.

15 The least common multiple is 60, then what is the next common multiple?

120, and the next is 180. 60 is the common multiple, so doubles and triples of that are also
16 common multiples.

17 There is a number called a prime number.

18 A prime number is a number that is not divisible by any other number.

For example, 1, 2, and 3 are no longer divisible; 4 is divisible by 2; 5 is not divisible; 6 is divisible
19 by 3 and 2; 7 is not divisible; 8 is divisible by 2; 9 is divisible by 3; and 10 is divisible by 2 and 5.

20 These undividable numbers, 1, 2, 3, 5, 7, etc., are prime numbers.

21 There are many prime numbers. Can you think of any other?

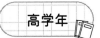

高学年

# 整数の性質

公約数

先生

1 倍数を学習しましたね。では、次に約数と数字を学習します。
2 ある整数をわり切ることができる整数をある数の約数といいます。
3 例えば、6 の約数は 1、2、3、6 の 4 つで、どの数も 6 をわり切ることができます。
4 同じように考えると、30 の約数は、1、2、3、5、6、10、15、30 の 8 つです。
5 どの数も 30 をわり切ることができます。
約数には必ずペアとなる相手がいるという性質を利用して、2 つ 1 組で求めていくと
6 より正確に求めることができます。
7 30 の約数は、かけて 30 になる組み合わせを 1×30 から順に求めていきます。
8 黒板に書きだしますよ。

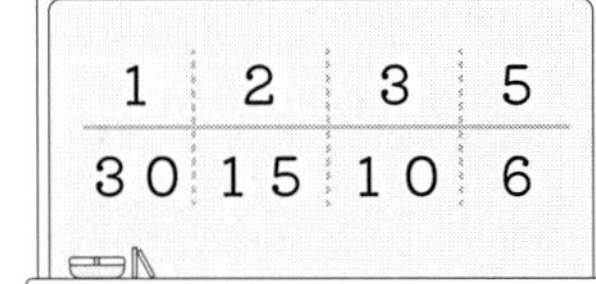

| 1 | 2 | 3 | 5 |
|---|---|---|---|
| 30 | 15 | 10 | 6 |

9 上下かけ合わせて 30 になり、書き出した数字がすべて 30 の約数です。
10 45 の約数はどうでしょう。

| 1 | 3 | 5 |
|---|---|---|
| 45 | 15 | 9 |

11 ですね。
よって、30 の約数は、1、2、3、5、6、10、15、30
12 45 の約数は、1、3、5、9、15、45　となります。
13 よって、公約数は、共通の約数だから 1、3、5、15 となります。
14 最大公約数は、公約数の中で最も大きい約数だから 15 です。

先生

1 大公約数を求める方法に連除法という方法があります。
2 どちらでも割ることのできる数（1 以外）を見つけて、次々に割っていく方法です。
3 30 と 45 でやってみます。まず、2 つの数字を並べます。

)30　45

4 次に、2 つの数字を素数で割っていきます。
割った素数の掛算した数が最大公約数です。

3)30　45
5)10　15
　　2　3

5 3×5＝15 ですから、答えは 15 です。

6 28、32、40 の 3 つの数字でやってみましょう。

)28　32　40

2)28　32　40
　　14　16　20

2)28　32　40
2)14　16　20
　　7　8　10

7 割った素数の掛算した数が最大公約数ですから、2×2＝4 で、答えは 4 です。

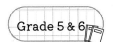

Grade 5 & 6

## Properties of Integers Commutative 2

### Common divisors

Teacher

1 You have learned about multiples. Now we will learn about divisors and numbers.
2 An integer that can divide another integer is called the divisor of the number.
3 For example, there are four divisors of 6: 1, 2, 3, and 6. Any of these four numbers can divide 6.
4 In the same way, there are eight divisors of 30: 1, 2, 3, 5, 6, 10, 15, and 30.
5 Any of these eight numbers can divide 30.
Using the property that divisors always have a pair of counterparts; it is possible to find them
6 more accurately by finding them in pairs.
7 For the divisors of 30, we will find the combinations that multiply to 30, starting with 1 × 30.
8 I will write them down on the blackboard.

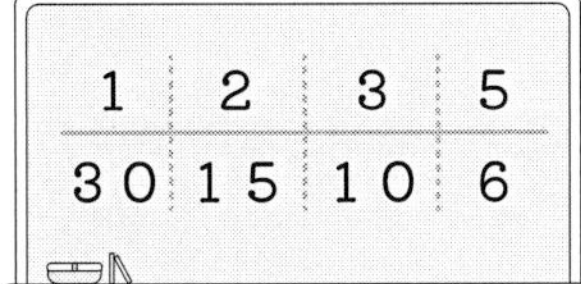

| 1 | 2 | 3 | 5 |
|---|---|---|---|
| 30 | 15 | 10 | 6 |

9 Multiply up and down to get 30, and all the numbers written out are divisors of 30.
10 What about the divisors of 45?

| 1 | 3 | 5 |
|---|---|---|
| 45 | 15 | 9 |

11 Yes
The divisors of 30 are 1, 2, 3, 5, 6, 10, 15, 30,
12 the divisors of 45 are 1, 3, 5, 9, 15, and 45.
13 Therefore, the common divisors are 1, 3, 5, and 15.
14 The greatest common divisor is 15 because it is the largest divisor among the common divisors.

Teacher

1 There is a method of finding the greatest common divisor called the prime factorization.
In this method, you find the divisors of a given number by dividing them completely and
repeating the process until no other divisors can be found. All the answers you get will also
2 be prime numbers. (other than 1)
3 Let's try this with 30 and 45. First, put the two numbers together.
Next, the two numbers are divided by the smallest prime number,
4 larger than 1, that gives an integer – in this case, 3.

```
 ) 30  45

3) 30  45
5) 10  15
    2   3
```

To find the greatest common divisors, we multiply the two prime numbers we used, 3 and 5.
5 3 × 5 = 15, so our greatest common divisor is 15 so the answer is 15.
6 Let's try again but this time it with three numbers: 28, 32, and 40.

```
 ) 28  32  40     2) 28  32  40     2) 28  32  40
                     14  16  20     2) 14  16  20
                                        7   8  10
```

Since the greatest common divisor is obtained by multiplying the prime numbers we used in
7 the division, the greatest common divisor, 2 x 2 = 4, the answer is 4.

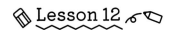

高学年

# 分数

## たし算

先生

1 整数、小数、分数を学習しました。
2 小数や分数の使い方を広げていきます。
これまで、割り切れる数字を学習してきました。そして割り切れないという場合、
3 余りとして書き出すということを学習しました。
4 例えば、10÷３＝３あまり１と表しました。
5 同じ計算式でもこれを分数で表すこともできます。１０÷３＝10/3と書きます。
線より下が分母、線より上が分子、これはすでに知っていますね。１０/3だと線より上
6 の数字が大きくてぐらぐらの感じです。これを仮分数といいます。

7 グラグラ感があるので、こういう分数は、３と１/3と表します。

この３というのは、分子の10は３+３+3+１と分けられ、3/3+3/3+３/3+１/3とわけて
あらわすことができ、分母と分子が同じ数字は１と同じですから、
8 １+1+１+１/3=3+１/3となります。

9 この分数を帯分数といいます。

逆に、１/3は1÷３と式をもとにもどすことができますし、3+１/3は、帯分数を元の
10 仮分数に戻して、10÷３と、式を戻すことができます。

分数同士の四則計算もできますから、学習しましょう。

11

12 1/4+1/4＝2/4です。

13 分母が同じなら $\frac{1}{4}+\frac{1}{4}=2$ となり、

14 分子の２と分母の４は、２が公約数なので、 $\frac{\cancel{2}}{\cancel{4}} \dashrightarrow \frac{1}{2}$ となります。

分数の加減算をする場合分母を合わせる、答えは公約数で約分するという規則を
15 覚えてください。分母を合わせることを通分といいます。

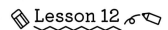

Grade 5 & 6

# Fractions

## Addition

Teacher

1 So far, we have studied integers, decimals, and fractions.
2 We will now expand on the use of decimals and fractions.
So far, we have studied numbers that are divisible. We have also learned that when a number
3 is not divisible, it is written down as the remainder.
4 For example, 10 ÷ 3 = 3 remainder 1.
5 The same formula can be expressed as a fraction, writing 10 divided by 3 = 10/3.
You already know that the denominator is below the line and the numerator is above the line, right?
When you see the number10/3, it might look strange because the numerator is larger than the
6 denominator. This is called an improper fraction.
7 To make it seem less strange, these fractions are expressed as 3 and 1/3.

This is based on the fact that the numerator, 10, can be divided into3+3+3+1 so the fraction
can be rewritten as 3/3+3/3+3/3+3/3+1/3 when the denominator is added. Since we know that
if the numerator and the denominator are the same number it is equal to one, we can rewrite
8 the equation as 1+1+1+1/3=3+1/3.
9 This fraction is called a mixed fraction.

Conversely, 1/3 can be restored to the original equation as 1 divided by 3, and 3+1/3 can be
restored to the equation as 10 divided by 3 by changing the mixed fraction back to the original
10 improper fraction.

You can also do four arithmetic operations, addition, subtraction, division, and multiplication
11 between fractions, so let's learn them.
12 Let's look at 1/4 + 1/4 = 2/4.

13 If the denominators are the same, then we can easily add the numerators $\frac{1}{4} + \frac{1}{4} = 2$

14 The numerator is 2, and denominator is 4, so $\frac{\cancel{2}}{\cancel{4}}$ is $\frac{1}{2}$

Remember the rule that when adding or subtracting fractions, the denominators must be
the same and the answer must be divisible by the common divisor. Finding the common
15 denominators is called reducing fractions to a common denominator.

高学年

## 分数 2

掛け算/割り算

先生

1 今日からは、分数の掛け算、割り算を学習します。

2 4×2/9 を考えてみましょう。

3 掛けられる数が整数、掛ける数が分数です。

このような場合は、整数を分数にしてしまいます。

4 4 を 4/1 と置き換えると、4/1×2/9 を計算することになります。

分数の掛け算というと難しく感じますが、4 は、4/1 と置きかえられるとわかると簡単に

5 わかるようになります。

6 4×3 はいくらですか。簡単ですね。12 です。

7 これを分数に置き換えたとすると、4/1×3/1 ですね。

8 4/1 の分子は 4、分母は 1、3/1 の分子は 3、分母は 1 です。

$$\frac{4\times3}{1\times1}$$

ですから、4×3＝4/1×3/1 つまり分子×分子、分母×分母で同じ数になりますから、

9 計算式を書いて計算します。

10 分数同士の計算も同じです。5/9×3/4＝です。

$$\frac{5\times3}{9\times4}=\frac{15}{36}$$

この約分は答えを一度出してから行ってもいいのですが、

11 計算の途中でやった方が早いですね。 $\frac{5\times\cancel{3}^{1}}{\cancel{9}_{3}\times4}=\frac{5}{12}$ です。

先生

では、分数の割り算を考えてみましょう。分数の割り算というと難しく聞こえますが、

1 半分のリンゴを二人で分けて食べるとしたら一人は何分の 1 食べますかという問題ですね。

2 もともとが 1/2 ですね。

3 それを二人つまり半分にしますから、1/2÷2＝1/4 ですね。割る数の 2 は、2/1 です。

1/2 を 2 で割るということは、分母が 2×2＝4 になることですから、割る数の分子と

4 分母を反対にして掛算にするとよいことがわかります。

$$\frac{1}{2}\div\frac{2}{1}=\frac{1\times1}{2\times2}=\frac{1}{4}$$

5 という式で置き換えられます。約分は割り算を掛け算の式に置き換えたから行います。

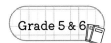

Grade 5 & 6

# Fractions

## Multiplication / Division

Teacher

1 Starting today, you will learn how to multiply and divide fractions.
2 Let's consider 4 × 2/9.
3 The number to be multiplied is a whole number and the multiplier is a fraction.
In such a case, the whole number should be turned into a fraction; replacing 4 with 4/1,
4 we would calculate 4/1 × 2/9.
Multiplying fractions may seem difficult, but it is easy to understand when you realize
5 that 4 can be replaced with 4/1.

$$\frac{4\times3}{1\times1}$$

6 What is 4 × 3 ? That's easy, right? 12.
7 If we were to replace this with a fraction, it would be 4/1 × 3/1.
The numerator of 4/1 is 4 and the denominator is 1;
8 the numerator of 3/1 is 3 and the denominator is 1.
Therefore, 4 × 3 = 4/1 × 3/1, in other words numerator × numerator and
9 denominator × denominator, are the same number, so the formula is written and calculated.
10 The same calculation applies to any fractions: 5/9 × 3/4 = 5/9 × 3/4.

$$\frac{5\times3}{9\times4}=\frac{15}{36}$$

You can do this reduction of the fraction once you have the final answer, but it is faster to do it
11 in the middle of the calculation.

$$\frac{5\times\cancel{3}^{1}}{\cancel{9}_{3}\times4}=\frac{5}{12}$$

Teacher

Now let's consider fraction division. You might think that dividing fractions sounds difficult,
but we often do it, for example if two people share half an apple, what fraction of the apple
1 does one person eat?
2 The original apple is 1/2. Since it is divided into two halves by 1/2 ÷ 2 = 1/4, right?
3 Now, like multiplication, we can turn our divisor into a fraction, so 2 becomes2/1.
We know that we want to divide 1/2 by 2 to get 1/4. Therefore, we can see that the numerator
and denominator of the number to be divided should be multiplied with the number opposite
4 to to each other

$$\frac{1}{2}\div\frac{2}{1}=\frac{1\times1}{2\times2}=\frac{1}{4}$$

In short, we are not really dividing but reversing the numerator and the denomination
5 and multiplying.

高学年

# 文字式

先生

1 文字式の文字として利用されている文字の代表的なものがxとyです。
2 皆さんも知っているように、英語には大文字と小文字がありますね。
3 小文字のxyだけでなく、大文字のXとYも代表的な文字です。
計算式を文字で表し、その文字がx、yなどとなりますから、面積を求める公式でも
三角形ならx×y＝面積、正方形ならx×y＝面積と表現でき、縦とか高さとか底辺と
4 いったそれまで別々に使っていた表現方法が簡単になります。

今、右辺は面積と漢字で書いていますが、当然この面積という言葉も、文字で表すこと
5 ができます。
ただ、すべてを文字で表すととても難しく感じるので、小学6年生では一つの式の中に
6 文字を二つまで使って学習することになっています。

中学生になると、文字の数が増えたり、文字を使った複雑な計算式を学習したりします。
今は、数字や漢字を使って学習してきた計算式をxとyを使って表現することに
7 慣れてください。

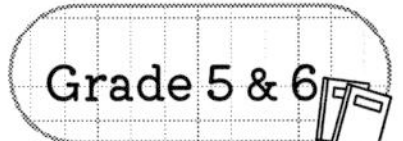


# Letter Expressions

Teacher

1 The typical letters that are used literal formulas by students around the world are x and y.
2 As you all know, the English language has upper and lower-case letters.
3 The lowercase letter x y as well as the uppercase letters X and Y are commonly used.
Since the formula is expressed in letters and the letters are x, y, etc., the formula for finding
area can also be expressed as X × Y÷2 = area for a triangle or X × Y = area for a square,
4 making it easier than the previous expressions such as length, height, and base.

The right side is now written in Chinese characters as “area,” but naturally, the word “area” can
5 also be expressed in English letters.
However, since it seems very difficult to represent everything in letters, sixth graders are required
6 to learn to use up to two letters in a single equation.

In junior high school, you will learn more complex formulas using more letters and more uses of
7 letters. For now, please get used to using x and y to express the formulas you have been learning.

高学年

# 比

先生

1 分数を使ったり、100 分率を使ったり割合という学習をしました。
割合では、太郎君が 200 円、花子さんが 300 円を持っていると、太郎君は花子さんの
2 2/3 の金額をもっているとか、花子さんは太郎君の 1.5 倍の金額を持っているという
答えでした。
これから学習するのは、割合の一つなのですが、これまでとは少し違う比較です。
3 それが比です。
これまで学習した割合は、太郎君は花子さんの何分の 1 とか何倍とかですが、比では、
4 二つ以上の大きさを何対何で表現します。
例えば、太郎君と花子さんの所持金の金額は、200 円と 300 円ですね。このとき、
太郎君と花子さんの持っている所持金は 200 :300 と書いて 200 対 300、最大公約数は
5 100 なので 2 :3 と書いて 2 対 3 になると表現します。

6 この表現が比です。

特に、比は同じ数を掛けても、同じ数で割っても等しい関係だということを覚えておきます。
7 これは分数の分子と分母に同じ数を掛けても割合が同じであることと同じ関係にあります。

つまり、2 ;3 の両方に 2 を掛けた 4 :6 も比は 2 :3 ですし、20 :30 の両方を 5 で割った
8 4 :6 も比は最大公約数で割った 2 :3 で同じです。
9 これが分かっていると、比のどちらかが分からない場合の数を簡単に求めることができます。

文字式で、$4:x=20:30$ の場合、$x$ は左辺の 4 と右辺の 20 が 5 倍、1/5 の関係ですから、
10 右辺の 30 の 1/5 の 6 が $x$ の値だと分かります。
同じように 3 つの比で二つの数字を求める場合も、$12:x:y=2:3:4$ で左辺の 12 が
11 右辺の 2 の 6 倍と分かるので、$x$ は 3 の 6 倍、$y$ は 4 の 6 倍で、12 :18 :24 となります。
この二つ以上の数の関係を比という割合で表現する方法はこれからの算数や中学校の数学
12 においてとても重要な表現です。
13 日常生活でもこの比という割合はよく使います。

14 地図には縮尺と書いてあって 1 :1000 とか 1 :500 と書いてあります。

15 地図の距離を定規で測ってその縮尺を掛けると実際の距離が出ます。

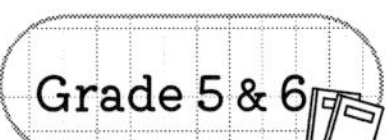


# Ratios

Teacher

1 In our study of fractions, we have used percentages, and proportions.
In terms of proportions, if Taro-kun has 200 yen and Hanako-san has 300 yen, then we can say
2 that Taro-kun has 2/3rds of Hanako-san's amount, or Hanako-san has 1.5 times as much as Taro.

What we are about to learn is one kind of proportion, but it is a slightly different comparison
3 than the previous ones. It is a ratio.
In ratios, we have learned that Taro-kun's amount is a fraction of Hanako-san's or a
4 multiple of Hanako-san's.
For example, the amounts of money that Taro-kun and Hanako-san have are 200 yen and 300 yen. In this case, we express the amount of money that Taro-kun and Hanako-san have as 200 to 300, written as 200:300. As the greatest common divisor is 100, it becomes a ratio
5 of 2 to 3, written as 2:3.

6 This expression is a ratio.

In particular, remember that ratios are equal whether you multiply by the same number or divide by the same number. This is the same as in a fraction when the numerator and
7 denominator are multiplied by the same number.
In other words, 4:6, which is both 2; 3 multiplied by 2, also has the ratio 2:3, and 4:6, which is
8 both 20:30 divided by 5, has the same ratio, 2:3 divided by the greatest common divisor.
9 Knowing this, it is easy to find the number in cases where one of the ratios is not known.

In the literal equation 4:x = 20:30, 4 on the left side is related to 20 on the right side by a factor
10 of 5 or 1/5. So, we know the value of x is 6, which is 1/5 of 30 on the right side.
Similarly for two numbers in a ratio of three, Since 12:x:y = 2:3:4 and we know that 12 on the
11 left side is 6 times 2 on the right side, x is 6 times 3 and y is 6 times 4, 12:18:24.
This method of expressing the relationship between two or more numbers in terms of a ratio
12 is a very important equation in future arithmetic and junior high school mathematics.
13 We often use this ratio in our daily lives.

14 On the map, there is a scale and it says 1:1000 or 1:500.
You can measure the distance on the map with a ruler and multiply by its scale to get the
15 actual distance.

高学年

# 比

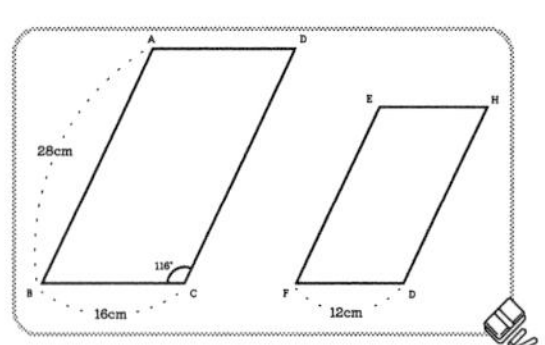

先生

1 比は縮尺で使われます。

2 相似という図形の学習をしました。

3 同じ角度で辺の長さの比が等しいと相似の図形です。

例えば、辺の長さが「6cm、4cm、4cm」の三角形は、辺の長さの比が「3：2：2」
4 ですね。

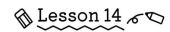

辺の長さが「3cm、2cm、2cm」の三角形も、辺の長さの比が「3：2：2」で、
5 上の三角形と、辺の長さの比は等しいです。

辺の長さが「12cm、8cm、8cm」の三角形も、辺の長さの比は「3：2：2」で、
6 これも上の２つの三角形と、辺の長さの比が等しい図形です。

7 ですから、これらの三角形は相似の関係で縮図と拡大図です。

8 四角形でも立体図形でも、辺の長さの比拡大図、縮図ができます。

9 縮図を使って実際の長さを求めてみましょう。

10 教科書の 97 ページを開いてください。そこに木を見上げて立っている図がありますね。

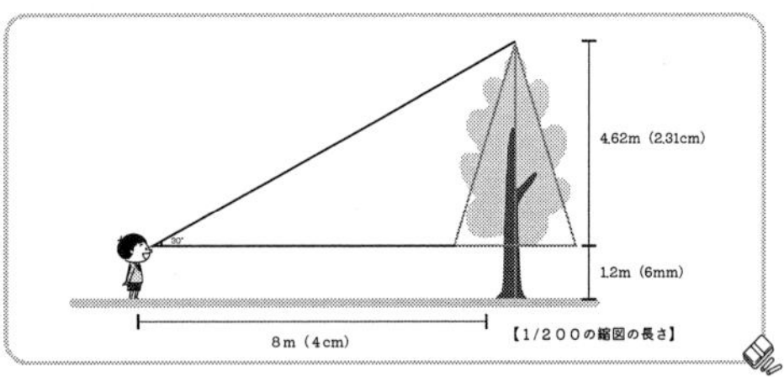


木から８m のところに立って木を見上げた角度をはかったら、30°でした。
11 目の高さは 1.2m です。縮図を利用して、木の実際の高さを求めましょう。

12 縮図は２００分の１です。

1/200 の縮図から目の高さから木の天辺までの高さは 2.31cm で表され、
13 実際の長さは、2.31cm×200＝462cm＝4.62m です。

14 これに、目の高さが 1.2m なので、実際の木の高さは 4.62＋1.2＝5.82（m）となります。

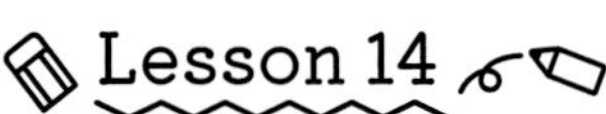




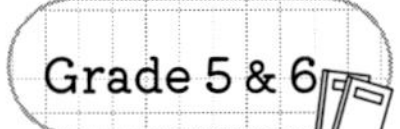


# Ratios

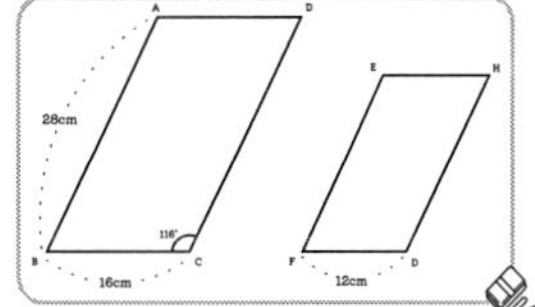

Teacher

1 Ratios are used in a reduced scale.
2 We've learned about shapes of similarity before.
Similarity is a figure in which the corresponding angles are equal in size and the ratio of
3 the lengths of the corresponding sides is equal.
4 For example, a triangle with side lengths of「6 cm, 4 cm, and 4 cm」has a side length ratio「3:2:2」.

Triangles with side lengths of「3 cm, 2 cm, 2 cm」also have side length ratios of「3:2:2」and
5 the ratio of side lengths is equal to that of the triangle above.

Triangles with side lengths of「12 cm, 8 cm, 8 cm」also have a side length ratio of「3:2:2」.
6 This is also the same as the two triangles above, and the ratio of the lengths of the sides are equal.
Therefore, these triangles are similar with one triangle being an enlargement and the other
7 a reduction of each other.
Ratio enlargement and reduction of side lengths can be done for both quadrilaterals and
8 three-dimensional figures.

9 Let's find the actual lengths using a reduced figure.
Open your textbook to page 97. There you can see a picture of a person standing and
10 looking up at a tree.

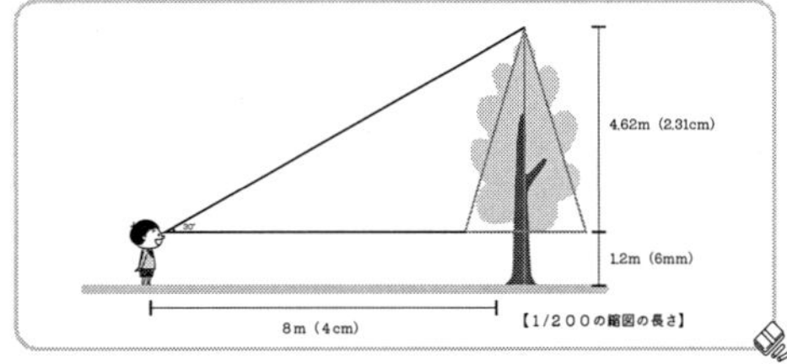


If you stand 8 meters from the tree and measure the angle from your eyeline to the top of
the tree, it is 30°.The height from the ground to your eyes is 1.2m. Let's use this
11 information to find the actual height of the tree.
12 The ratio for this diagram is 1:200.

The height of the tree from the person's eyeline to the top of the tree is 2.31cm. Knowing that
13 a scale of 1:200, we can calculate the actual length: 2.31cm × 200 = 462cm = 4.62m.
Then because the length between the ground and the person's eyeline is 1.2 m, the actual
14 tree is 4.62 + 1.2 = 5.82 (m).

高学年

# 速さ

先生

車に乗って道路を走っている時、道路の脇にこんな標識が
1 立っていることを見たことがありますね。

2 この道路は時速 50 ㎞が制限速度ですという意味です。
時速 50 ㎞というのは、1 時間に 50 ㎞走る速さ
3 という意味です。

4 他の速さを知っていますか。
5 音速と光速があります。
6 音速とは 1 秒間に音が伝わる距離を元に速さを測り、飛行機の速さに使います。

光速とは光の進む距離を元に速さを測り、光速という言い方よりも光年と言って、
光が 1 年間に進む距離をもとに、宇宙空間の惑星と惑星の間の距離を示すときに 3 光年
7 とか使います。

音速はマッハという単位を使い、環境の状況によりますが、概ね 1 秒間に 298m 進む
速さです。マッハ 1 以上のスピードというのは音が伝わる速さ以上に速いスピードで
8 飛んでいることになります。

9 教科書の問題を解いてみましょう。
問題は、「分速 84m で歩くと家から学校まで 25 分 46 秒、分速 90m で歩くと学校から
駅まで 24 分 4 秒かかります。家から学校までと学校から駅までの道のりはどちらが
10 何m長いですか」ですね。

11 分速 84m は秒速 14m です。25 分 46 秒は 1546 秒です。14m×1546＝21644m です。

12 分速 90m は秒速 15m。24 分 4 秒は 1444 秒です。

13 15m×1444＝21660m です。
14 21660m-21644m＝16m　答え学校から駅までの道のりの方が 1.6m長い。

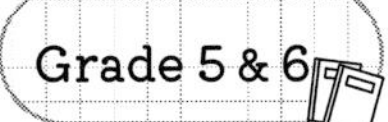


# Speed

Teacher

1 When you are in a car driving down the road, you often see this sign on the side of the road, right?

2 It means that 50 km/h is the speed limit on this road.

3 Which means that if we drive for one hour, we will travel 50km.

4 Do you know other speeds?

5 There is the speed of sound and the speed of light.

6 The speed of sound is measured based on the distance sound travels in one second and is used to measure the speed of airplanes.

7 The speed of light is based on the distance that light travels in one year, and is used to measure the distance between planets in space, for example, 3 light years.

8 The speed of sound uses the unit Mach, and is generally the speed at which sound travels which is 298 meters per second, depending on environmental conditions. Speeds above Mach 1 means that the aircraft is flying faster than the speed at which sound is transmitted.

9 Let’s try another question from the textbook.

10 The question is: 「If you walk at a speed of 84 meters per minute, it takes 25 minutes and 46 seconds to get from home to school and walking at 90 meters per minute, it takes 24 minutes and 4 seconds from school to the station. Which is longer, the walk from home to school or the walk from school to the station?」

11 For part one, the speed of 84 meters per minute is 14 meters per second. 25 minutes and 46 seconds is 1546 seconds. 14m × 1546seconds = 21644m.

12 For part two, the speed of 90 meters per minute is 15 meters per second; 24 minutes and 4 seconds is 1444 seconds.

13 15m × 1444 seconds = 21660m.

14 Subtract 21644m from 21660m and you get 16m. Therefore, the path from the school to the station is 16m longer.

高学年

# 比例と反比例

先生

1 今日から比例、反比例という学習をします。
2 分速 80m で歩く場合、2 分後、4 分後、6 分後に歩いている距離は何mになりますか。

3 160m, 320m, 480m です。
それを表にしてみましょう。時間と距離が出てきますから、時間を x 分、距離を y m と
4 します。
このように、x が 2 倍、3 倍、4 倍となると、y も 2 倍、3 倍、4 倍となる関係を
5 「y は x に比例する」といといい、今回は $y = 80 \times x$ の式となります。

距離を縦軸、時間を横軸とします。これをグラフにすると、比例の特色が分かります。
6 同じ割合で増加する関係比例です。

この $y = 80 \times x$ の式の 80 を比例定数と言います。また、比例定数と x は必ず掛算
7 しますから、× を省略して、$y = 80x$ と式を書きます。

8 では、もう一つ学習します。
9 面積が 12 平方cm の長方形があります。
縦が 1cm なら横は 12cm、縦が 2cm なら横は 6cm、縦が 3cm なら横は 4cm、
10 縦が 4cm なら横は 3cm、…と、縦が大きくなると横は逆に小さくなっていきます。

11 このときの縦と横の関係が反比例です。表にしてみましょう。

| 縦（cm） | 1 | 2 | 3 | 4 | 6 | 12 |
|---|---|---|---|---|---|---|
| 横（cm） | 12 | 6 | 4 | 3 | 2 | 1 |

12 式で表すと、縦をy、横を x とすると、$y = 12 \div x$ ですね。図で書いてみましょう。

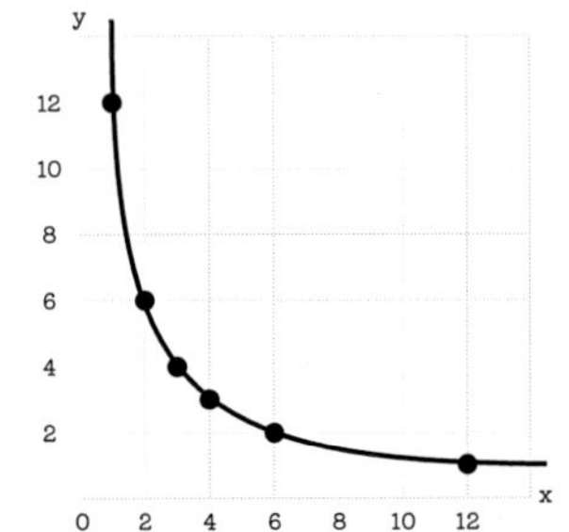


13 縦がy、横が x です。
X と y が交わる点を順につけていき、
14 それを線で結ぶと、ほら、曲線になりますね。

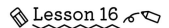

# Proportions and Inverse Proportions

Teacher

1 Today we will start learning about proportions and inverse proportions.

If you walk at a speed of 80 meters per minute, what is the distance you will have walked
2 after 2, 4, and 6 minutes?

3 That's 160m, 320m, and 480m.

4 Let's put it in a table. Let time be x minutes and distance be y meters.

If x is doubled, tripled, or quadrupled, y is also doubled, tripled or quadrupled.
To describe this relationship we say 「y is proportional to x」. In this case, the equation is
5 y = 80 times x.

If we put this on a graph, with distance on the vertical axis (y) and time on the horizontal
6 axis (x) you can see the proportionate relationship.

It is a relational proportion where both sides increases at the same rate.
The 80 in the equation $y = 80 \times x$ is called the proportionality constant.
Also, because the proportionality constant and x always multiply,
7 You can simplify the equation by omitting × and writing the equation as $y = 80x$.

8 Now we will learn one more thing.

9 There is a rectangle with an area of 12 sq. cm.

If the height is 1 cm, the width is 12 cm; if the height is 2 cm, the width is 6 cm.
If the height is 3 cm, the width is 4 cm, if the height is 4 cm, the width is 3 cm, and so on.
10 As the height increases, the width conversely decreases.

The relationship between length and width in this case is inversely proportional.
11 Let's look at the table.

| 縦（cm） | 1 | 2 | 3 | 4 | 6 | 12 |
|---|---|---|---|---|---|---|
| 横（cm） | 12 | 6 | 4 | 3 | 2 | 1 |

As an equation, we can express this relationship as $y = 12 \div x$, where y is the height
12 and x is the width. Let's draw a diagram.

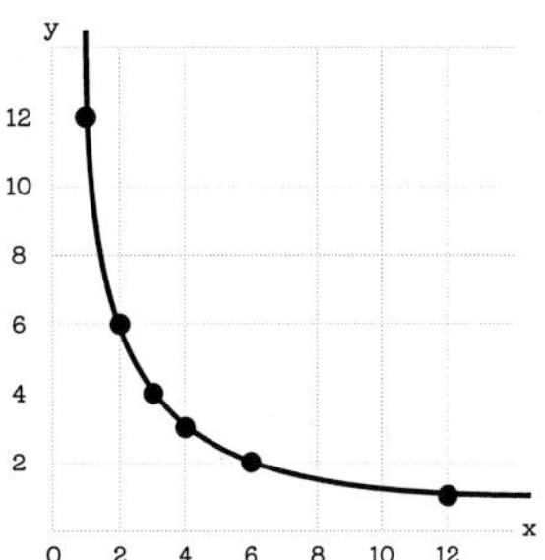


13 The vertical axis is y and the horizontal axis is x.

If you plot the points and connect the dots with
14 a line, you get a curved line.

高学年

# 組合せ

先生

5枚のカードの並べ方の組み合わせを考えてみましょう。
全部で何通りになりますか。

5×4×3×2×1＝120　120通りです。

5枚のカードの中に0のカードがあった場合は
4×4×3×2＝96　96通りです。

0のカードは1番目のカードに選べないので、第1番目の選択が4通りだからです。

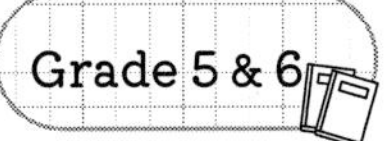

# Lesson 17

算数 Mathematics

Grade 5 & 6

## Combinations

Teacher

1 For example, let us consider the combination of the five cards.

2 How many ways are there in total?

3 $5 \times 4 \times 3 \times 2 \times 1 = 120$ 120 ways.

4 How many ways are there for a card with 0 among the 5 cards?

5 $4 \times 4 \times 3 \times 2 = 96$ 96 ways.

6 The 0 card cannot be chosen as the first card, so there are only 4 options for the first card.

## 図表の英語

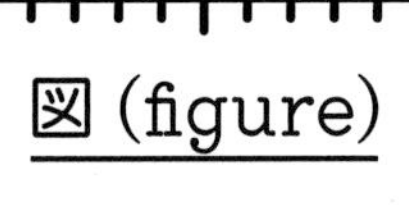

# 図 (figure)

通常、下記のような表形式のものは、"table"、グラフや、図は "chart" と表現しますが、図やグラフ、表すべてに使えるのが、この "figure" という言葉です。論文や、プレゼンテーションのフリップで使う 図、表、グラフすべてを "Figure 1, Figure 2, Figure 3…" という風に表記していきます。勿論、"Table 1" や、"Graph 1" という風に表記しても構いません。

### 表 (table)

表で使われる用語

表題 : title　列 : column
項目 : item　単位 : unit
行 : row

| Year | 2020 | 2021 | 2022 | 2023 |
|---|---|---|---|---|
| Class A | 75 | 61 | 34 | 11 |
| Class B | 86 | 55 | 67 | 78 |
| Class C | 88 | 75 | 84 | 74 |
| Class D | 53 | 57 | 48 | 61 |

### グラフ (graph)

主なグラフの英語名

棒グラフ ・・・bar graph / bar chart
折れ線グラフ ・・・line graph
円グラフ ・・・pie chart / circle chart 単に "chart" といいます。
帯グラフ ・・・bar graph
分布図 ・・・distribution
柱状グラフ ・・・histogram 棒グラフとの違いは、グラフの間が空いていないこと！

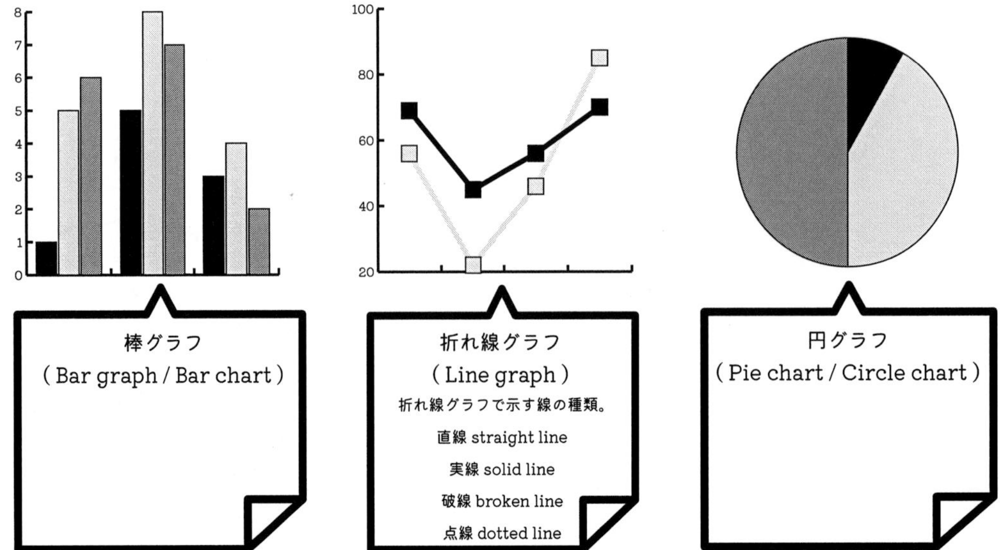


棒グラフ
( Bar graph / Bar chart )

折れ線グラフ
( Line graph )
折れ線グラフで示す線の種類。
直線 straight line
実線 solid line
破線 broken line
点線 dotted line

円グラフ
( Pie chart / Circle chart )

# 算数

subject 1

Mathematics

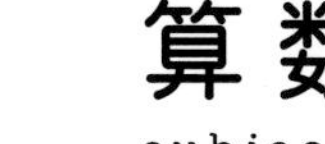
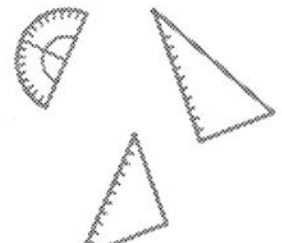

第二章　図形



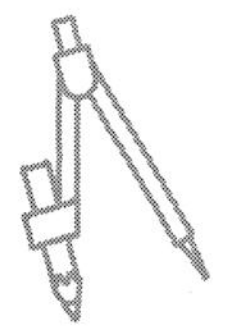

低学年

## かたち/図形

先生

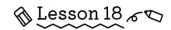

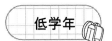

1 こちらを見てください。今、先生が持っている紙の形を四角形といいます。4つの辺と4つの角がある形を四角形、3つの辺と3つの角がある形を三角形といいます。辺も角もない丸い形は円といいます。

2 4つ以上の辺と角をもつ形は、辺と角の数によって、5角形、6角形・・・などと増えていき最後には、角がない円となります。

3 角は、二つの辺の向きで決まりこれを角度といいます。この角度で、皆さんが覚えておかなければならない角度が、直角という角度です。

4 皆さんの教科書の角を見てください。この角度が直角です。

5 教科書の4つの角度は、全て直角になっています。

6 このように、4つの角の角度が全て直角な四角形を、長方形といい、4つの辺の長さも同じ場合、正方形といいます。

中学年

## かたち/図形

先生

1 先生が、黒板にコンパスを使って円を描きます。

2 針を立てて、コンパスの足を広げて、円の大きさを決めます。

3 コンパスの頭の持ち手をもち、時計周りにクルッと一周させます。

4 上手に円を描くコツは、針を動かさないこと、コンパスをまっすぐに立てないで、すこし進行方向に倒しながら回すことです。

5 黒板に円ができましたね。事前に円の説明をしておきます。

6 コンパスの針からコンパスの先までの距離を円の半径といいます。

7 コンパスの針があった部分を中心といいます。

8 中心からは半径はどこも同じ長さです。円の弧から中心を通った直線を直径といいます。

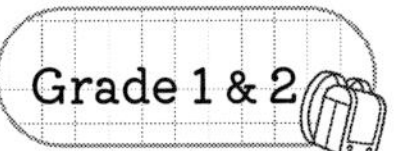


## Shapes

Teacher

Everyone, attention please. This paper hat I'm holding right now is called a square. A square always has four sides. Shapes with only 3 sides are called triangles. If there are no straight sides
1 to it, then that's called a circle.

Ones with five sides are called, pentagons and those with 6 sides are called hexagons. If we keep adding sides, when there are too many angles that you can't see a straight side
2 anymore, it becomes a circle.

An angle is determined by two straight lines. Think of it as the space in between the lines. They also have different names to it, but the most important one that I want you to remember
3 is called a right angle.

4 Please look at the four corners of your textbook. Those are right angles.
A sharp corner with a line going totally horizontal, which meets a line that is perfectly vertical.
5 All of the four corners of the textbook are right angles.
And a shape with only right angles is called a rectangle. Also, if a rectangle has four sides of
6 equal length, then that is called a square.

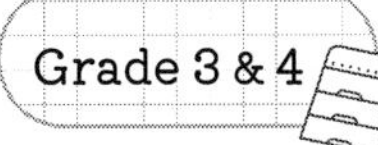


## Shapes

Teacher

1 I will draw a circle on the blackboard using a compass.
2 Set up the needle and spread the legs of the compass to determine the size of the circle.
3 Hold the handle at the head of the compass and circle it clockwise.
The trick is to keep the needle still and to turn the compass in the direction of travel, rather
4 than holding it straight up.

5 I have made a circle on the blackboard. I will explain the circle in advance.
The distance from the needle of the compass to the tip of the compass is called the radius
6 of the circle.
7 The area where the needle of the compass was is called the center.
From the center, the radius is the same length everywhere. A straight line from the arc of
8 the circle through the center is called the diameter.

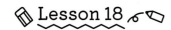

中学年

## かたち/図形

先生

1 このボールの形は何と言いますか。
2 そうですね。球といいます。
球の特色は、どこを輪切りにしても円であることと、球の中心から球の表面までの距離は
3 どこでも同じことです。
4 球の直径をどうやったら測れると思いますか。球だと測るのが難しいですね。
5 アイデアありますか。
6 そのままでは測るのが難しいですね。
7 そこで、このような、球がピッタリ入る箱を準備します。
8 先ほど言いましたね。球は中心からの半径はどこでも同じです。
9 中心から表面までは半径二つで直径でしたね。
10 だから、球がピッタリ入るということは、その箱の幅を測れば、球の直径が分かります。

角度は、2本の直線が交差しないと測ることができません。角度には、基本となる角度
として、180°があり、180°というのは、2本の直線が全く重なった状態です。
11 面でいえば、まっ平らな平面をいいます。
横にかさなっている2本の直線のうち、1本の直線をだんだん立てていくと、30°、45°、
90°120°、150°等と2本の直線の交差がだんだん広くなっていき、最後に、
12 2本目の直線の右端が左端に回転して1本目の直線に重なると180°になります。
2本の辺が直角に交わるという表現をしましたね。この直角というのは、2本の直線が
13 90°の角度で交差することです。

# Shapes 3

Teacher

1 What is the shape of this ball?

2 It is called a sphere.

The special feature of a sphere is that no matter where you slice it, it is a circle, and the distance
3 from the center of the sphere to the surface of the sphere is the same everywhere.

4 How do you think you can measure the diameter of a sphere?

5 Do you have any ideas?

6 It is difficult to measure as it is.

7 Therefore, we prepare a box like this one, in which the sphere fits perfectly.

8 As I said earlier. A sphere has the same radius from the center to everywhere.

9 From the center to the surface the diameter is two times the radii, right?

So, if the ball sphere fits perfectly, we can determine the diameter of the sphere by measuring
10 the width of the box.

An angle can only be measured when two straight lines intersect. The basic angle is 180°, which
is the angle at which two straight lines completely overlap. In terms of surfaces, 180° is
11 a perfectly flat plane.

The intersection of the two lines becomes wider and wider as one of the two overlapping lines
is gradually raised, 30°, 45°, 90°, 120°, 150°, etc. Finally, the right end of the second line rotates to
12 the left end and overlaps the first line to form 180°.

You have expressed that two sides intersect at a right angle. This right angle means that two
13 straight lines intersect at a 90° angle.

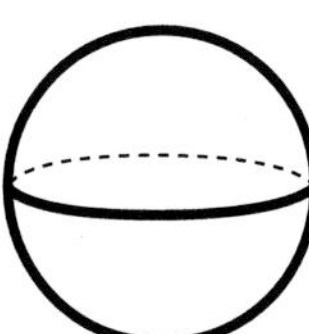

先生

1 図形についての学習を深めます。

まず、黒板に貼った２枚の三角形を見てください。この二つは双子の三角形です。
2 双子ですから全く同じです。重ねてみましょう。全く同じですね。

3 合わせると同じでしょという意味で「合同」といいます。

4 もう一枚、三角形を貼ります。この三角形は前のより小さいですね。

小さいですが、大きい三角形と形が同じですね。このような、形が同じなことを
5 「相似」といいます。

6 相似は、辺の長さが違うだけで角度が同じ図形同士を言います。

7 また、二つの図形のどの角度とどの角度が同じかを確認する必要が出てきます。

8 まず、三角形の角度が合計 180°ですね。

これは正確には内角の和、三角形を作っている３つの辺で囲まれている角度の合計が
9 180°です。各辺を伸ばします。すると辺の直線上に内角でない角度ができますね。

10 これが外角です。

外角は直線から内角を引いた角ですね。ですから、ひとつの外角はその内角以外の
11 内角の和と等しいことがわかります。

12 三角形の三つの角を∠あ、∠い、∠うとします。

13 内角の∠あ+∠い+∠う＝180°です。

14 ∠あの辺の一つを延長すると外角の∠あができます。

15 外角の∠あ+ 内角の∠あ＝直線になりますから、合わせて 180°です。

だから、内角∠あ+ 外角∠あ＝180°＝内角の∠あ+∠い+∠うですから、
16 外角∠あ＝内角の∠い+∠うとわかります。

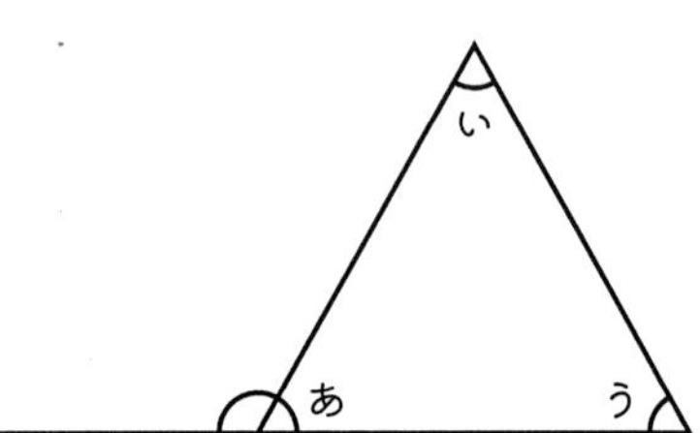

# Shapes

Teacher

1 We will deepen our study of shapes.
First, look at the two triangles on the blackboard. These two are twin triangles. Since they are twins, they are exactly the same. Let's put them on top of each other. They are exactly
2 the same, right?
They are called congruent triangles, which means that they are the same when they are put
3 together.
4 Let's add another triangle. This triangle is smaller than the previous one.
5 Although it is smaller, it has the same shape as the larger triangle. This is called similarity.

6 Similarity refers to figures that have the same angles but different side lengths.
7 Also, you will need to check which angles of the two figures are the same.
8 First, we know that the three angles of a triangle is equal to 180°.
This is precisely the sum of the interior angles, the sum of the angles enclosed by the three sides making the triangle is 180°. If you draw a straight line to extend each side of the triangle, then
9 you will notice an angle on the straight line of the sides that is not an interior angle.
10 This is the exterior angle.

The exterior angle is the angle obtained by subtracting an interior angle from the straight line.
11 So, we see that one exterior angle is equal to the sum of all interior angles.

12 For example, Let the three angles of a triangle be ∠a, ∠b, and ∠c.
13 The interior angle, angle a + angle b + angle c = 180°.
14 ∠a Extending one of the sides of angle a creates angle a at the exterior angle.
Since the exterior angle angle a + the interior angle angle a = a straight line, the angles are
15 180° together.
So, internal angle angle a + external angle a = 180° = internal angle a + angle b + angle c.
16 Therefore, we know that external angle a = internal angle b + angle c.

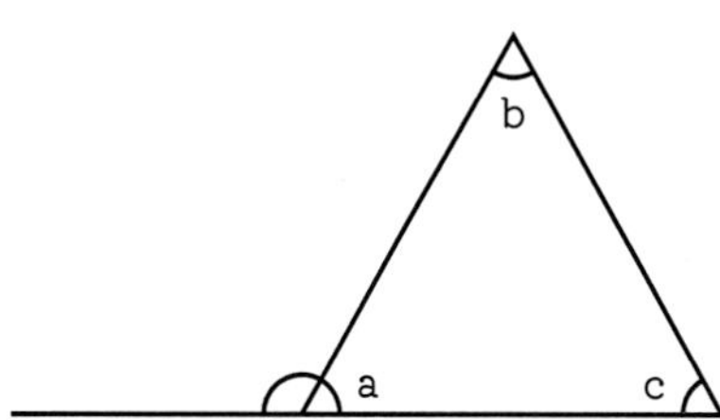

中学年

# 角度

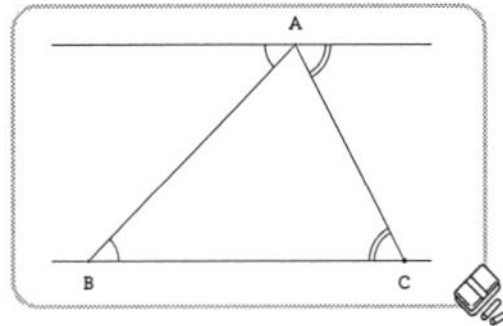

先生

1 角度の学習では、基本ルールを覚えてください。
それは、三角形、つまり3つの角と3つの辺からなる
図形の3つの角の角度を合計すると、必ず180°になるということ、
2 四角形は4つの角の角度の合計は360°になるということです。
直角で二つの辺が同じ三角形を直角2等辺三角形、辺の長さが違う三角形を
3 不等辺直角三角形と言います。
4 4つの辺の長さが同じで、4つの角が直角つまり90°の四角形を正方形と言います。
角度の呼び方ですが、90°より小さい角度は鋭角、大きい角度は鈍角、180°つまり平らに
5 なった角度を平角といいます。
6 角度のことが理解できると、図形への理解が広がります。
4つの辺の長さが同じでも、向かい合う角度2つずつが夫々同じ場合、図形はひし形に
7 なります。
8 向かい合う辺が2つずつ同じ場合の図形は、平行四辺形になります。
この角度が同じ、線の長さが同じという場合、決められた印があります。この印も
9 覚えてください。
10 正方形、長方形、ひし形、平行四辺形の向いあった頂点を、定規を使って結んで下さい。
11 同様に、もう一方の向かいあった頂点も同じように結んでください。
この直線を対角線といい、四角形には2本の対角線が引けて、この2本が交差します。
12 その対角線は、四角形によって特徴があります。

13 ・　2本の対角線が、それぞれのまん中の点で交わるのは、
平行四辺形、ひし形、長方形、正方形。
14 ・　2本の対角線の長さが等しいのは…長方形、正方形。
15 ・　2本の対角線が直角に交わるのは…ひし形、正方形となります。

先生

対角線とは一つの頂点と他の頂点を結ぶ直線です。隣同士の頂点はすでに辺として
1 結ばれているので、一つの頂点と隣り合う頂点は対角線で結べません。
だから、一つの頂点から引ける対角線の数は、全部の頂点の数から、出発点となる頂点
と隣同士の頂点2つを引いた数となり、(頂点の数－3)×頂点の数、そして、出発点と
なる頂点と繋ぐ頂点の対角線は反対側から引いても同じですから1/2となり、
2 (頂点の数－3)×頂点の数÷2となります。

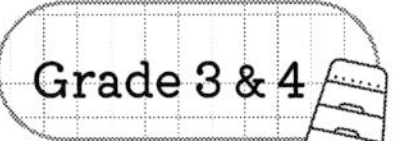

Grade 3 & 4

# Angles

Teacher

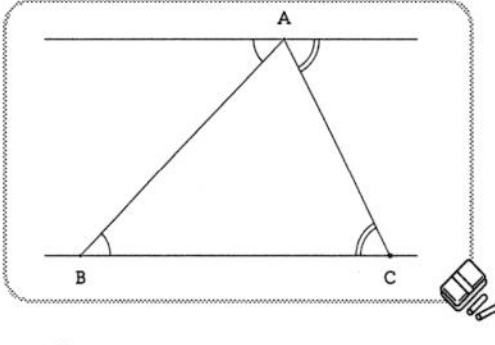


1 When learning angles, please remember the basic rules.
That is, the sum of the angles of the three angles of a triangle,
a figure consisting of three angles and three sides, will always be 180°,
2 and the sum of the angles of the four angles of a square will be 360°.
A triangle with right angles and two equal sides is called a right-angled isosceles triangle, and
3 a triangle with different side lengths is called an unequal right-angled triangle.
4 A rectangle with four sides of equal length and four corners at right angles, i.e., 90° is called a square.
Angles smaller than 90° are called acute angles, larger angles are obtuse angles, and 180°,
5 or flattened angles, are called flat angles.
6 When you understand angles, your understanding of shapes will expand.
If the four sides have the same length but two opposite angles are the same for each side,
7 the figure is a rhombus.
8 A figure with two equal opposite sides is a parallelogram.
If the angles are the same and the lengths of the lines are the same, there is a marker. Please
9 remember these marks as well.
10 Connect the opposite vertices of a square, rectangle, rhombus, or parallelogram using a ruler.
11 Similarly, connect the other facing vertex in the same way.
This line is called a diagonal, and two diagonals can be drawn in a square, These two intersect.
12 Their diagonals are characterized by quadrangles.

13 ・ The two diagonals intersect at their midpoints：
Parallelograms, rhombuses, rectangles, and squares.
14 ・ Two diagonals are equal in length...rectangle, square.
15 ・ Two diagonals intersect at right angles...a rhombus and a square.

Teacher

A diagonal is a line connecting one vertex to another. Since adjacent vertices are already
1 connected as edges, one vertex cannot be connected to an adjacent vertex by a diagonal line.
Therefore, the number of diagonals that can be drawn from a vertex is the number of vertices
minus the starting vertex and two adjacent vertices,
which is (number of vertices - 3) × the number of vertices, and the number of diagonals from
the starting vertex and the connecting vertex is 1/2, since it is the same
if drawn from the opposite side, which is (number of vertices - 3) × the number of vertices 1/ 2.
2 The result is (number of vertices - 3) × the number of vertices divided by 2.

中学年

# 面積

先生

1 長さ、重さ、角度等の単位を学習してきました。

2 今回から広さの単位を学習します。

広さは、縦の長さ×横の長さで計算し、単位は、cm×cm の時は、平方センチメートル
3 といいcm²、m×m のときは平方メートルといい、m²と書きます。

4 面積は、いろんな図形の大きさを比べるために欠かせません。

図形が、正方形や長方形のように、縦と横の長さを掛けて出すと簡単ですが、
形が凹凸だったり、三角形だったりとすると、計算の方法を工夫して答えを出す必要が
5 出てきます。

6 この工夫として図形に引く線を補助線といいいいます。

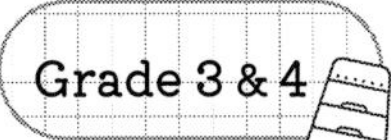


# Area

Teacher

1 We have been learning units of length, weight, angles, and so on.
2 From now on, you will learn how to measure area.
3 Area is calculated as length x width, and is written in units of $cm^2$ (cm x cm), which is called square centimeters, and $m^2$ (m x m), which is called square meters.
4 Area is essential for comparing the size of various shapes.

5 However, if the shape is uneven or triangular, it is necessary to devise a calculation method to obtain the answer.
6 The lines that are drawn on the figure in this method are called additional or auxiliary lines.

中学年

## 面積

先生

1 少し難しくなります。プリントを見てください。

この図は、もちろん方眼紙に書き写してマスを数えてもよいですが、かなりマスを数えることが必要になります。そこで、このような問題の場合は、計算がしやすいように、図形の中に補助線を引いて、図形を分割して計算をして、後で合算する方法と取ります。

2 やってみましょう。

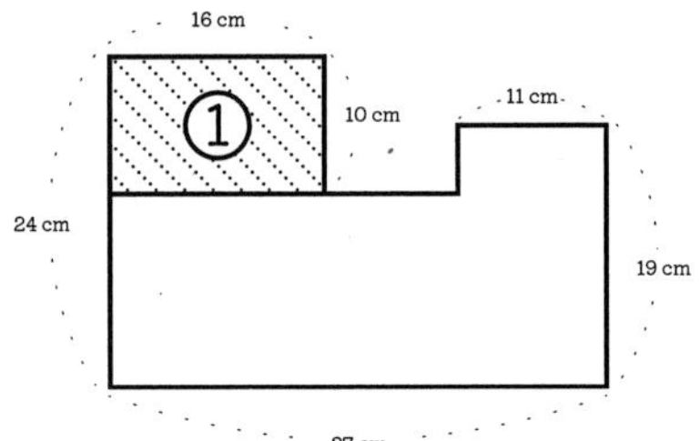


3 部分①は、最初から 縦・横 の数値がわかっていますので、簡単ですね。

4 ( 部分①)10 × 6 = 160 ㎠です。

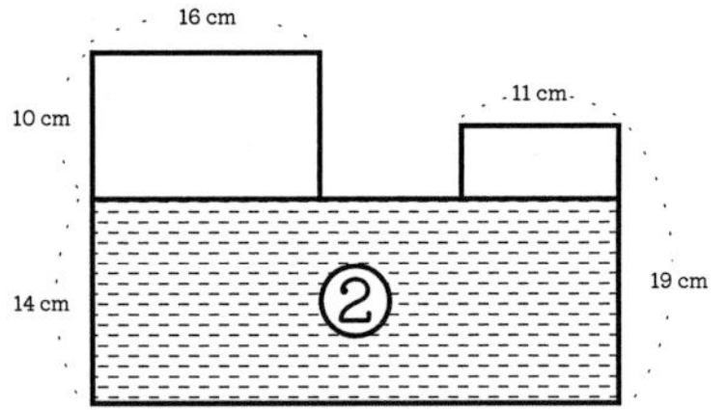


5 次に、部分②です。

もともとの図からは、緑色の縦の部分の長さがわかりません。しかし、先ほどの赤色の四角の縦部分が 10 ㎝ですので、( 部分②)長い左辺の 24cm から その 10 ㎝を引けば、 (薄い緑) の縦辺の長さがわかります。

6 (24 - 10) × 37 = 518 ㎠

これも、最初は縦辺の長さがわかりませんが、先ほどの (薄い緑) の縦辺が 14cm だったので、右辺の 19cm から引けば、 (薄い青) の縦辺が求められます。よって、

7 求める図形の面積は

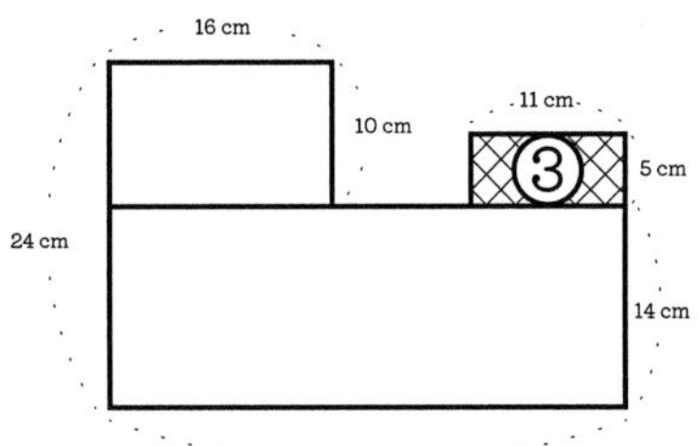


8 160 + 518 + 55 = 733 ㎠となります。このように、補助線により、計算が容易になります。

なお、面積計算では、大きな単位が出てきます。長さなら、1 ㎞ = 1000m ですね。

9 これが面積となると 100m×100m = 10,000 ㎡になります。

10 このため、10,000 ㎡は 1 a 、1 a ×1 a は 1ha という単位を使います。

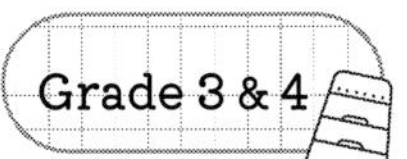


# Area

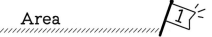

Teacher

1 This is going to be a bit difficult. Please take a look at the handout.
This figure can, of course, be copied on a piece of graph paper and the squares counted, but it requires quite a bit of square counting. So, for this kind of problem, draw additional or auxiliary lines in the figure to make the calculation easier. The idea is to divide the figure into
2 pieces, perform the calculation, and then add them together later. Let's try it.

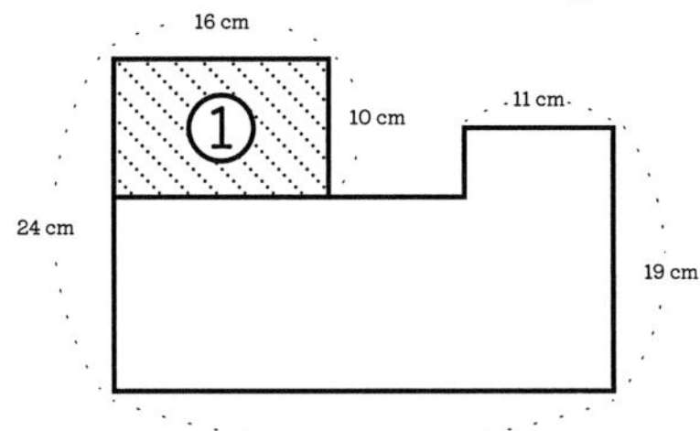


3 For part (1), the values of height and width are known from the beginning. So, it is easy.

4 Red area(Part 1) 10 × 6 = 160 ㎠

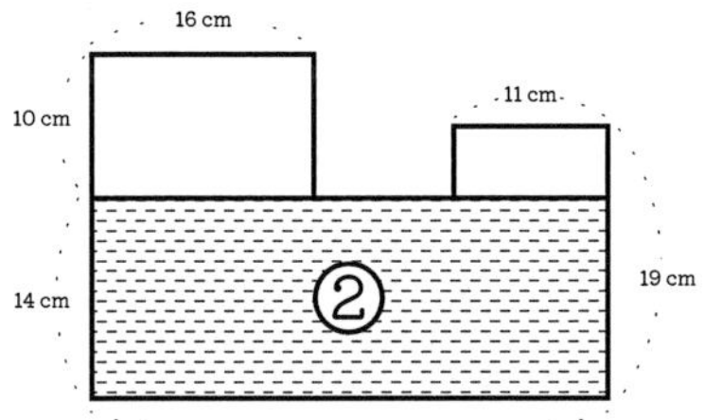


5 Next is part (2).
In the green section, it doesn't exactly say the height of the area. However, since we know the measurement of part 1 (the red area) we can subtract 10 cm from the long left side (24 cm),
(light green) The lengths of the vertical sides of the

6 (24 - 10) × 37 = 518 ㎠
The length of the vertical side is not known at first, but since the vertical side of the previous (light green) was 14 cm, it can be subtracted from the right side (19 cm),
7 (light blue) vertical sides are required. Therefore, the area of the figure we are checking is

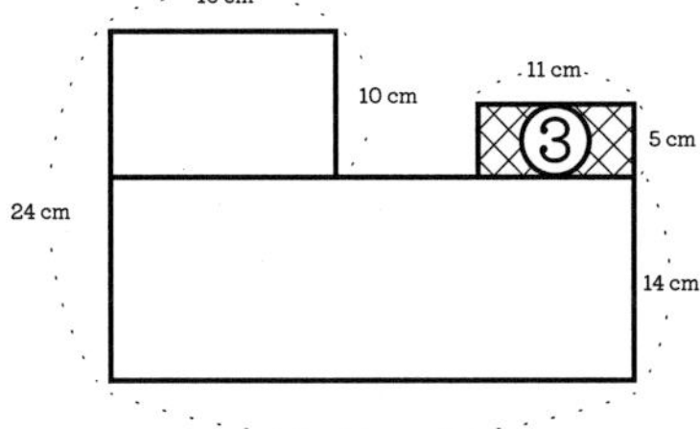


8 In this case, the auxiliary line mades the calculation 160 + 518 + 55 = 733 ㎠
In addition, large numbers are used when we calculate areas. For length, 1 km = 1,000 m right?
9 When it comes to area, 100 m x 100 m = 10,000 ㎡.
10 "hectare". We can write this as 1 a x 1 a = 1 ha.

高学年

# 面積

先生

1 いろいろな図形の面積を学習します。
2 正方形や長方形が縦× 横で面積が求められることは学習しました。

3 今日は、三角形、平行四辺形、台形の面積の求め方を学習しましょう。
4 紙に書いた図形で考えるのがわかりやすいです。
三角形の場合、底辺を方眼紙のマスに合わせて、底辺の二つの頂点からもう一つの頂点の
高さまで直線を引き、長方形を作ると、その三角形が長方形の半分の大きさであることが
5 わかりますね。だから、三角形の面積は、底辺× 高さ÷2 で求めます。

もう一度、念を押しますが、図形の面積を求めるときに高さというのは、直角で測る
6 長さです。
7 直角かどうかは図形に“L”(直角を表す記号)が記してあります。
8 必ずしも下から上に引いてある直線が高さとは限らないので、引っかかってはだめですよ。
9 では、平行四辺形を方眼紙に描いて面積の出し方を調べてみましょう。
平行四辺形とは、下辺と上辺が平行で、右辺と左辺も平行になっていて、頂点の角度が
10 直角でない四角形ですね。
11 下辺と上辺のそれぞれ出っ張ている頂点から直線を対辺の高さまで直角に引いてください。
12 そこにできる三角形がもう一方にできている三角形と合同であることがわかりますね。
合同ですから、その三角形の部分を切り取って、もう一方の三角形の部分に移動しても
13 同じ面積で、そこに移動すると長方形になることがわかります。
14 だから、底辺× 高さで平行四辺形は面積を求めることが出来ます。
15 では、台形を同じようにして調べてみましょう
16 台形は、下辺と上辺、左辺と右辺の長さも異なり、頂点の角度もバラバラな四角形です。

方眼紙に底辺をそろえて台形を描きます。その横に上下を逆にした台形を描くと二つを
17 合わせると平行四辺形になっていますね。
さすがに台形一つだけでは面積をもとめることはできませんが、台形と逆台形を
18 組み合わせて平行四辺形を作ると底辺× 高さで求めることが出来ることがわかります。

ただ、気を付けないといけないのは、底辺というのは、台形と逆台形を組み合わせた
19 長さつまり、下辺＋上辺の長さです。
20 そして、底辺 (下辺＋上辺)× 高さで台形二つ分ですから、1/2 します。

算数

Mathematics

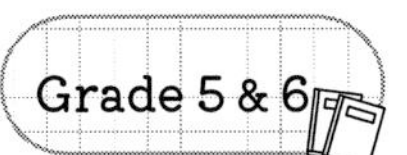


# Area

2

Teacher

1 We will study how to measure the areas of various shapes.

We have learned that the area of a square or rectangle can be obtained by multiplying its
2 length by its width.

3 Today, we will learn how to find the areas of triangles, parallelograms, and trapezoids.

4 It is easier to understand if we draw them on graph paper.

In the case of a triangle, if you align the base of the triangle with the square of the grid paper
and draw a straight line from the two vertices of the base to the height of the other vertex to
form a rectangle, you can see that the triangle is half the size of the rectangle, right? So, we see
5 that the area of the triangle is found by dividing (the base) x (the height of the triangle) by 2.

Again, as a reminder, when determining the area of a shape, height is the length measured
6 from the base at a right angle.

7 Whether it is a right angle or not is marked on the figure with "∟ "(the symbol for a right angle).

8 Not all lines that is drawn vertically on the paper is the height so don't be tricked.

9 Now, let's draw a parallelogram on the graph paper and find out how to get the area.

A parallelogram is a rectangle in which the lower and upper sides are parallel, the right and
10 left sides are also parallel, and none of the angles are at right angles.

11 Now, please draw vertical and horizontal lines from the parallelogram's vertices.

12 You can see that the two triangles formed are mirror images or congruent to each other.

Since it is congruent, if you cut out one of the triangles and move it to the other triangle the
13 area will be the same and if you put the cut triangle on the other side of the triangle.

14 So, we can find the area of the parallelogram by the formula base × height.

15 Now let's examine the trapezoid in the same way.

A trapezoid is a rectangle with different lengths at the bottom and top sides, left and right sides,
16 and different angles at the vertices.

Draw a trapezoid on your graph paper with the bottom edges aligned. If we draw an identical
17 trapezoid but upside down the two together form a parallelogram.

One trapezoid alone is not enough to determine the area of a parallelogram but if we combine
a trapezoid and an inverted trapezoid to form a parallelogram, we can find the area of
18 the parallelogram by multiplying the base by the height of the trapezoid.

However, please be careful, the base is the length of the trapezoid combined with the
19 inverted trapezoid, i.e., the combined trapezoid.

And since base (lower side + upper side) x height is equal to two trapezoids, we have to
20 divide it by 2.

高学年

# 面積

先生

1 今日は円について学習します。

2 円はコンパスで中心からグルッと一周させて弧を描きますね。
中心点を通って円周まで直線を引くと直径、中心点から円周までを半径といい、
3 直径は半径の２倍ということはすでに学習しました。

4 これまでの図形では頂点の角度を学習してきましたが、円には頂点がありません。

5 円の学習ではまず中心の角度と円周の長さが重要です。

中心の角度は、中心を通る直線で半円を作ると半円の底辺が二つでき、
6 底辺は 180°ですから２倍することになり 360°です。

7 円の中心角度は 360°ですね。

8 円周の長さですが、求め方が決まっていて、直径 x 3.14 です。

9

10 では、同じく半径５㎝で、中心角度 90°の場合の弧の長さと周りの長さはどうですか。

11 円周が角度によって切り取られると弧の長さと表現し、半径は辺として表現します。

12 そして、半円より小さいものを扇形と表現します。

13 周りの長さですから、弧の長さ+2 辺を足します。

14 よく、この２辺の足し算を忘れることがありますから注意しましょう。

15 では、プリントで練習しましょう。

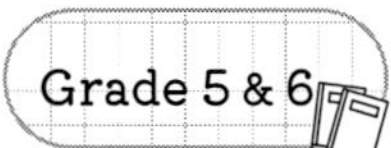

# Lesson 20

算数 Mathematics

Grade 5 & 6

## Area

**Teacher**

1 Today we will learn about circles.
2 A circle is an arc that is drawn by going around a center point with a compass.
We have already learned that a straight line drawn from one side of the circumference,
through the center point and then to the other side of to the circumference is called a diameter.
Also the line from the center point to any points on the circumference is called a radius, and
3 the diameter is twice the radius.
4 We have studied angles at vertices in previous figures, but a circle does not have vertices.

5 In the study of circles, the center angle and the length of the circumference are important.

If you draw a straight line passing through the center you will make a semicircle and,
two sides of the semicircle will be formed. Each semi-circle is 180 degrees so if you multiply
6 it by 2 it is 360°.

7 The angle at the center is 360°.
8 The length of the circumference is determined by multiplying the diameter × 3.14.
9 The central angle of the circle is 360°.
Now, what is the length of the arc and the circumference of the arc, when the radius is also
10 5 cm and the central angle is 90?
When the circumference is cut by an angle, it is described as an arc length and the radius are
11 described as an edge.
12 Anything smaller than a semicircle is called a sector.
When you are asked to derive the circumference of a sector or circle, make sure that you
13 add the length of the two radii.
14 Note that many people often forget to add these two sides.
15 Now, let's practice with the handout.

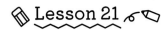

高学年

# 体積

先生

1 竹の筒に入った空気が押し棒でされて筒の先端に詰めていた紙玉を飛ばしました。

この時、筒の中にあった空気の体積が押されて小さくなり、元の大きさに戻ろうとする
2 力が働いて、紙玉を押し出しましたと説明しました。
3 このある大きさの中に入っているかさの単位が体積です。
4 先ほどの紙鉄砲のように、かさの大きさや形はいろいろあります。
5 ただ、かさは縦×横の面積に高さや深さといった立体です。
6 今回はこの立体ということと、かさの大きさである体積を学習します。
7 まず、かさの体積は、縦×横×高さで求めます。これを公式とよびます。
8 このような３辺の長さが同じ形を立方体といいます。
9 どれかまたはいずれも３辺の長さが違う立体を直方体といいます。
10 立体には、竹筒のような円柱、ピラミッドのような四角すい等があります。

11 縦５㎝、横５㎝、高さ５㎝の立方体の体積は、5×5×5＝25 ㎤となります。
12 直方体も同じ計算式で体積を求めます。
計算式では、単位は必ず合わせます。一辺は㎝、他の辺はｍ、残りの辺は㎜など単位が
13 異なると計算ができません。
14 また、面積の場合と違って、単位がちがうとちょっと驚く数字となります。
15 例えば、一辺が 1m の立方体の場合、1 ㎥ですね。これを㎝の単位で表すと、
16 100 ㎝×100 ㎝×100 ㎝で 1,000,000 ㎤となります。
17 こんな数字すぐには読めないですよね。
18 ２年生の学習でかさの単位をℓで表すことを学習しましたね。
この１ℓというかさは、1 辺 10 ㎝の立方体の体積ですから、
19 1ℓ＝1000 ㎤となります。1 ℓ＝1000ml ですから 1ml＝1 ㎤となります。
20 1ℓ＝10 ㎝×10 ㎝×10 ㎝ということは、メートルで表示すると 0, 001 ㎥です。
だから、1000ℓでようやく 1 ㎥となります。体積という場合、このように数字が単位に
よってかなり大きな数や小さな数になってきますから、何度も練習をしないと身につき
21 ません。
体積に似た単位として容積があります。
22 体積とはもののかさですが、容積とはかさが入る容器の空間の大きさです。
直方体の底の面積は縦×横で求められてこれに高さを掛けると直方体の体積が求まりま
23 すね。これを半分に切り取ると、三角形の柱になります。この角柱を三角柱といいます。

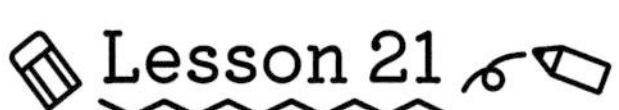




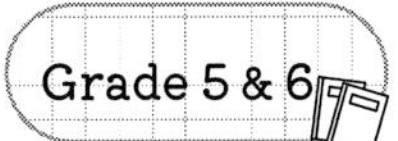


# Volume

Teacher

With the bamboo gun, the air in the bamboo tube was pushed out by a stick, sending the paper
1 ball stuffed in the tip of the tube flying.
At that time, I explained that, the volume of air in the tube was pushed down to make it smaller,
2 and the force exerted to return it to its original size pushed the paper ball out.
3 The unit of air contained within a container of a certain size is called the volume.
4 Like the paper guns mentioned earlier, there are many different sizes and shapes of containers.
5 However, the volume of any of this three-dimensional object is length × width, height, and depth.
6 In this lesson, we will learn about this three-dimensionality and volume.
7 First, the volume of a solid is determined by its length × width × height. This is called the formula.
8 Shapes like these with three sides of equal lengths is called a cube.
9 A cube where any or all of its three sides are of different lengths is called a rectangle.
There are a wide variety of three-dimensional objects including cylinders like bamboo tubes,
10 square pyramids, etc.
11 The volume of a cube 5 cm long, 5 cm wide, and 5 cm high is 5 × 5 × 5 = 25 ㎤.
12 The same formula is used to find the volume of a rectangular body.
In formulas, units must match. If one side is in cm, the other side is in m, and the remaining
13 side is in mm, etc., the calculation will not be possible.
14 Also, unlike the case of area, the numbers are a bit surprising when the units are different.
15 For example, a cube with one side of 1 meter is 1 ㎥
16 If we express this in units of cm, 100 cm × 100 cm × 100 cm would be 1,000,000 ㎤.
17 You can't read these numbers right away, can you?
18 You learned in second grade to express volumes liquid in ℓ.
This 1 liter of liquid is the volume of a cube with 10 cm on each side,
19 1 ℓ = 1000 ㎤. 1 ℓ = 1000ml, so 1ml = 1 ㎤.
20 1 ℓ = 10cm × 10cm × 10cm, which is 0,001 ㎥ when expressed in meters.
Therefore, 1,000 liters is equivalent to 1 ㎥. In the case of volume, this number can be quite
large or small depending on the unit of measure, so, you will have to practice many times to
21 learn it.
A concept similar to volume is capacity. While volume is the amount of space an object
22 takes up, capacity is the maximum amount a container can hold when full.
Let's look at this cuboid. I can find the area of the base of this cuboid by the formula
length × width and multiply this by the height to get the volume of the cuboid.
23 If we cut this in half, we get a triangular shaped prism. This prism is called a triangular prism.

高学年

# 対称

1

## 線対称

先生

1 折り紙を二つに折って三角形をつくります。そして広げます。

2 二つに折った線からわかれた二つの三角形は同じ形ですね。

しかも同じ形というだけでなく、折った線から重ねると必ず角も辺の長さも同じに

3 なりますね。

4 このように線を挟んで重ねると同じ図形になることを線対称の図形といいます。

折り線は、縦横ななめいずれでも構いません。

5 折り線で折ったらきちんと重なる、このような関係を線対象といいます。

6 線対称の図形の特色を掴みましょう。

7 黒板にはった図の場合、点線で折り返すと頂点Ａと頂点Bが重なります。

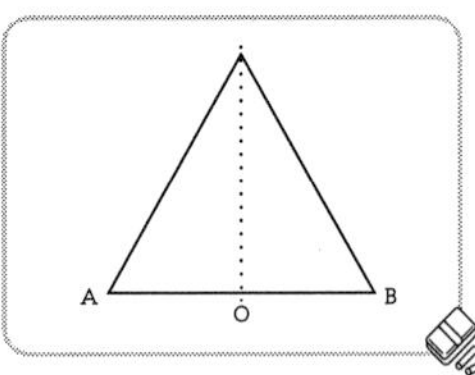


8 この時、「点Ａと点Bは線対称の関係にある」と言います。

9 折れ線を対称軸といいます。

10 そして重なる点を対応する点、重なる線を対応する線といいます。

11 つまり、頂点Ａと頂点Ｂが対応する点、線分ＯＡと線分ＯＢが対応する線となります。

対称軸で折り返すと線対称となるというためには、

①対応する２つの点（この場合点Ａと点B)を結ぶ直線は、対称軸と垂直に交わって

いなければなりません。

12 直線AB と点線が垂直になるということです。

②そして対応する２点までの距離が等しくなければ対称になりませんから、

13 線OA＝線OB となります。

14 では、図形を対称軸から線対称で図形を描いてみましょう。

線対称ということは、対称軸から距離が一緒ということですから、各頂点を結んだ直線が

15 対称軸から同じ長さとなるように両方の図形を描きます。

16 同じ長さとなるように両方の図形を描きます。

17 この時、対称軸との交点は必ず直角になっていないと線対称になりません。

18 直角に交差していることを示す「L」を交点に書きます。

19 そして対称軸からの各直線が同じ距離であることを示す記号を書きます。

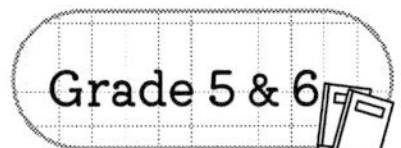


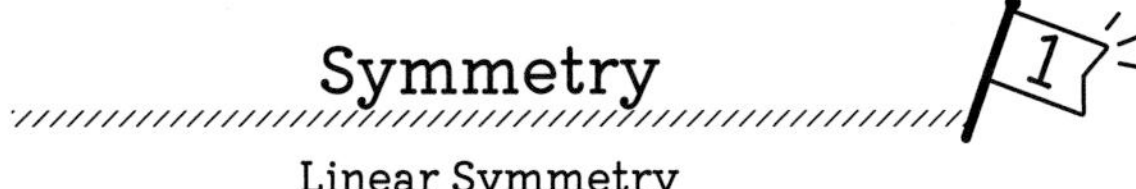

# Symmetry

## Linear Symmetry

Teacher

1 Fold the origami paper in two to make a triangle. Then unfold it.

2 Two triangles separated by a line folded in two are the same shape, right?

Moreover, not only are they the same shape, but if you put them on top of each other,
3 they also have the same lengths and angles.

This kind of shape that becomes the same when superimposed across lines is called a figure
4 with line symmetry.

It doesn't matter where or which direction you fold. As long as when you make the fold,
5 each side perfectly matches the other then you have line symmetry.

6 Let's take a look at the characteristics of a figure with line symmetry.

In the case of the diagram on the blackboard, vertex A and vertex B overlap when folded along
7 a dotted line.

8 At this point, we say that "point A and point B have line symmetry".

9 The dotted line where the fold is made is called the axis of symmetry.

And overlapping points are called corresponding points and
10 overlapping lines are called corresponding lines.

That is, vertex A and vertex B are corresponding points and line OA and line OB are
11 corresponding lines.

In order for a line to be said to be line symmetrical when it is folded back on the axis of symmetry, the line connecting the two corresponding points (in this case point A and point B) must intersect the axis of symmetry perpendicularly.

12 This means that the straight-line AB and the dotted line are perpendicular.

13 The distance to the two corresponding points must be equal, so, the line OA = line OB.

14 Now let's draw a figure with line symmetry from the axis of symmetry.

Linear symmetry means that the distance from the axis of symmetry is the same to the edge
15 of both sides of your shape should be the same.

16 Draw both figures so that they are the same length.

17 In addition, make sure that the lines connect at right angles.

18 Write「∟」at the intersection to indicate that they intersect at right angles.

19 Then write a symbol indicating that each line from the axis of symmetry is the same distance.

高学年

## 対称

### 点対称

先生

1 点対称な図形とはある点を中心にして 180°回転した場合に重なる図形のことです。

2 トランプの絵札カードを使って説明しましょう。

3 トランプの中心に回転の中心点があると想定します。
すると 180°回転（つまりこの場合は上下反転）したらぴったり絵柄が重なりますよね！

4 これが点対称です。

点対称とは、対称の中心となる点から、180 度回転させたときにもとの図形と重なる
5 図形です。

ですから、回転させて重なる点や線は、対称の中心から直線で結ぶと同じ距離にある
6 ことになります。

7 この重なる点や辺を、線対称の場合と同じく、対応する点、対応する辺といいます。

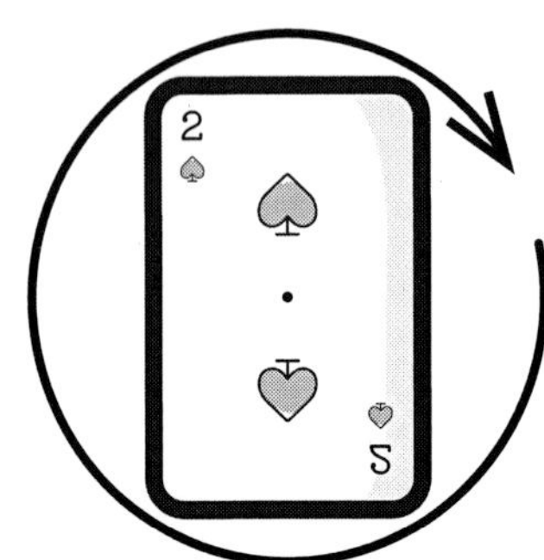

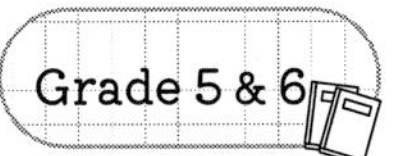

Grade 5 & 6

# Symmetry

## Point Symmetry

Teacher

1 A point-symmetrical figure is a figure that overlaps when rotated 180°around a certain point.

2 I will explain using a deck of playing cards.

3 Imagine that at the center of the playing cards there is a point.

Then, if we rotate the cards 180° (i.e., flip them upside down in this case), the patterns will
4 overlap exactly, right? This is point symmetry.

Point symmetry occurs when a shape or object overlaps the original figure when rotated
5 180 degrees from the point at the center of symmetry.

Therefore, points and lines that overlap when rotated are the same distance from the center of
6 symmetry when connected by a straight line.

These overlapping points and sides are called corresponding points and corresponding sides,
7 as in the case of line symmetry.

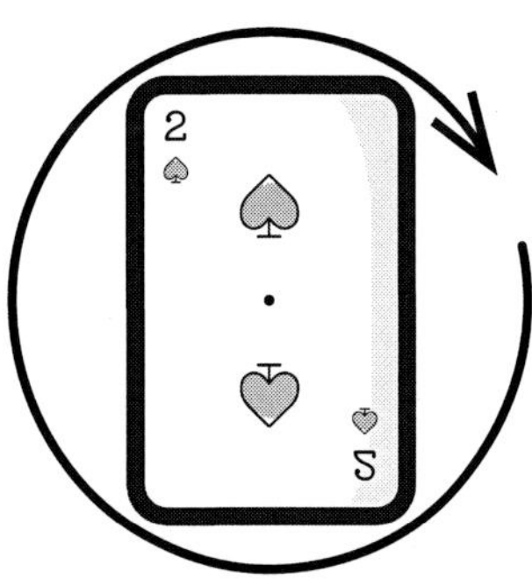

高学年

# 円の面積

先生

1 今日は円の場合の面積の求め方を学習します。
円の場合は、辺も角度もありません。ですから、これまで習った計算式では面積が
2 求められませんね。
3 皆さん、コンパスを出してください。
4 コンパスの幅が３㎝になるように定規で測って、ノートに円を描いてください。

5 描いたら、コンパスの軸の横にＯと書いてください。
この軸を中心にしてぐるっと円を描きました。この点を中心点といいます。
6 Ｏと記号を書きましたが、これは、原点とかここが始まりという意味を表す
英語のorigin の頭文字のＯです。
7 ですから、円の中心をＯと書くのは、世界共通です。

8 はい、みなさんよく見てください。田中さんの引いた軸となる線はどこを通って、
どこまで伸びていますか。
9 中心点を通って、円の線まで伸びていますね。
10 ノートに描いた円にこの対象となる軸を書いてみてください。たくさん書けますよね。

11 そうです。円の線対称の軸の数は無数にあります。
12 円の特徴で他の図形と違うところの一つです。
13 この線対称の軸の数はたくさんある。これを覚えておいてください。

14 円は丸ですね。
でも、この線対称の軸が多数あるということは、この軸の数を使って、
15 円を四角にできるということです。
16 実際にやってみましょうね。
17 先生が持っている画用紙の円は直径 10 ㎝の円です。
18 この円に対称軸を書いてみますよ。9 本書きます。角度は何度で書けばよいですか?

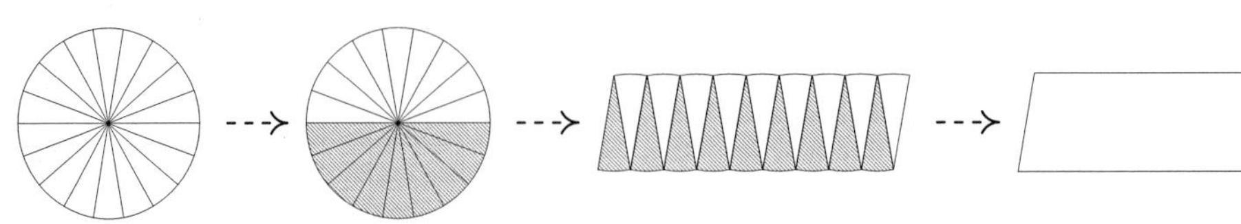

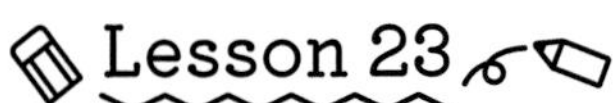




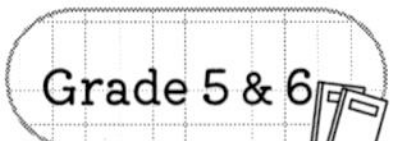


# The Area of a circle

Teacher

1 Today we will learn how to find the area of a circle.
In the case of a circle, there are neither sides nor angles. Therefore, we cannot find the area
2 using the formulas we have learned so far.
3 Everyone, please get out your compasses.
Measure with a ruler so that the width of the compass is 3 cm and draw a circle in your
4 notebook.
5 After drawing, write O next to the axis of the compass.
You drew a circle around this axis. This point is called the center point, and the symbol O
6 is the first letter O of the English word origin, which means origin or this is the beginning.

7 Therefore, it is universal to write the center of a circle as O.

8 Please look closely. Where does the axis line drawn by Mr. Tanaka extend to?

9 It extends through the center point to the line of the circle.
Try to draw this target axis on the circle you drew in your notebook.
10 You can draw many axes, can't you?
11 That's right. The number of axes of line symmetry of a circle is innumerable.
12 This is one of the characteristics of a circle that makes it different from other shapes.
13 There are many axes of this line symmetry. Please remember this.

14 A circle is a circle.
But the fact that there are many axes of this line symmetry means that we can make a circle
15 into a square by using this number of axes.
16 Let's actually try it.
17 The circle on the drawing paper that the sensei is holding a circle with a diameter of 10 cm.
18 I'm going to draw an axis of symmetry on this circle, 9 lines. What is the angle in degrees?

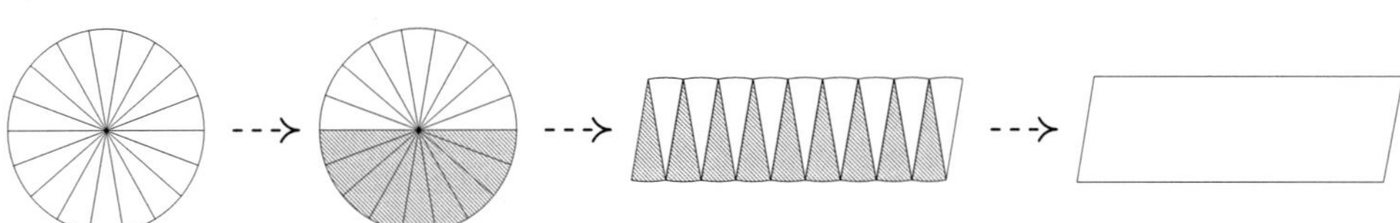

高学年

# そろばん

先生

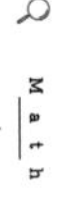

いまから、そろばんを皆さんに配ります。列の一番前の人の机に置きますから、

1 うしろに順番に回してください。みんなに行きわたりましたか。

2 では、説明します。黒板の図を見て下さい。

枠は、そろばんの周りの淵のことをいい、梁（はり）五珠と一珠との間にある

3 横のさんのことです。

4 桁（けた）は、縦の棒で珠を貫いている軸をいいます。

定位点（ていいてん）
五玉（ごだま）
梁（はり）
桁（けた）
枠（わく）
一玉（いちだま）

各けたに、梁から上に、玉一個で５を意味する５玉があり、梁から下に、

5 玉一個で１を意味する１玉が４個あります。玉を動かすことを「おく」といいます。

6 各けたの玉は、梁に近づけると加える、離すと減らすことを表すルールになっています。

7 玉を動かす時は親指と人差し指を使います。

１珠の増やし方（おく）と減らし方ですが、増やすのは、親指の腹で上げ、

8 減らすときは人差し指の腹を使って。

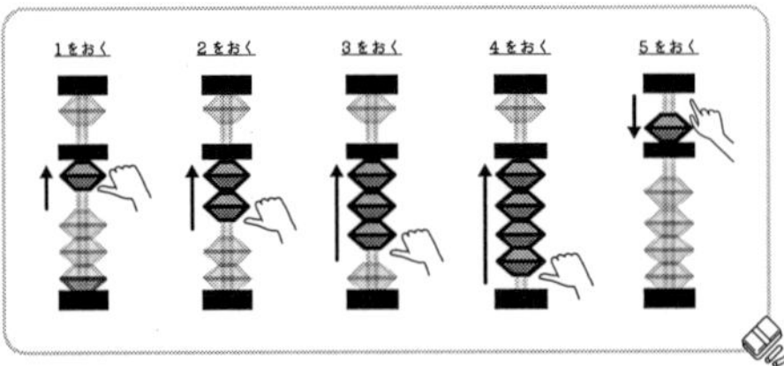


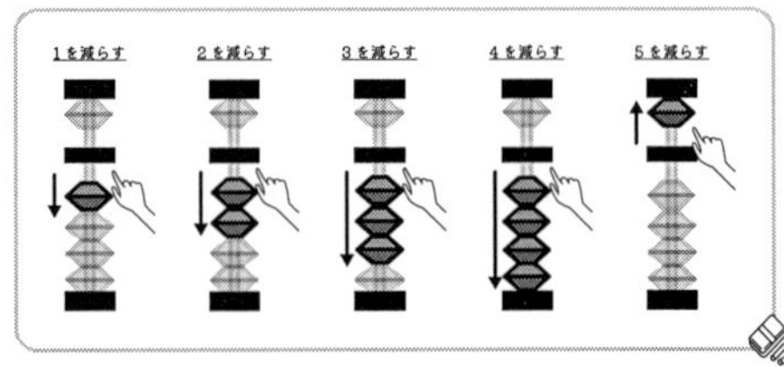


9 梁の上にある五珠のおき方ですが、人差し指だけをつかいます。

10 増やすときは人差し指の腹で下げ、減らすときは人差し指の爪の方で上げます

梁の上にある点を定位点といい、３桁ごとに打ってあります。

11 定位点は計算するときの桁確認になります。

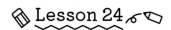

Grade 5 & 6

# Soroban (Abacus)

Teacher

I am going to hand out abacuses to you now.　I will give them to the person in the first row.
1 Please pass them back to everyone. Does everyone have one?
2 Now, let me explain. Look at the diagram on the blackboard.
The outside area is called the frame. There is a horizontal bar called the Beam which separates
3 the lower beads from the upper beads.
4 The vertical poles that run through the beads are called rods.

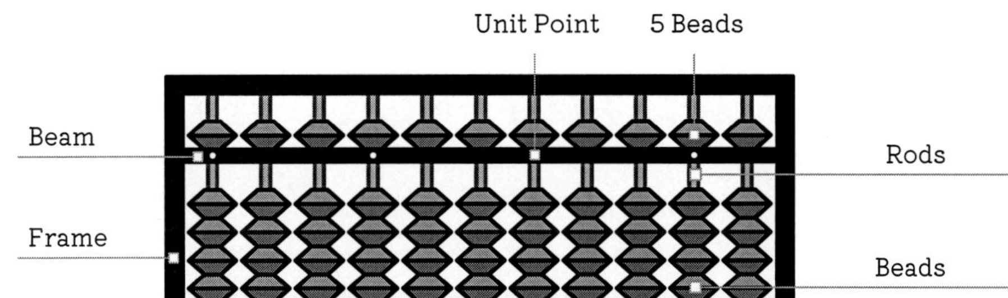


In each column, there are 5 beads (go-dama). Four beads are below the Beam and 1 is above
5 the beam (ichi dama). Moving the balls is called "Oku". When we move a bead, we say we 'place it'.
The rule is that when we slide a bead towards the Beam, that means the number is increasing.
6 Conversely, when we move the bead away from the Beam it means the number is decreasing.
7 Use your thumb and index finger to move the beads.
Raise the bead with the ball of your thumb to increase, and use the belly of your index finger
8 to decrease.

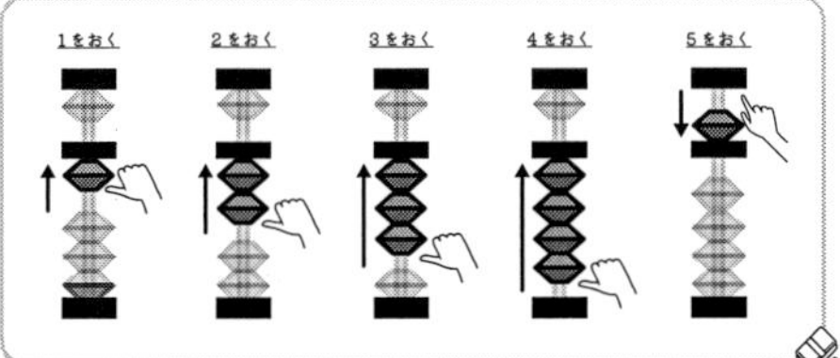


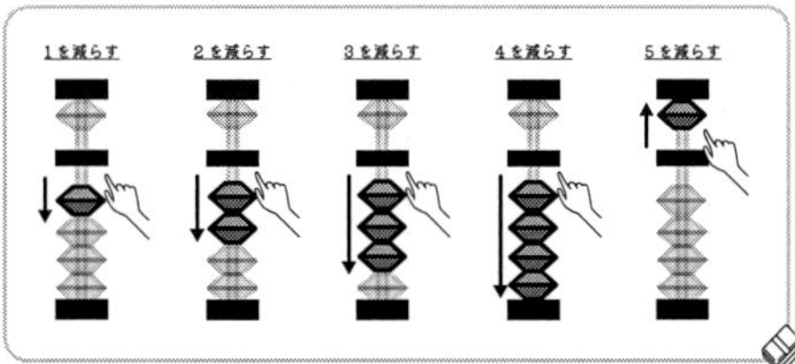


9 How do you place the five beads on the beam? For the go-dama we only use our index fingers.
When increasing, lower with the ball of the index finger, when reducing, raise it with the index
10 fingernail.
On the Beam, every third column has a dot. These are called unit points and they represent
11 the last digit of a number when calculating.

高学年

# そろばん

先生

1 では、実際にソロバンを使ってみましょう。
2 まず、そろばんの端を左手でしっかりおさえます。ステップ１です。
次に、そろばんを上の方を持ち上げて、五珠も一珠も下に揃えて、
3 五珠を右手の小指ではらいます。ステップ２です。
一珠を上にあげる時は親指を使い、下げる時は人差し指を使いますが、
4 使わない３本の指は軽く握ります。ステップ３です。

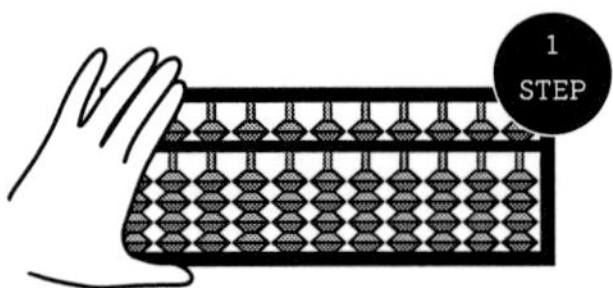

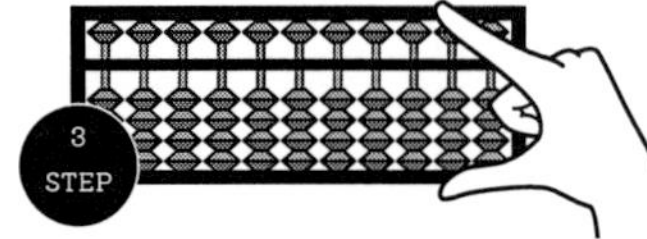


5 4+8＝12 を、そろばんでやってみましょう。
6 黒板に図を貼りますから、顔をあげてください。

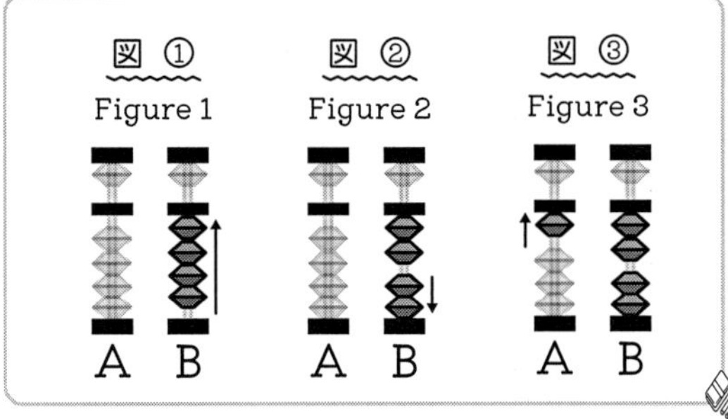


まず、「4」は一の位が４ということですから、B のけたの１玉を４つ、
7 はりに近づけます。(図①)
次に、「8」は一の位が８ということなのですが、B のけたには、残りは５を表す５玉
しか残っていませんから、計算ができません。そこで、8 は、10 から ２ を引いた数です
8 から先程、はりにちかづけた１玉４個のうち、2 個をはりから遠ざけて（図②)、

9 十の位を表すA の桁の１玉１個を梁に近づけます（図③)

すると、A のけたで１玉１個が加わりましたので 10、B のけたで最初１玉４個が加え
られていましたが、2 個が減りましたから ２となり、A とB のけたを併せると 12 と
10 なります。

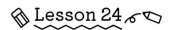

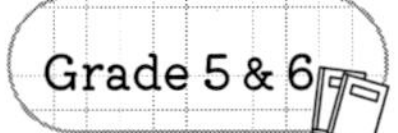


# Soroban (Abacus)

Teacher

1 Now, let's actually use the Soroban.
2 First, hold the edge of the abacus firmly with your left hand. Step 1.
Next, lift the abacus up so all the beads fall to the bottom of the center and use your pinky
3 to move all the go-dama to the top. Step 2.
Use the thumb to raise the single bead up and the index finger to lower it, but lightly grip
4 with the three fingers that are not used. Step 3.

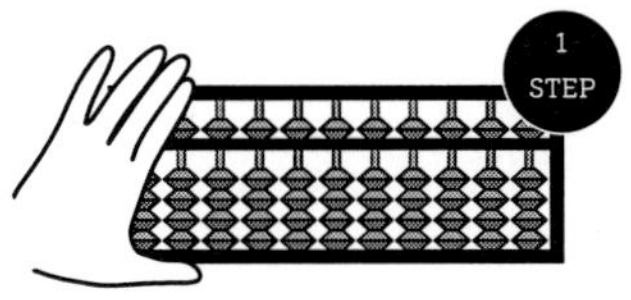

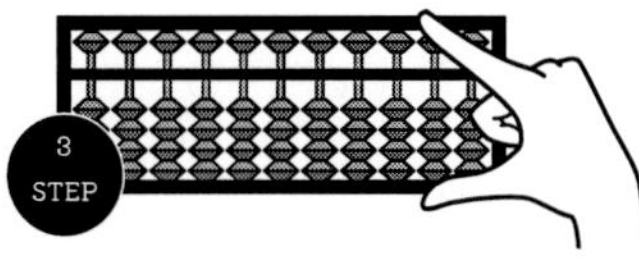


5 Let's try 4 + 8 = 12 on the abacus.
6 I will put the diagram on the blackboard, so everyone please look up.

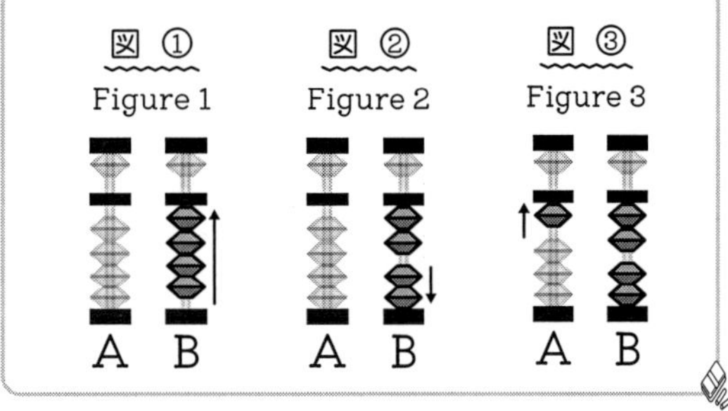


First, the "4" means that we use the ichi-dama so move four beads, which has a value of 1 each,
7 in column B closer to the Beam. (Figure 1)
Next, "8" means that we add 8 but if you look at column B, only the go-dama, which has a value
of 5 is left, right? We can't calculate it only using column B. To calculate it then, we have to carry
it over to column A, which represent tens. We first know that 8 is a number that you get by
8 subtracting 2 from 10, so first we slide 2 beads down from the four beads we just slid up. (Figure 2)
We now have 10 that we need to add in. Since the first column of beads, column B represent
single digit numbers and column A represent tens, for the remaining ten we move 1 bead from
9 column A closer to the Beam. (Figure 3).
In other words, 1 bead gets added to column A, and the 2 beads in column B stay the same
10 since we carried two over from the four beads we had before. Finally adding A and B we get 12.

## いろんな図形の表現

正三角形

Equilatetal Triangle

二等辺三角形

Isosceles Triangle

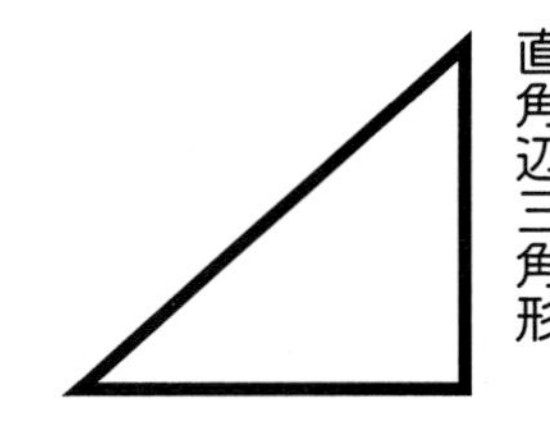

直角辺三角形

Right Triangle

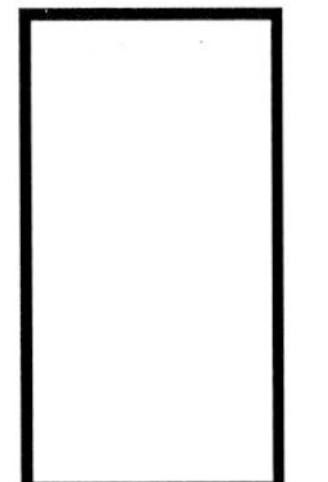

長方形

Rectangle

平行四辺形

Parallelogram

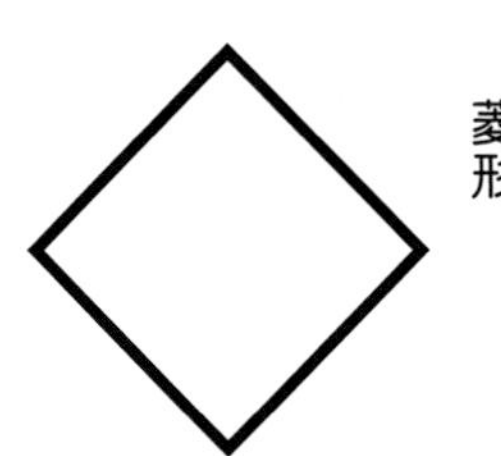

菱形

Diamond

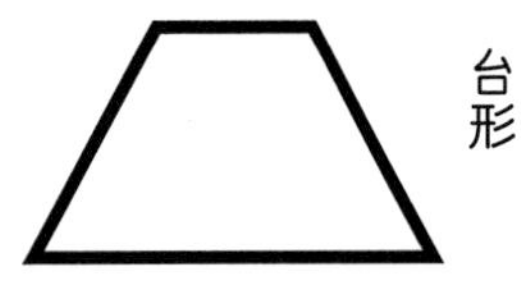

台形

Trapezoid

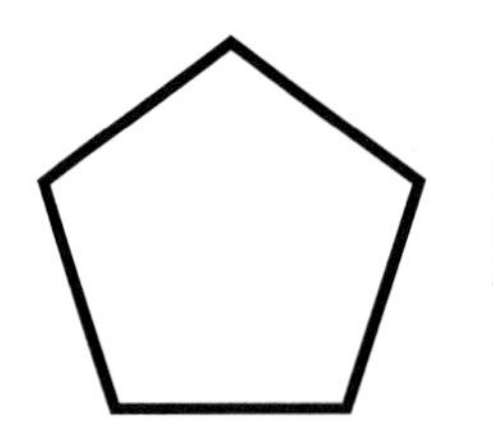

五角形

Pentagon

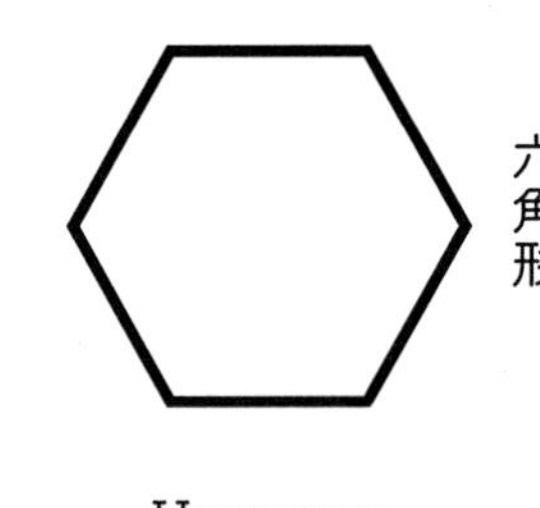

六角形

Hexagon

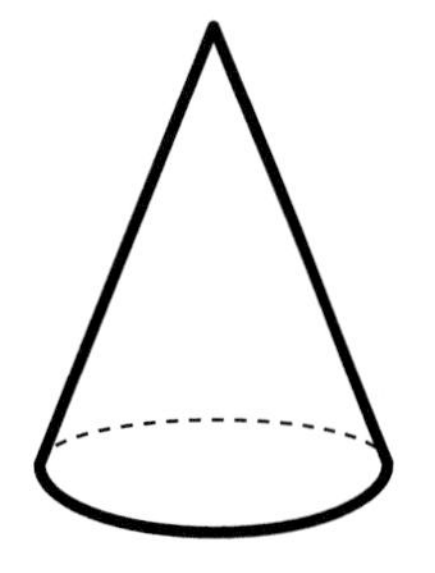

円柱

Cone

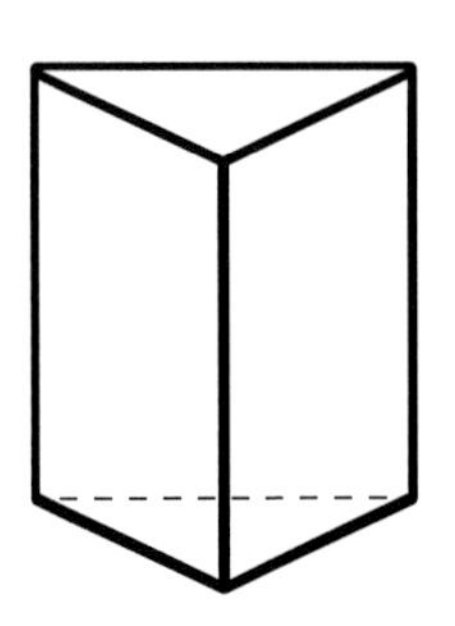

三角柱

Triangular Prism

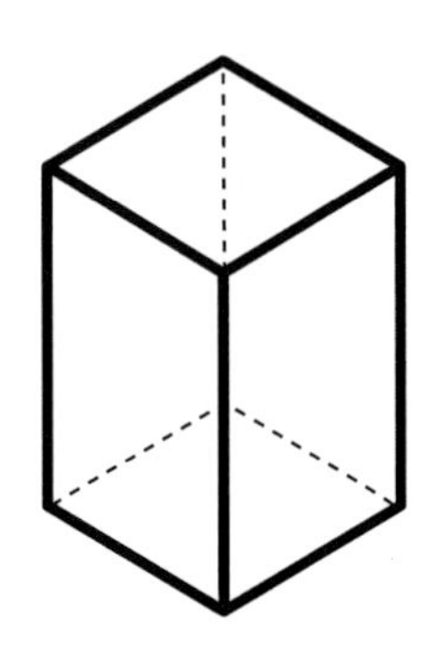

四角柱

Quadrangular Prism

# 国語
subject 2
Japanese

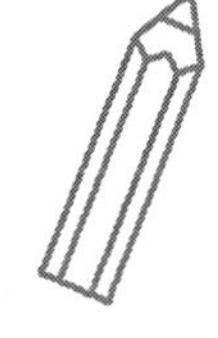

低学年

# 書き方の基本

先生

1 小学生になると、毎日、鉛筆で文字や数字を書くことになります。
2 正しい姿勢で、正しく鉛筆をもって、書けるようにしましょう。
まず、背中をまっすぐ伸ばして、体と机の間を少し開けます。お腹が、机に触れない
3 くらいに開けます。
両足を床につけます。足の裏が、床につかない人はいますか。
4 では、鉛筆を一本出してください。
5 鉛筆を、親指と人差し指で挟むようにして持ち、中指で支えます。こんな感じです。

中指、薬指、小指を軽く丸めて、小指は、ノートにつけます。
6 指に力を入れすぎないようにします。

先生

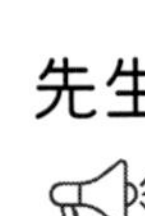

1 私たちが使っている日本語には、ひらがなとカタカナと漢字という 3 種類の文字が
2 あります。教室の前の壁に、50 音ひらがな表と 50 音カタカナ表が、貼ってありますね。

3 ひらがなとカタカナは、文字としては違いますが、同じ発音です。
右端の一番上にある文字は、ひらがなでは「あ」、カタカナでは「ア」と書いてありますが、
4 どちらも「a」という発音です。
ですから、50 音ひらがな表で発音の順番を覚えると、50 音カタカナ表も簡単に覚える
5 ことができます。
皆さん、先生が、「あいうえお」を、ゆっくりと発音しますから、先生の口を見ていて
6 ください。
7 発音するときに、口の形が違います。「あ・い・う・え・お」。わかりますね。
8 では、先生の口の形を見ながら、発音してみましょう。準備はいいですか。
9 大きな声で、一緒に始めますよ。続けて、かきくけこを発音してみましょう。
10 先生が、かきくけこを発音しますから、先生の口を、また見ていてください。
11 「か・き・く・け・こ」。わかりましたか。
12 あれ、先生の口の動きが、「あいうえお」と、かなり似ているのに気が付きましたか。
そうなんです。「あ」と「か」、「い」と「き」、「う」と「く」、「え」と「け」、「お」と「こ」は、
13 形が同じなんですよ。なぜかわかりますか。
「か」を長く発音してみてください。「か・あー」となるでしょ。「き」は「き・いー」
14 となりますね。「く」は「く・うー」ですね。
「かきくけこ」からは、発音の最後が、「あいうえお」になるんです。だから、口の形が
15 同じになるんですよ。

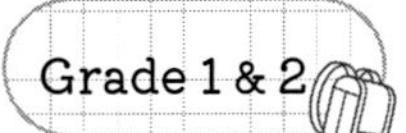


# Basics of Writing

Teacher

1 In elementary school, you will start to use a pencil to write letters and numbers every day.
2 So, let's learn how to write while sitting up properly and holding the pencil correctly.
First, sit with your back straight and keep a little space between your body and the desk,
3 so your stomach is not quite touching the desk. Your feet should be touching the floor.
Is there anyone whose feet cannot touch the ground?
4 Now, take out your pencil.
You should hold the pencil with your thumb and your index finger, and your middle finger
5 should be supporting it. Like this.
Bend your middle, ring, and pinky finger slightly, and your pinky should touch the paper.
6 Try not to put too much pressure on your fingers.

Teacher

1 There are three types of characters in the Japanese language that we use: "hiragana", "katakana", and "kanji".On the wall in front of the classroom, there is a 50-syllable hiragana
2 chart and a 50-syllable katakana chart, right?
3 Hiragana and katakana are different characters, but they are pronounced the same.
The character at the top right corner in hiragana is written あ, and on the katakana chart
4 it's written ア, but both are pronounced "a".
This means that if we remember how to pronounce all the words in hiragana in order,
5 you can memorize the katakana chart easily as well.
Listen, I'm going to slowly pronounce "あ, い, う, え, お" (a, i, u, e, o) so please watch
6 my mouth carefully.
7 The shape of my mouth is different when I pronounce each one. "あ, い, う, え, お". You see?
8 Let's now pronounce them together, watch the shape of my mouth. OK, ready?
9 Together in a loud voice. Let's continue to pronounce "か, き, く, け, こ", now.
10 I'll pronounce"か, き, く, け, こ", so watch my mouth again.
11 "か, き, く, け, こ". Is it clear?
12 Did you notice, my mouth moved quite similar to "あ, い, う, え, お"?
Indeed, あ and か, い and き, う and く, え and け, お and こ have the same mouth shapes.
13 Do you know why?
Try to hold か for a long time. It becomes "かあー", right? And for き, it becomes "きいー".
14 く becomes "くうー".
Yes, from "か, き, く, け, こ", the ending sound will actually be the same sound
15 as "あ, い, う, え, お". That is why the shape of the mouth is the same.

低学年

## ひらがな

先生

1 今日から、ひらがなの勉強をはじめます。

2 「あ」を学習します。

3 では、次に、「あ」の書き順を練習してみましょう。

4 書くときは、書く順序がとても大事です。

5 先生の方を見てくださいね、いいですか。

6 皆さん、鉛筆を持つ方の手の人差し指を立てて、手を上げてください。

7 いいですか。まず、①と書いてあるところからです。→の方向を見てくださいね。
左から右に横に伸ばして、止めます。

8 次に、②と書いてある部分です。
今、引いた横棒の真ん中の少し上から、→の方向を見て、上から斜め右下に、少し曲げて

9 下ろします。

最後に、③と書いてある部分です。最初の横線の右端の少し下から、斜め左下に、少し曲げて下ろして、それからクルッと回します。

10 鉛筆を持たない方の手は、上に出して、ノートが動かないように押さえてください。

11 はい、「あ、い、う、え、お」の書き順の練習が終わりましたね。

12 では、続けて、「か、き、く、け、こ」の書き順の練習をしましょう。

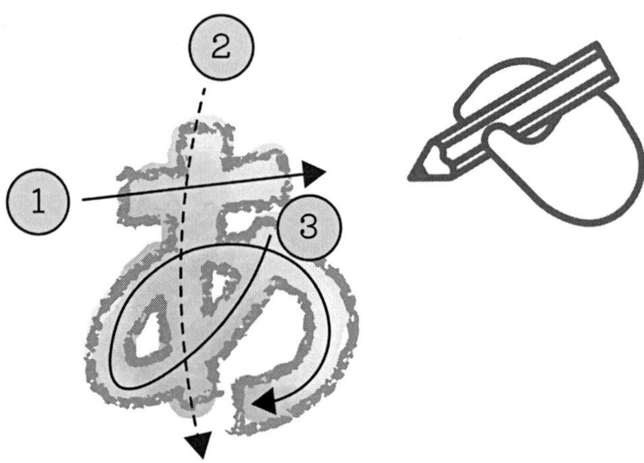

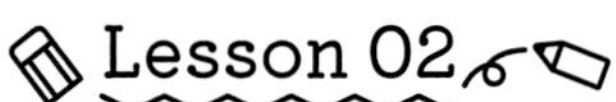

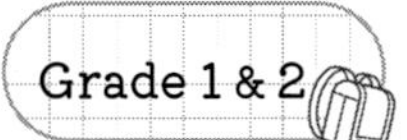


# Hiragana

Teacher

1 Starting today, we are going to begin learning hiragana.

2 We are going to start from あ.

3 Let's practice how to write あ.

4 When you write, stroke order is very important.

5 So please watch what I do carefully, OK?

6 Put up the index finger of your writing hand.

7 Ready? First of all, let's start from the place where it says ①. Please look in the direction of →.
Move horizontally from left to right and then stop.

8 Next is the part marked ②.
From a little above the middle of the horizontal bar you just drew, look in the direction of →,
and make a downward stroke. Please notice that it curves slightly sideways from the top to

9 the bottom.
Finally, the part marked ③. From just below the right end tip of the first horizontal line,
make a stroke down but slightly toward the left. Then bring it around to the right, drawing a loop.

10 Use your free hand to hold the worksheet so it won't move.

11 Alright, we have now finished practicing writing " あ, い, う, え, お".

12 Now, let's continue and practice the stroke orders of " か, き, く, け, こ".

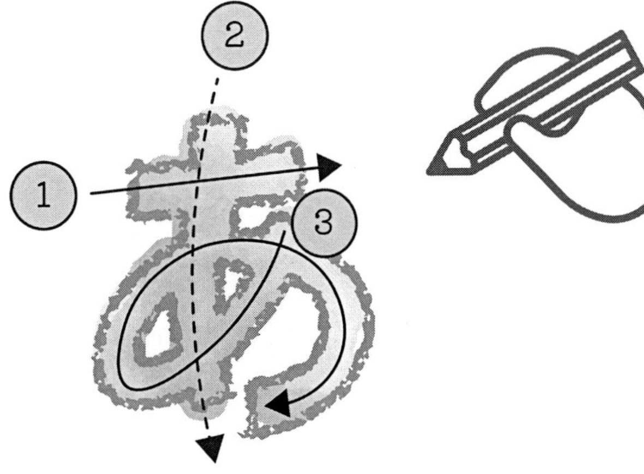

低学年

## 表現

先生

1 ひらがな50音表とカタカナ50音表は、みなさん、覚えましたね。ひらがなやカタカナの
2 練習をしながら、お話をしたとき、覚えたひらがなやカタカナでない言葉が、ありましたね。

3 例えば、チョウチョのチョ、ダンスのダ、という言葉です。
4 言葉を文字にしてみましょう。
5 黒板に書いてみますね。　チョウチョ、パン、ダンス
6 このように、「゛」（濁点）や「゜」（半濁点）、「ョ」のように捨て仮名があります。

7 50音表の左側を見てください。その文字が書いてあります。
8 ゛（濁点）がついて発音する文字は、か行, さ行、タ行, ハ行です。
9 ゜（半濁点）がついて発音する文字は、ハ行です。
捨て仮名は、表に載っているのはヤ行です。ただ、捨て仮名については、従来日本語に
10 なかった外国語の発音のために、捨て仮名として、母音が使用されるようになってきました。

ところで、「゛」（濁点）の書き順は、その文字を書き終えた最後で、左の点、右の点の順で
書きます。「゜」（半濁点）も最後に書きます。
11 どちらも、マスの中に書き、マスからはみ出さないようにしてください。
12 捨て仮名は、ひとマス使って、普通の文字の大きさの半分の大きさで、マスの右上に書きます。

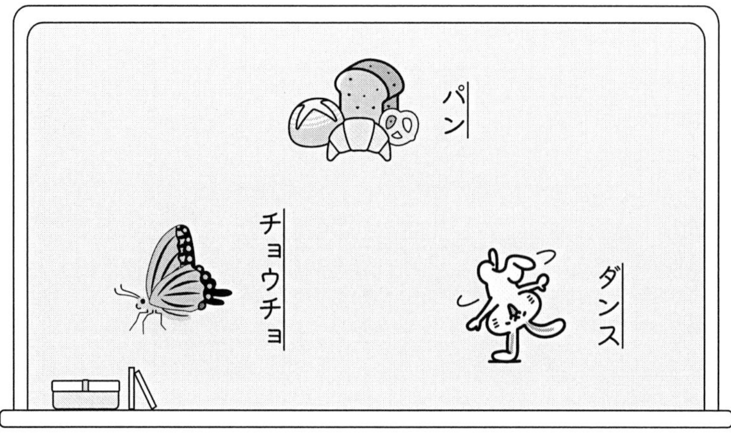


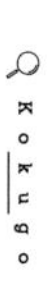

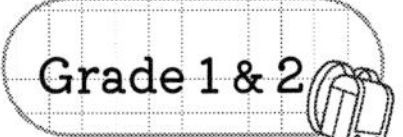

Grade 1 & 2

# Expressions

Teacher

1 You have all memorized the hiragana 50-syllable chart and the katakana 50-syllable chart, right?
As we practiced practicing hiragana and katakana, we came across some hiragana and katakana
2 that we haven't learned yet, right?
3 For example, “cho” in “choucho” (butterfly), and “da” in “dansu” (dance).
4 Let's try to write these words.
5 I'll write them on the blackboard: チョウチョ、パン、ダンス
Like this, we use two small lines 「゛」(dakuten) and a small circle 「゜」(han-dakuten) or
6 sometimes small characters like「ョ」discarded pseudonym(sutekana).
7 Those are written on the left side of the characters, as you can see.
8 The「゛」(dakuten) is used with the カ column, サ column, タ column, and ハ column.
9 The「゜」(han-dakuten) is used only with the ハ column.
Only the characters in the ヤ column are made discarded pseudonym(sutekana).
These small vowel letters are used to make foreign sounds which originally did not exist
10 in Japanese.
By the way, the order of how you write 「゛」is to start writing from the lower one then
the upper one, and always write it after you write the character. The same is true for「゜」.
11 Be careful not to go out of the box.
For the small letters like ャ , ュ , and ョ , you should use a new box, and write them about
12 half of the size of the normal size letters at the top right corner of the box.

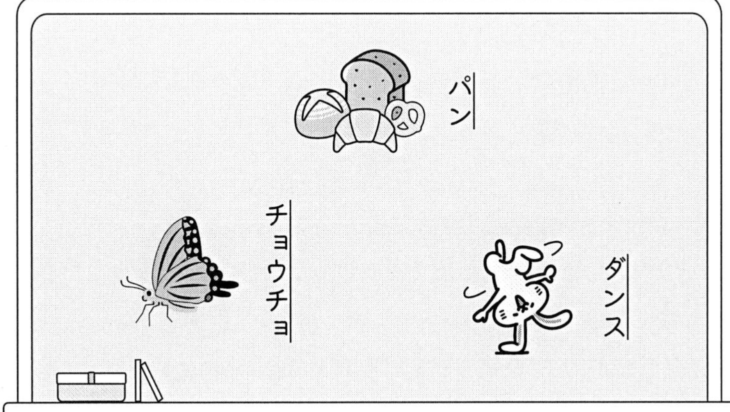

低学年

## 書いてみよう

先生

1 ひらがなとカタカナを書けて、読めるようになりましたから、いろんな文章が読めて、
楽しめるようになりましたね。
2 いろんな本を読んで、新しいことをどんどん、吸収していきましょう!
本を読むときは、背中を伸ばして、両方の腕も伸ばして、本を両方の手で握って、
本を立てます。
3 机の上に置いたままで、背中を丸めて、目の近くで読むと、目が悪くなります。
4 みんなで、大きな声をだして読みますよ。

クラス

5 くまさんが、ふくろをみつけました。

6 「おや、なにかな。いっぱい、はいっている。」

先生

皆さん、「くまさんが」の後に「、」がついていて、「みつけました」の後に「。」がついていますが、
7 これを読まなかったのは、正しいです。
「、」(句点)ところで、一度読むのを止めてから読み出し、「。」(読点)までが、一つの文章
8 ですから、そこで、また読むのを止める、ことを表す記号です。
9 おや、なにかな。いっぱいはいっている。の前後に「　と　」がついていますね。

10 これは、「かぎかっこ」といって、誰かが話している言葉である記号です。
文章には、このような記号を付けるルールがあります。これは重要ですから、覚えて
11 おいてください。
また、文章には、誰がや何がといった、文章の主人公がいて、主人公であることは、
12 主人公の言葉のあとに、「が」か「は」を付けるルールになっています。

13 だから、くまさんが、ふくろをみつけました。
14 では、くまさんが、この文章の主人公であることが分かります。

では、続けて、文章を読みます。同じように、先生が読みますから、続けて、皆さんが読んで
15 ください。さっき、読む声が小さかったので、今回は、もっと大きな声で読んでくださいね。
16 鉛筆を握っている人がいますね。今は鉛筆を握る時間ではありません。
17 筆箱にしまってください。

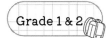

Grade 1 & 2

## Let's Write

**Teacher**

1 Now that we have learned hiragana and katakana, we can enjoy reading many kinds of sentences.

2 Let's read many kinds of books and learn even more new things!
When you read, you need to sit with your back straight, both of your arms stretched out,
and hold the book up with both hands. If you leave the book on your desk and read with
3 your back bent forward, your sight can get worse because the book is too close to your eyes.
4 Now, let's read together out loud.

**Class**

くまさんが、ふくろをみつけました。
5 (A bear found a bag.)
「おや、なにかな。いっぱい、はいっている。」
6 ("Oh! What's this! It's really full.")

**Teacher**

Well done everyone. After『くまさんが』, there is「、」a comma and「。」is period after
7 『みつけました』. You all did a good job because you didn't read those.
When you see a comma, you take a short pause. And when you see a period, you pause
8 longer because that is the sign for the end of a sentence.
We can also see that there are brackets containing
9 the「おや、なにかな。いっぱいはいっている。」sentence.
10 These are like quotation marks. It means that somebody is talking.
In written Japanese, there are rules like this for punctuation. It's very important, so please
11 don't forget.
Also, in sentences, there are main subjects and objects. There is a rule to put「が」or「は」
12 after the subject of the sentence.

13 So for a sentence like「くまさんが、ふくろをみつけました」(the bear found a bag).
14 You can see that くまさん (bear) is the main character of this sentence.

OK, let's keep reading. Like last time, I will read first so please follow after me. Last time
15 I didn't hear enough of you reading, please read it out loud this time, OK?
16 I see some of you are holding pencils. It's not time to have your pencils now.
17 Please put them away in your pencil cases.

低学年

## 助詞

先生

1 「ぼく(　　)、ちょうしょくにバナナ(　)たべました。」
2 Boku wa,　choushoku ni banana o tabemashita、と言いました。

この発音ですと、「ぼくわ」となりますし、「バナナお」となりますが、日本語の文章は、
3 「ぼくは」、「バナナを」と書いて、「は」を「wa」、「を」を「o」と発音します。

この使い方は、くっつきの「は」、くっつきの「を」といい、言葉を文字であらわすときで、
4 文字に「wa」、「o」を発音するときに使います。
ほかに、がっこう(　　)いく。というときも、発音は「e」ですが、
5 へ (he)と書いて、えと発音します。
「は」を「wa」、「を」を「o」、「へ」を「e」と発音して、文章に使う場合というのは、
6 たくさんの本を読んで、知っていくことが必要です。

### 「わ」と発音する「は」

＋one

主語につく助詞（格助詞）は、「わ」と読んでも「は」と書きます。と教えがちですが、副助詞（係助詞）においても「は」を使い、接続詞や「は」を語源とする語句も「わ」と発音しても、「は」と書きます。

接続詞・・・
あるいは、または、もしくは、では、それでは、とはいえ

他・・・
いずれは、さては、恐らくは、願わくは、こんにちは、こんばんは、これはこれは

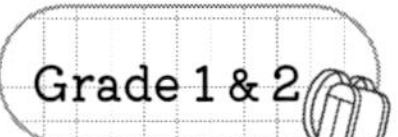


# Particles

Teacher

1 ぼく（　）、ちょうしょくにバナナ（）たべました。

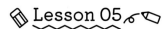

2 I've just said, "Boku wa, choushoku ni banana o tabemashita."

From the pronunciation, you hear ぼくわ (boku wa) and バナナお (Banana o), but in Japanese,
write「ぼくは」(boku ha) and「バナナを」(banana wo) .「は」(ha) is pronounced "wa", and
3 「を」(wo) is pronounced "o".

We call these "くっつき"の「は」and "くっつき"の「を」particles and when used in
4 sentences they are pronounced "wa" and "o".

Another example is がっこう（へ）いく (go school). We pronounce this "e" the same
5 as「え」(e), but we write「へ」(he).

6 So we need to read a lot and get familiar with「は」-wa,「お」-o and「へ」-e.

低学年

# 漢字の基本

先生

1 ひらがなとカタカナを学習したので、今回から漢字の学習をします。

漢字というのは、中国大陸から入ってきた文字で、ひらがなやカタカナより古くから
使われてきた文字で、ひらがなは、漢字から作られました。カタカナについては、
2 ひらがな同様に漢字から作られたという説と全く別で作られたという説があります。
3 現在使われている漢字は、昔より随分簡略化されています。
4 漢字は、日本語の発音を文字として表すのに、大変、役立っています。
例えば、はしとひらがなで書くと、食事の時のはし(箸)なのか、
川にかかっているはし(橋)なのか、隅のはし(端)なのかわかりませんよね。
5 漢字で、橋と書くと、川にかかっているはしのことだとわかります。
6 漢字には、いくつかルールがあります。
7 一つは、漢字を書く時の書き順です。書き順は、漢字ごとに決まっています。
8 ひらがなやカタカナでも、書き順がきまっていましたね。
9 もともと、中国大陸や日本では、文字は、毛筆で書いていました。
書き順は、毛筆で書きやすい順に決まって、鉛筆やボールペンで書くことが多い現代でも、
10 その順を守って書いています。

11 二つ目に、画数です。画数とは、漢字を構成する「画」の数のことです。
「画」とは、漢字を書く時に、ペンを紙に下してから、離すまでに描かれた線や点のことで、
12 漢字は、複数の画数で構成されています。
13 三つ目に、はね、とめ、はらいです。これは後程、説明します。
14 四つ目に、一つの漢字に、読みが二つかそれ以上あることです。
これも、今後、新しい漢字を学習するたびに説明しますが、読みは、音読みと訓読みの
15 2つがあります。
16 教科書の裏ページを見てください。
17 1年生で習う漢字の一覧があります。
その一覧の一つ一つのマスに、漢字が書いてあって、左上に画数、その下に書き順が
18 載っていますね。
漢字の下に、カタカナとひらがなで書いてあるのが、その漢字の読みで、カタカナの読みが
音読み、ひらがなの読みが訓読みです。音読みは、中国大陸から漢字が伝わったときに、
その漢字の読みがもとになった読み、訓読みは、漢字が伝わる前から日本で使われていた
19 発音に、漢字を当てはめた読みです。
20 このように、漢字は、日本語を文字として表すために大変重要です。

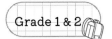

# Basics of Kanji

Teacher

So far we've learned hiragana and katakana, and from today, we are going to learn about
1 kanji.
Kanji comes from China. It's much older than hiragana and katakana, and actually
hiragana was formed from kanji. With katakana, we are not sure. Some people think that
2 katakana came from kanji, like hiragana, but others think it has no relationship to kanji.
3 The kanji we use today are much simpler versions of the kanji used in olden times.
4 Kanji is very useful for expressing the pronunciation of Japanese as characters.
For example, if we write はし (hashi) in hiragana, you don't know if it means
chopsticks（箸）, or a bridge（橋), or the edge of something,（端)right? But if you write
5 a bridge 橋 in kanji, you know right away that it is something over a river.
6 There are several rules for writing kanji.
7 One is the stroke order when writing kanji. The stroke order is determined for each kanji.
8 Hiragana and katakana also have a certain stroke order.
9 This is because people used to use brushes to write in China and Japan.
The order of writing was determined by the order in which the characters could be easily
written with a brush, and even today, when pencils and ballpoint pens are often used
10 for writing, the order is still followed.
11 Second, the numbers of strokes. A stroke is counted after your pencil leaves the paper.
The moment the pencil touches the paper until the moment the pencil leaves the paper
12 is one stroke. Kanji are formed by these lines and dots.
13 Third, there are the hooks, stops, and sweeps. I will explain these to you later.
14 Fourth, there are often two or more ways of reading the same kanji.
I will explain more about this as well once we learn a new kanji, but there are two ways to
15 read; there is an 音読み (onyomi) and a 訓読み (kunyomi) for each kanji.
16 Please look at the back of the textbook.
17 There's a chart of all the kanji you will learn in first grade.
In each box, there is one kanji, and at the top left corner it says the number of strokes and
18 below it shows the order of strokes. Got it?
And at the bottom of the box, there are the different pronunciations of the character in
both hiragana and katakana. The katakana is the 音読み (onyomi) while the hiragana is
the 訓読み (kunyomi). 音読み is based on the pronunciation from China, and 訓読み is
19 the pronunciation Japanese people attached to the characters a long time ago.
20 As you can see, Kanji are very important characters for expressing Japanese.

低学年

# 漢字の基本

先生

1 数字にも、漢字があります。まず、数字を表す漢字から学習します。
教科書 58 ページを開いて、そこが閉じないように指を挟んで、教科書の裏ページの
2 1年生で習う漢字の一覧を見てください。

3 数字を表す漢字は、一、二、三、四、五、六、七、八、九、十です。
4 先ほど説明したように、数字を表す漢字も漢字ですから、読みが、音読みと訓読みの
二つあります。
5 訓読みの方を見てください。訓読みの下に「つ」が書いてありますね。
これを送りがなといいます。漢字の訓読みでは、漢字そのもので意味がある場合と、
6 送り仮名と一緒になって意味がある場合があります。
7 音読みでは、他の漢字と組み合わせて意味があることが多いです。
8 数字を表す漢字は、画数は少ないですが、書き順を見て、しっかりと練習します。

書くときは、黄金の決まりがあります。それは、横線を引く場合は左から右、縦線を引くとき
9 は上から下です。
縦書きの文章では、漢字の数字を使い、数字は使いません。横書きの文章では、数字を使い、
10 漢字の数字は使いません。
11 数字は、アラビア文字と呼ばれています。もともとは、厳格に使い分けがされていましたが、
12 今はあいまいで、縦書きの場合も、数字を使うことがあります。

数字を表す漢字を使って数を書きますが、その下に数え方と書いてあります。数え方は、
13 日本語独特のものです。
リンゴやミカンは何個、猫や犬は何匹、車は何台、本やノートは何冊、紙や新聞は何枚、
14 鉛筆は何本、人は何人と数えます。

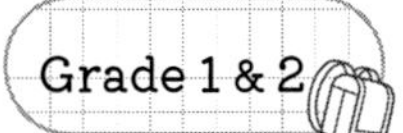

Grade 1 & 2

## Basics of Kanji

Teacher

1 There are also ways to express numbers with kanji. That is what we will study today.

Please open to page 58 and hold the place with your fingers so you can quickly look at
2 the back of the textbook.

3 As you can see, the way to express numbers in kanji is 一, 二, 三, 四, 五, 六, 七, 八, 九, 十.
4 Like I explained just now, there are also onyomi and kunyomi for each of these characters.

5 Look at the kunyomi here. There is also「つ」(tsu) following the kunyomi, right?

This is needed to complete the word. With kunyomi, there are cases where the kanji
6 itself has a meaning, and cases where you need to use other characters to make a word.
7 With onyomi, often kanji are combined with other kanji to create meaning.

OK now, we are going to practice writing numbers in kanji. There aren't many strokes
8 but I want you to focus and practice as seriously as usual.

When writing kanji, we have a golden rule. That is, we always write horizontal lines from
9 right to left, and we always write vertical lines from top to bottom.

In vertically written sentences, use kanji numbers and not numerals. However,
10 in horizontal writing, use numerals and not kanji numbers.
11 These numbers are actually called Arabic numbers. Before, this rule used to be very strict.
12 But nowadays, it's not so strict and both are used.

There are numbers written in kanji, but then below them, it says counter. Counters are
13 something very specific to the Japanese language.

Apples and oranges are こ (ko), cats and dogs are ひき (hiki), cars are だい (dai),
notebooks and books are さつ (satsu), papers and newspapers are まい (mai),
14 pencils are ほん (hon), and people are にん (nin)

低学年

## 漢字の基本

先生

1 では、数字以外の漢字の学習を行います。
2 テレビを見る、手のひらを見るといった、見るの見という漢字からです。
3 先生の方を、「見」てください。カードを一緒に 「見」ながら、学習しますよ。

見という漢字の右側にみると、ひらがなが書いてあって、「み」と「る」は、文字の色が
4 違いますね。
5 これは黒色のひらがなは、漢字の読み、赤いひらがなは、送りかなです。
6 漢字の下にマスが3つあって、その左側に、書き順が書いてありますね。
その下に7画と書いてあります。これは、見という漢字を書くには、縦や横やななめに、
7 線を7回、書いては止めて、また書き始めるということです。

8 練習しましょう。人差し指を立ててください。
始めますよ。まず、左の線を上から下に引きます。次に、一番上の横線を左から右に引いて、
止めないでそのまま下におろしますよ。2画目は、横線から続けて縦線を引いて、これで
9 二画目です。

10 教科書の横線から縦線に折れるところの角を見てください。少し斜めになっていますね。
11 これは、習字で、筆を使って書くときに、方向を変更しやすいようにしているものです。
一画ずつ、書いてみますよ。
見るの漢字の下の部分のはねは、左は少し曲がってますね、右は最後に少し跳ね上げて
12 います。よく見て練習します。

続けて、学校の「学」と「校」を練習しますよ。2つの漢字を併せて読むと「がっこう」ですが、
13 別々に読むときは、「がく」と「こう」です。
14 学の5画目は、横線から曲げて、はねていて、これで5画目です。
15 また、6画目と7画目は続いていませんよ。

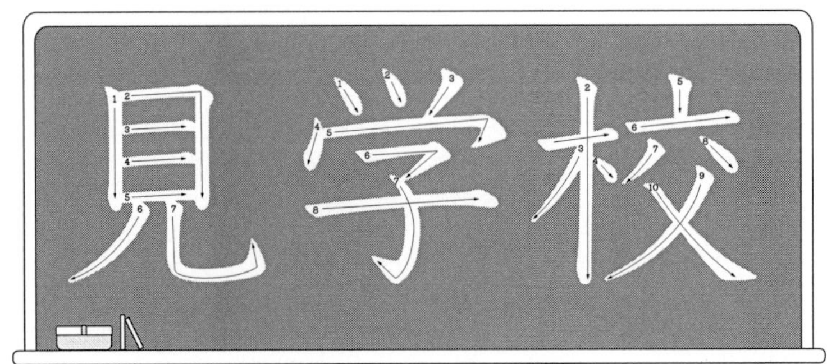

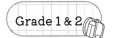

# Basics of Kanji

Teacher

1 Today, we are going to practice kanji other than numbers.
2 In this lesson, we are going to learn 見 (mi), it means "see"or "watch".
The mi here is used in situations like, テレビを見る (watch TV) or
3 手のひらを見る (look at your palm). Look here and please study this card.

4 On the rig3ht side of the kanji, 「み」(mi) and 「る」(ru) are written in different colors.
The one written in black is the pronunciation for the kanji and the one in red completes
5 the word.
6 There are three squares below the kanji and on the left; they show the stroke order, right?
Below that, it says 7 strokes. This means that the kanji 見 has 7 strokes, so writing all
7 the horizontal, vertical, and diagonal lines should be a total of 7 strokes.
8 Let's now practice this all together in the air with your index finger.
Alright, first, we are going to write this straight line on the left, from the top to the bottom.
And then, the second line will start from the top of that stroke. Draw a line straight to the
9 right, then make a sharp turn down without lifting your pencil from the paper.

By the way, in the textbook, the corner is not sharp, but rather it comes down at an angle,
10 right? This is just because when we write it with a brush, it is hard to make a sharp turn.
11 We are going to practice stroke by stroke.
Also, looking at the 見 kanji, do you see this bottom part where it curves outwards?
Notice that there is a hook at the end. It flips up! So you should all try to pay attention to
12 such details. It will make your handwriting much nicer.

Continuing on, let's practice the two kanji for "school"; putting 学 and 校 together
13 makes "gakkou" or school. Separately, 学 reads as "gaku" and 校 reads as "kou".
14 The 5th stroke in 学 has a hook at the end.
15 Also, the 6th and 7th strokes look like one stroke, but there are two strokes there.

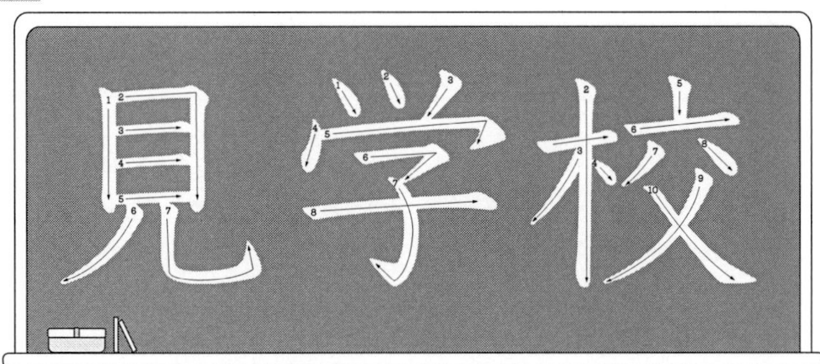

低学年

## 並び替え

先生

1 黒板を見てください。
2 私　本屋　絵本　一冊　買う
という言葉が、並んでいます。意味の通る文章にしてください。なお、このままでは、
3 日本語の文章になりませんから、適切な助詞を加えてください。

この文章の[誰が]は私で、[どこで]は本屋で、[何を]は絵本を、[どうする]は買うという
ことです。そして、主語のくっつき言葉で[は]を加え、どこでのくっつき言葉[で]、本屋で
4 を加え、何をのくっつき言葉で[を]を加えて文章の完成です。
5 もう1問やってみましょう。
6 私の　お弁当　母さん　作る　毎日　　語順もばらばらになっています。
7 私の母さん（は)、毎日、お弁当（を)作る　です。

8 それでもいいですし、この毎日という言葉は、先頭に持ってきて、
9 毎日、私の母さん（は)、お弁当（を)作る
10 毎日、お母さんは、私のお弁当（を)作る
11 とも、語順を変えることができます。どちらも正解です。
日本語は、このように、述語となる動詞が一番後ろにあって、主語が[が]あるいは[は]の
12 くっつき言葉ではっきりしていれば、意味を変えないで、語順を変えることができます。

先生

1 いまからプリントを配ります。

| | |
|---|---|
| カード1 | みんなで、じゃんけんをして、オニを決め、鬼は走り回って、<br>みんなの背中や手にタッチします。 |
| カード2 | オニの数が、4人以上になると、2人ずつの単位で分裂して、オニが増えていき、<br>逃げた人みんながオニの仲間になったら、初めからやり直して遊びます。 |
| カード3 | 鬼ごっこは、1人の鬼を決めて、鬼が、みんなを捕まえる遊びです。 |
| カード4 | オニがタッチして捕まえたら、その人もオニの1人となり、みんなを追いかけます。 |

このプリントは、文章がバラバラです。正しい順番に、文章をつなげていきます。
2 はさみで、カードを切り取ってください。切り取りましたか。
では、正しい順番に文章を並び替えてみましょう。みんな、それぞれで考えてみてください。
3 わからない時は、カードを色々と入れ替えてみてください。

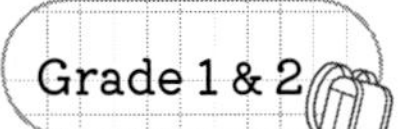

# Changing the Order of Words

Teacher

1 OK, please look at the blackboard.

2 Here, it says, 私 本屋 絵本 一冊 買う (I bookstore picture book one buy)

These words alone do not make any sense because, first of all, the order is messy and also

3 the particles are missing. I want you to correct this so that it is proper Japanese.

In this sense, the 'who', or the subject of the sentence, is 私, and the 'where' is 本屋,

4 'what' is 絵本 and the verb is 買う. To connect all these は, で, and を serve a certain purpose.

5 Let's try another one.

6 私の お弁当 母さん 作る 毎日 (My bento mother make every day)

7 [私の母さん (は)、毎日、お弁当 (を)作る]

(Watashi no okaasan wa, mainichi, obento o tsukuru - My mother makes a bento everyday).

8 Alternatively, you can also say

9 「毎日、私の母さん (は)、お弁当 (を)作る (Everyday, my mother makes a bento).

10 「母さん (は)毎日、私のお弁当 (を)作る (Everyday, mother makes my bento.).

11 Of course, all of these are correct expressions.

In Japanese, the verb is at the end while the subject is connected with particles like は or

が to show the relationship with the verb, so sometimes we can change the word order and keep

12 the same meaning.

Teacher

1 I am going to hand out a worksheet now.

| | |
|---|---|
| Card 1 | Everyone please play rock-paper-scissors to decide who will be "it" or the Oni, and the Oni will run around to catch the others by touching them. |
| Card 2 | Once there are over 4 "its", then they must chase in groups of two. Finally, when everyone gets caught then the game will be over. |
| Card 3 | Tag is a group game where one person, "it", tries to catch others. |
| Card 4 | Once "it" catches a person, then that person will also become "it". |

As you notice, the order of the cards is not correct. We need to rearrange them in a way that

2 makes sense. Please cut out each card with scissors. Done?

Now then, let's put these into the right order. I want everyone to think about it by yourself.

3 If you are not sure, try to shuffle around the cards randomly and see what makes sense.

中学年

# 書写

先生

1 3年生になると、時間割に書写という時間があります。

2 書写の時間は、文字を整えて書く方法を学ぶ時間です。

1年の時から、教科書や練習問題に、薄く書いてあったり、点線で書いてあったりした漢字やひらがな、カタカナをなぞって、文字の形を学んだり、書き順を練習してきまし
3 たね。

4 初めて学習する文字は、こうして、なぞって、書き順を覚えて学習していきます。

これまでと同じことをやるのに、なぜ国語の時間でなく、書写の時間となっているかというと、国語の時間での文字の学習は、その意味を知り、使い方を学習することに重点があります。いろいろな文字を習ってきました。

5 今度は、その文字自体のきれいな書き方を学習しますというのが、書写の時間です。

6 この時間は、墨を使います。絵の具と同じように、注意しないと洋服を汚します。

図工の時間と同じよ うに、スモックを着て構いませんよ、むしろ慣れるまでは着たほうが
7 よいと思います。

8 はい、黒板に注目してください。

9 右から、硯です。この中に墨を入れます。

10 その横が筆です。筆は、文字を書く太筆と、名前を書く小筆があります。

11 白い紙は、半紙といい、上に載っているが、文鎮というおもりです。

12 その下が黒に布でできていて、下敷きです。

13 左端に置いてあるのが、お手本です。

Grade 3 & 4

# Calligraphy

Teacher

1 In grade 3, we will  start calligraphy class.
2 The main focus of the lesson is to learn how to write characters neatly.
Since first grade, we have been practicing writing kanji, hiragana, and katakana by tracing dotted
3 lines and grey lines in textbooks and workbooks and learning their shapes and stroke order.

4 In this way, we could learn the order of strokes by tracing them.
Although we learn characters in both calligraphy and kokugo class, we have different purposes
5 for each.

In this calligraphy class, we will use this special black ink, sumi. Similarly to when you use paints,
6 you must be careful not to get your clothes dirty.
You can wear a smock if you want...actually, maybe it's better to just wear one for now until you
7 get used to using sumi.
8 OK. Now, please look at the blackboard.
9 On the right, there's an inkstone. We pour sumi into this inkstone.
Now place your brush next to it. There are two types of brushes, one is for writing larger
10 characters and the other is for smaller characters, like when you write your names.
11 The white paper is called hanshi. On top of it is a paperweight called a bunchin.
12 Below the paper, you'll see a cloth called a shitajiki, a desk pad.
13 And at the very left, you have an example to copy from.

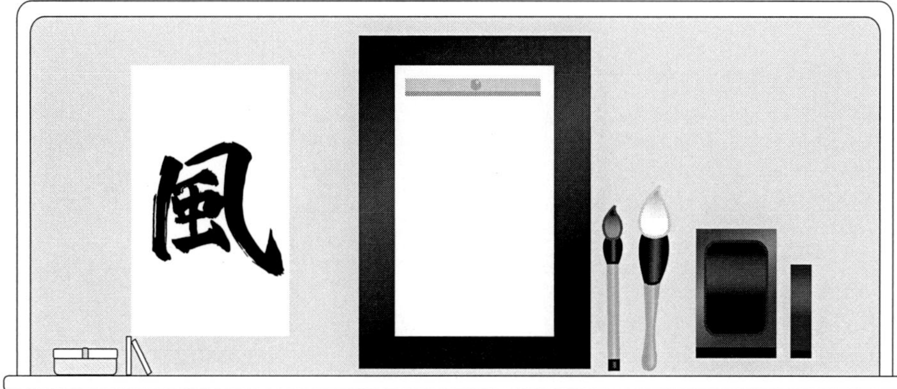

中学年

## 書写

先生

筆と墨は、鉛筆やボールペンが使われるようになった以前の古い時代から、文字を書
1 くために用いられてきました。
鉛筆やボールペンを使うことが多い現代で、小学校から筆と墨を使った習字を学習するのは、一つ目に、日本の多くの古い書物が、筆と墨で書かれていて、筆を使って書いてある文字は、私たちが 使っている文字の形とかなり違っているものもあるので、
2 それを理解していないと、古い書物が読めないことになります。

もう一つは、墨と筆を使うと、線を細くしたり、太くしたり、薄くしたり、かすれたりと、
3 文字を書くというより、芸術作品を作ることができるようになるからです。

黒板を見てください。これは皆さんも書くことのできる「風」という漢字を書いたものです。このように、墨と筆を使った文字で芸術作品を作ることを書道といい、日本
4 の伝統文化です。

5 では、書写セットを開いて、黒板に貼ってあるように並べてください。

6 文鎮は一本ですから、半紙の上の端に横に置いてください。
7 筆で使うときは、鉛筆で文字を書く時と、体の姿勢も、筆の持ち方も違います。

まず、背中をぴんと伸ばし、背もたれに触れず、机にお腹が触れないように椅子を
8 移動します。
次に、筆は、まっすぐ立てて、人差し指から３本をそろえて、親指と挟んで持ちます。
9 先生の持ち方をよく見てください。
10 そして、筆を持たない方の手で、半紙の下の部分を押さえます。

Grade 3 & 4

# Calligraphy

Teacher

1 A brush and black ink used to be the main tools for writing before pencils and pens were used.

In today's world of pencils and ballpoint pens, the reasons for learning calligraphy with a brush
and ink from elementary school is so that we can read old books. Old books were written using
brushes and ink and the characters have quite different shapes from what we are used to now.
2 They can be difficult to read without knowing about how characters were written in those days.

Another purpose is that, by using brushes and black ink, you can not only write characters that
deliver a message, but also create artistic works by making parts of a character thicker or thinner,
3 or even jagged.

Look at the blackboard here. This is the character '風' (wind) written in the kanji that we learned
before. As you might know, creating an artistic work with black ink and a brush is called shodou
4 (the art of calligraphy), and it's part of Japanese traditional culture.

Now, please open your calligraphy set and prepare the items inside just as I've shown
5 on the blackboard.
6 The paper weight should be placed on top of the paper horizontally.
When you write with a brush, your posture and how you hold your brush is different from when
7 you write with a pencil.
First, sit up straight so your back doesn't touch the back of your chair. Adjust your chair so that
8 your stomach is not touching your desk.
Next, hold the brush, keeping it straight up with your first, second, and third fingers in a row,
9 and use your thumb to support the brush. Look at how I am holding my brush.
10 Then hold the bottom of the paper with the hand not holding your brush.

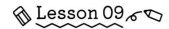

中学年

## 短歌と俳句

先生

毎年、春と秋に全国交通安全運動があります。毎年、学校に警察の方に交通安全指導に
1 来てもらっています。交通安全運動の一つとして、毎年、標語の募集があります。

2 歩道橋や道路のガードレールに書いてある標語をみた人がいるかもしれません。
3 有名なもののひとつに『気をつけよう、車は急には止まれない』というのがありました。
4 たぶん, これはみなさんの ほとんどが知っていると思います。
多くの人がこの標語をおぼえているのは、メッセージがみなさんのような学校に行く子ども
5 から会社員、お年寄りまで幅広く当てはまるからです。

こういうスローガンをつくるとき、印象に残り、テンポよくするため「５・７・５」で全
6 部で１７音のリズムにします。俳句というのは日本の古くからの韻文です。

先生

学習した通り、俳句というのは、日本で 昔から伝わる短文の詩です。この俳句をつくるとき
1 にはいくつかのきまりがあります。
2 ５・７・５のきまり以外に、17 音の中に季節を表す季語をいれるというきまりがあります。

例えば、ゆきだるま（５音）は冬の季語です. 雪は冬に降りますから, これはそんなに
難しくないです。でも, すこしピンとこないものもあります。七夕といえば、今では
季節が夏と思いますが, たなばたや（５音　たなばたでは４音なので、
3 一音付加）は秋の季語です。400 年前は秋の季節とされていました。

今日は, みんなで「夏」をお題に俳句を考えてみましょう。季語をいれることを忘れて
はいけません。夏の季語は、キャンプ・プール・海水浴・花火大会・扇風機・風鈴・蚊
4 取り線香・かき氷・蚊・ホタル・ひまわり等があります。
5 気持ちや情景が伝わるものをつくってくださいね。

今日, 私たちは国際化の世界にいます。そして, フランスやアメリカの多くの学生が学
6 校で俳句をつくっています。そこで今日は英語で俳句を作ってみましょう。
英語で作るときは３行にして書きます。１行目は５音節の語句を書き, ２行目は７音節,
7 ３行目は５音節です。

Grade 3 & 4

# Tanka and Haiku Poems

Teacher

Every spring and autumn, we have a traffic safety campaign nationwide. A few police officers come to our school and explain traffic safety every year. They also take applications for
1 the slogan of the year.
2 You might see these slogans on pedestrian bridges or along safety barriers.
3 One popular one was, “Watch out, cars can’t stop quickly”.
4 I’m sure most of you know this.
One reason a lot of people remember this is because the message of the slogan can be applied to a wide range of people, from elementary school kids like you to company employees or
5 the elderly.
When creating a slogan like this, the entire slogan should have a 17-note rhythm with "5, 7, 5" to leave a lasting impression and make the tempo more attractive. The rhythm of
6 the 17 syllables is used in all parts of the slogan. Haiku is an ancient Japanese rhyming text.

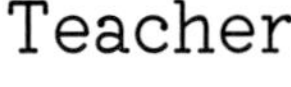

Teacher

As we learned, haiku is one of Japan's oldest traditional forms of poetry, and when you make
1 one yourself,
In addition to the 5-7-5 rule, today, we’re going to learn another rule. You have to use a word
2 that represents a season, which is called a “seasonal word.”
For example, 雪だるま(yukidaruma - snowman) (5 syllables) is a seasonal word for winter. We have snow in winter, so it’s not so difficult. But there are some tricky ones. You probably associate たなばた(Tanabata - Star Festival) with summer now; however, until 400 years ago, it was considered to be an autumn event, so
3 たなばたや (Tanabataya - Star Festival) (5 syllables) is a seasonal word for fall.
Today, I want you to think of a haiku representing summer. Make sure your haiku has a seasonal word. Seasonal words for summer are—camp, pool, swimming, summer
4 festival, fan, wind chime, mosquito coil, ice cream, firefly, sunflower, and so on.
5 I’d like you to make one that conveys your emotions and the scene.

Nowadays, we live in a very international world, and many students in the United States
6 or France make haiku at school. Today, let’s make a haiku in English.
When we make one in English, we write it on three lines. The word or phrase in the first
7 line should be 5 syllables, the second one 7, and the third 5.

中学年

# 短歌と俳句

先生

1 今日は、五・七・五に七・七を加えた日本の伝統的な短歌を学習します。

短歌といえば、皆さんが知っているのは、百人一首だと思います。みなさんは百人一首は知っています よね。カルタの一種で、正月に開かれる全国大会は日本の風物詩の一つ
2 ですし、テレビでもその様子が放映されています。

短歌の形式の話に戻りましょう。短歌は、五・七・五・七・七の音数で、五・七・五の部分を上の句、七・七の部分を下の句といいます。俳句は、もともと短歌の上の句の部
3 分を切り出したものです。
4 短歌は、俳句のように、季語を必ずいれなければならないという決まりがありません。ただ、上の句があって、それで下の句が続くという詩でなければ文章としての流れに
5 なりません。



天智天皇
秋の田の
かりほの庵の
苫を荒み
我衣手は
露にぬれつつ

持統天皇
春過ぎて
夏来にけらし
白妙の
衣ほすてふ
天の香具山

柿本人麿
あし引きの
山鳥の尾の
しだり尾の
ながながし夜を
ひとりかも寝む

在原業平朝臣
ちはやぶる
神代もきかず

水くくるとは

小野小町
花の色は
移りにけりな
いたづらに
わが身世にふる
ながめせし間に

紀貫之
人はいさ
心も知らず
ふる里は
花ぞ昔の
香ににほひける

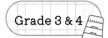

# Tanka and Haiku Poems

**Teacher**

Today, we're going to learn about "tanka"—a traditional Japanese poetry style. One tanka
1 is made up of a set syllable pattern 5-7-5-7-7 syllables.
I believe you all know Hyakunin Ishu, a traditional card game where one person reads a line and the other people compete to take the card that the line is written on. Hyakunin Ishu is very popular, and there is a national competition held every year.
2 It's usually broadcasted on TV.
Okay, let's go back to how tanka are structured. Tanka poems have a syllable construction of 5-7- 5-7-7, and we call the initial 5-7-5 part the first verse, and the final 7-7 part the last verse.
3 As a matter of fact, haiku came from the first verse of tanka poetry.
4 Tanka don't have to have include seasonal words like haiku do.
However, the tanka must have an upper clause followed by a lower clause in order to flow
5 as a sentence.

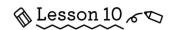

高学年

# 言葉のきまり

## 敬語

先生

1 私たちは、話す相手によって、同じことでも表現を違えています。
2 これが、日本語の表現の特徴です。
3 同じことを伝えるとしても、どのように表現するのが正しい使い方かを学習します。
4 使い方でもっとも重要なのは、尊敬語と謙譲語と丁寧語の区別です。

5 急に使い方に区別がありますといわれると戸惑いますね。
4 でも、そんなに難しいことではないです。
それは、これまでいつも使っている言葉や本で読んだり、おうちの人に教えてもらったり
6 して、自然に身についていることが多いからです。
ただ、自然に身についている表現が、使い方として正しいとは限りませんね。だから、
7 授業で、正しい表現を学習するわけです。
8 皆さんは、成長していくと、どんどんいろんな人と関わることが増えてきます。
中学校になればクラブ活動を通じて、先輩、後輩という関係ができますし、今でも目上
9 の人との関わりがあります。
10 大学を卒業して、社会にでると、上司とかお客さんなどとの関わりも出てきます。

そのときに、自分が使っている日本語の使い方が間違えていると、とても恥ずかしい思い
11 をするだけでなく、常識のない人だと思われてしまいます。
12 だから、正しい使い方を身に付けておきましょう。

先生への挨拶は「おはようございます。」そして、友達には、「おはよう」と言います。
13 どこか違うかというと、分かりますね、「ございます」という言葉がついているかどうかです。
14 この「ございます」という言葉を加えた表現を丁寧語といいます。
15 表現には、このような丁寧語のほかに、尊敬語と謙譲語があります。
尊敬語、謙譲語、丁寧語、黒板に漢字で書きましたが、まだ習っていない漢字もあるし、
画数も多いし、とても難しいように見えますが、何度も言いますが、実際は、皆さんが
16 日常使っている表現を整理することが多いですから、それほど難しいものではありません。

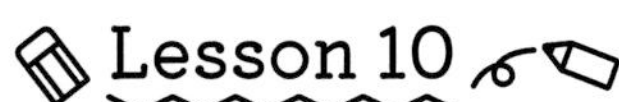




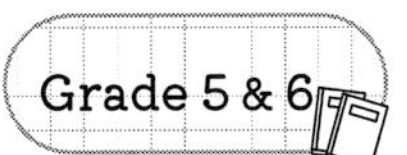


## Language Rules

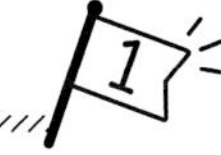


Honorific

Teacher

1 In this way, we express the same thing differently depending on who we are talking to.

2 This is a characteristic of the Japanese language.

3 Even if you try to communicate the same things, you will learn how to express it properly.

The most important distinction in usage is the distinction between honorific language,
4 humble language, and polite language.

5 If you are suddenly told that there are these different and distinct usages, you may feel confused.

4 But it is not that difficult.

This is because many of these expressions have become second nature to us through the words
6 we have always used, read in books, or learned from our family members.

However, the expressions that come naturally to us are not always the correct ones. That is why
7 we will learn about choosing and using correct expressions in class.

8 In the future, you will be involved with more and more people.

In junior high school, you will have relationships with your seniors and juniors through
9 club activities, and even now you have relationships with your elders.

When you graduate from university and enter the workforce, you will have to deal with bosses
10 and customers.

At that time, if you use Japanese incorrectly, you will not only be embarrassed but also
11 be thought of as a person without common sense.

12 So, you should learn how to use it correctly.

Greeting to the teacher is Ohayo gozaimasu. Greeting a friend is ohayo
13 Can you see the difference? It is whether or not the word "gozaimasu is added.

14 The expression Ohayo' with the word "gozaimasu" added is called polite language.

15 In addition to these polite words, there are also respectful and humble words.

Respectful, humble, and polite words are written in kanji on the blackboard, but there are some kanji that you have not yet learned, and there are many strokes. The kanjis may look very difficult, but as I have said many times before, it is actually not that difficult because they are
16 a combination of parts that you use in your daily life.

高学年

# 言葉のきまり 1

## 敬語

先生

1 では、使い方を見ていきましょう。尊敬語というのは、自分より年齢が高い人つまり
2 目上の人に対して使う表現で、相手を敬む意味合いで使います。

例えば、お客さんが家に来るとは言いません。お客さんがいらっしゃるといいます。これは、
3 「来る」という動詞を、「いらっしゃる」という尊敬語の表現にしています。

謙譲語というのは、目上の人に対して、自分をへりくだって使う表現で、相手を立てる
4 意味合いで使います。
謙遜するという言葉を知っていますね。この謙遜を態度でなく言葉で表現する使い方が
5 謙譲語です。
例えば、先ほどの「来る」という動詞は、謙譲語では「参ります」と表現します。
同じ、来るという動詞が、「いらっしゃる」という尊敬語の表現と、「参ります」という
8 謙譲語の表現になります。使い分けが分かりますか？
6 誰の行為かで使い分けます。
7 尊敬語は、主語が目上の人で、謙譲語は、主語が自分や自分の関係している人です。

つまり、皆さんのお母さんが学校に来るという場合、お母さんは皆さんより目上の人で
8 すね。だけど、お母さんが学校にいらっしゃるとは使いません。
それは、お母さんは目上の人ですが、自分の関係している人、仲間ですから、自分と同じ
9 立場の人とみなして、お母さんが参りますと表現します。

10 いくつかの尊敬語と謙譲語を黒板に書きだしますから、ノートに書き写してください。

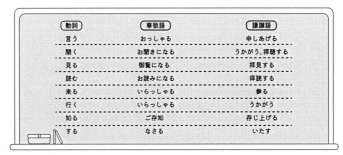

| 動詞 | 尊敬語 | 謙譲語 |
|---|---|---|
| 言う | おっしゃる | 申しあげる |
| 聞く | お聞きになる | うかがう、拝聴する |
| 見る | 御覧になる | 拝見する |
| 読む | お読みになる | 拝読する |
| 来る | いらっしゃる | 参る |
| 行く | いらっしゃる | うかがう |
| 知る | ご存知 | 存じ上げる |
| する | なさる | いたす |

11 使い方として、間違えやすい例を挙げてみましょうね。
先生が申されることは･･･　→ ○先生がおっしゃっていることは
一緒に参られますか　→ ○一緒にいらっしゃいますか
12 話していると、ついつい間違えがちになります。気をつけてください。

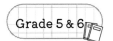

Grade 5 & 6

# Language Rules

Honorific

Teacher

1 Now, let's look at usage more closely. Honorifics are expressions used for people who are older
than you, in other words, for people who are your superiors and it shows that you respect
2 the other person.
For example, if you want to say that a customer is coming to your house. You would not express
the verb to come as 来る(kuru) but instead as いらっしゃる(irassyaru). In this case the verb 'kuru'
3 is converted into the more respectful expression 'irassyaru'.
Humble language is an expression used to humble oneself to one's superiors, and is used with
4 the meaning of elevating one's superior.
You know the word "humility", right? Humble language is used to show humility, not in attitude
5 or actions, but in words.
For example, the verb "kuru"(to come) is expressed as " mairimasu" in humble language.
The verb "to come" can be used in two different ways: as a honorific expression "irasharu" or
4 as a humble expression "mairimasu". Do you understand the difference?
6 You can use them according to who is doing the action.
In honorific language, the subject is your superior, and in humble language, the subject is you
7 or someone in the same group as you.
In other words, if your mother is coming to school, she is a superior person to you. However,
8 we do not use "irasharu" when we say "your mother is coming to school".
Although your mother is a superior person, she is someone you are related to, so you regard
her as someone in the same position as yourself and use the expression 'mairimasu' when you
9 say "your mother will come".
I will write out some honorific and humble words on the blackboard, and you can copy them
10 into your notebooks.

| 動詞 | 尊敬語 | 謙譲語 |
|---|---|---|
| 言う | おっしゃる | 申しあげる |
| 聞く | お聞きになる | うかがう、拝聴する |
| 見る | 御覧になる | 拝見する |
| 読む | お読みになる | 拝読する |
| 来る | いらっしゃる | 参る |
| 行く | いらっしゃる | うかがう |
| 知る | ご存知 | 存じ上げる |
| する | なさる | いたす |

11 Let me give you examples of common mistakes.

先生が申されることは・・・ → ○先生がおっしゃっていることは

一緒に参られますか → ○一緒にいらっしゃいますか

12 It is easy to make mistakes when speaking so please be careful.

高学年

## 言葉のきまり

### 敬語

先生

1 敬語には、もう一つ、丁寧語があります。

2 これはいわゆる『ですます調』の言葉使いです。

丁寧語は、目上の人とかに限らず、クラスで発表や意見を言ったりするときも使って
3 いますね。

「発表する」とは言わず、「発表します」といいますね。「食べる」といわず「食べます」と
4 言いますね。

最初に話をした「ございます」という表現は、この「ですます調」の丁寧語をより丁寧に
5 表現したものです。



尊敬語
Honorific

丁寧語
Polite Form

謙譲語
Humble Words

Grade 5 & 6

## Language Rules

Honorific

Teacher

1 There is another form of honorific expression called the polite form.
2 This is using sentences with desu and masu.
Polite speech is not limited to superiors, but is also used when giving presentations or
3 opinions in class.
Instead of saying "happyousuru" we say "happyoushimasu" Instead of saying "taberu,
4 "we say "tabemasu".
5 The previous expression I mentioned, “gozaimasu” is a more polite version of "desu-masu".

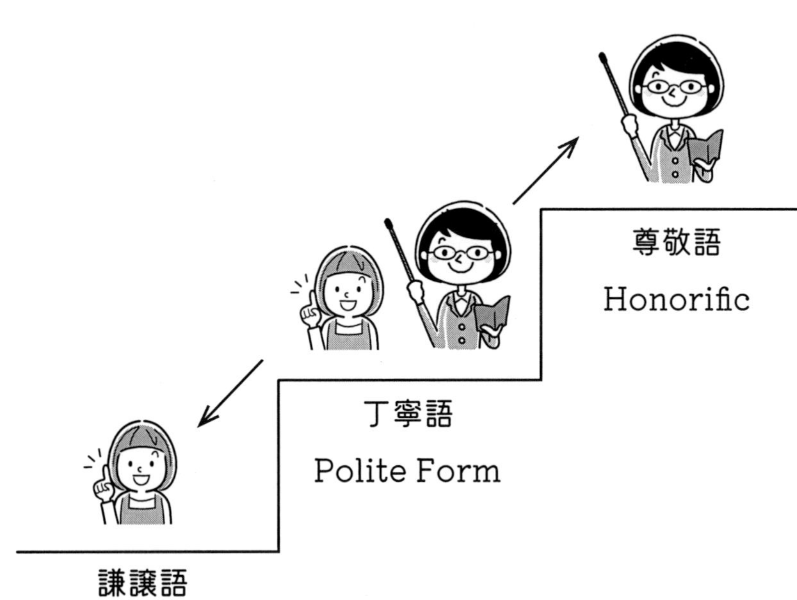

高学年

# 言葉のきまり 2

## 品詞

先生

1 私たちが話したり、書いたりする言葉には、それぞれ役割があって、その役割を
2 グループ分けすることを品詞といいます。
3 例えば、私、自動車、窓、服などは、名詞という品詞です。走る、食べる、着るなどは、動詞という
品詞です。他に、美しい、高い、青いなどの形容詞、ゆっくり、とても、ちょっと等の副詞、
4 そして、しかし、ところで等の接続詞などがあります。
品詞は、話をしたり、文章を作るうえで必要な表現を分担していますから、間違えた品詞を
5 使うと、会話が通じなかったり、文章がおかしくなったりします。

品詞は、算数のグループ分けの経験を生かして考えます。また、文章を品詞ごとに区切って
6 考えるという習慣をつけると、早く身 につきます。

7 具体的にやってみましょうね。
太郎君は、毎朝、お父さんと一緒に、自宅の回りを走っています。品詞に分けてみますよ。
8 太郎君/ は/ 毎朝/ お父さん/ と/ 一緒に/ 自宅/ の/ 周り/ を/ 走っ / て/ います。
9 「太郎君」は、名詞です。「は」は、助詞です。「毎朝」は、名詞です。「お父さん」は、名詞です。
「と」は、助詞です。「一緒に」は、副詞です。「自宅」は、名詞です。
「の」は、助詞です。「周り」は、名詞 です。「を」は、助詞です。「走っ」は、動詞です。
10 「て」は、助詞です。「います」は、補助動詞です。
すごいですね。たった一行の文章の中に、名詞が５つ、助詞が５つ、副詞と動詞と補助動詞が
11 それぞれ１つ入っていました。
これだけの品詞の種類と数で構成されている文章を、私たちはごく自然に、当たり前の
12 ように言葉にできて、書いたり、読んだりして理解できるのです。
品詞の学習を始めるにあたって、あと二つ、一緒に学習して知っておく必要があることが
13 あります。その一つは、文の種類です。黒板を見てください。

| | 例文 | 説明 |
|---|---|---|
| ① | 太郎君は走ります。 | この文章には主語と述語がひとつずつです。 |
| ② | 太郎君は走るので、足が速い。 | この文章は主語と述語が二つずつです。 |
| ③ | 太郎君は走りますが、お父さんは歩きます。 | この文章は、主語と述語が二ずつです。 |

14 ②と③は、両方とも主語と述語が二つずつですが、どこか違いますね。
分かりますか？　②は前の文章と後ろの文章が関係ありますが、③はそうではありません。
15 ①のような文章を単文、②のような文章を複文、③のような文章を重文といいます。

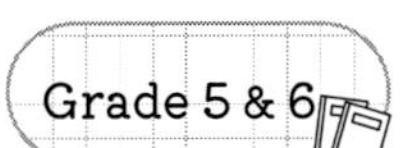

# Language Rules

## Parts of Speech

**Teacher**

1 Each of the words we speak and write has a role, and the grouping of these roles is called
2 part of speech.
3 For example, "I, automobile, window, clothes, etc." are nouns. "Run, eat, and wear" are verbs.
We also have adjectives like "beautiful, tall, blue, etc.", adverbs such as "slow, very, a little, etc.",
4 and conjunctions such as "but, by the way, etc."
The parts of speech are important for making the sentences necessary for speaking and writing,
so using the wrong part of speech can result in miscommunications during conversations and
5 illogical sentences when writing.
The parts of speech can be thought of by using the experience of grouping we learned in math
class. You will also learn quickly if you get into the habit of thinking of sentences in terms of
6 parts of speech.
7 Let's look at it in concrete terms.
太郎君は、毎朝、お父さんと一緒に、自宅の回りを走っています。
8 Taro and his father run around their home every morning. I'll break it down into parts of speech.
9 太郎君 / は / 毎朝 / お父さん / と / 一緒に / 自宅 / の / 回り / を / 走っ / て / います.
太郎君 is a noun. は is a particle. 毎朝 is a noun. お父さん is a noun. と is a particle. 一緒 is an
adverb. 自宅 is a noun. の a particle. 回り is a noun. を a particle. 走っ is a verb. て is a particle.
10 います is an auxiliary verb.
Wow. In just one sentence, there were five nouns, five particles, one adverb, one verb, and one
11 auxiliary verb.
Without even thinking about it, we are able to naturally understand and use a large variety and
12 number of parts of speech while reading and writing.
There are two more things we need to take a look at together before we start learning about
13 parts of speech. One of them is sentence type. Look at the blackboard.

| | Sentence | |
|---|---|---|
| ① | Tarou-kun runs. | This sentence has one subject and one predicate. |
| ② | Tarou-kun is fast because he runs. | This sentence has two subjects and two predicates. |
| ③ | Tarou-kun runs, but his father walks. | This sentence has two subjects and two predicates. |

14 Both ② and ③ have two subjects and two predicates, but they are somehow different.
Do you understand why? In sentence ② there is a casual relationship between the two parts
however number ③ does not. sentences like ① are called simple sentences, sentences like
15 ② are called complex sentences, and sentences like ③ are called compound sentences.

高学年

# 言葉のきまり 2

品詞

先生

1 品詞と文の種類を学習しました。もう一つは、修飾ということです。

2 誕生日のお祝いに食べるケーキを思い出してください。
ケーキには、上にローソクや「おめでとう」と書いた板チョコ等、いろいろ飾っていますね。
この「飾る」ということを、言葉や文では、「修飾する」、「修飾される」といいます。
3 この修飾が、言葉や文章に意味を持たせています。
文の種類と修飾語は、グループが違いますよ。だから、単文でも、複文でも、重文でも
4 修飾語を使います。
小学５年生の太郎君は、毎日、お父さんと一緒に、自宅の周りを走ります。
5 この文章は、太郎君は走りますという文章より長いですが、単文ですよ。
6 主語と述語がひとつずつしかありませんからね。
「小学５年生の」というのは、太郎君の修飾語です。「毎日、お父さんと一緒に、自宅の周りを」
7 は、どれも、「走ります」の修飾語です。
8 太郎君は、毎日、自宅の周りを走っているので、クラスの中で、一番速いです。
9 この文章は、複文ですね。
そして、「毎日、自宅の周りをが、走っているので」を修飾していて、「クラスので」と、
10 「一番」が、「早い」を修飾しています。
最初に学習した品詞というのは、文の種類を区別したり、修飾と深い関係にあります。
11 だから、まとめて学習しています。

品詞の種類や役割、文の種類、修飾語などは、私たちの使っている日本語の基本となる
12 ことですから、これをきちんと理解することは、国語という科目だけでなく、算数や理科
などのすべての科目の学習にも大変重要です。
13 では、これらの学習を深めていきましょう。

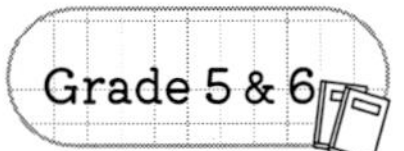

Grade 5 & 6

# Language Rules

## Parts of Speech

Teacher

We learned about parts of speech and sentence types. Another thing we need to
1 consider is modifiers.
2 Try to imagine the cake you eat at birthday celebrations?
On top of the cake, there are many decorations such as candles, a chocolate plaque with congratulations written on it, etc. These are called modifiers and help to make your sentences
3 more beautiful.
There are different groups of modifiers for different types of sentences. So, we use mdifiers in
4 simple sentences, compound sentences, and complex sentences.
小学５年生の太郎君は、毎日、おとうさんと一緒に、自宅の周りを走ります。
5 This sentence is longer than the sentence, 太郎君は走ります。but it is a simple sentence.
6 There is only one subject and one predicate.
小学５年生 is a modifier for 太郎君. 毎日、お父さんと一緒に、自宅の周りを is a modifier for
7 走ります.
8 太郎君は、毎日、自宅の回りを走っているので、クラスの中で、一番速いです。
9 This sentence is a compound sentence, right?
And 毎日、自宅の回りを is a modifier for 走っているので,
10 クラスの中で and 一番 is a modifier for 速い.
The part of speech we learned at the beginning of this unit are used to differentiate types of sentences, and therefore are closely connected with modifiers. That's why we are learning
11 them together.
Understanding the parts of speech, their roles, sentence types, modifiers, etc., is very important
12 not only for the Japanese language but also for other subjects such as math and science.

13 Now, let's take a closer look.

高学年

# 言葉のきまり 

## 品詞

先生

1 まず、品詞から学習を深めましょう。まず、①「助詞」です。
太郎君/は/毎朝/お父さん/と/一緒に/自宅/の/回り/を/走っ/て/います。この文章の
2 中で、は、と、の、を、てという言葉が助詞ですね。
助詞は、それだけで使うことはありません。必ず他の品詞と一緒に使います。しかし助詞が
3 ないと意味が分からないことがあります。助詞は、他の品詞と一体で文節を構成します。

4 次が、②「動詞」です。動詞は、文章の主語と述語のうちの述語として使います。

5 走る、書く、見る、起きる、あける、閉める、来る、する、勉強するなどです。
6 表現の中で、大変重要です。日本語 では、主語が明らかなときは省略することがありますね。

「私は走る。」の「私は」を省略したり、「あなたは食べる？「の「あなたは」を省略したりする
ことはよくありますね。でも、走るとか食べるなどの動詞ー述語が省略されることはあまり
7 ありませんね。
8 それから、③「形容詞」と④「形容動詞」です。
9 形容詞は、状態を表現し、名詞の修飾語となります。
美しい、楽しい、すがすがしい、赤い、高い、深い、暗い、丸い など、また、状態を表現するとき
10 は文章の述語となることもあります。
例えば、「この花は、美しい。」と表現します。形容詞が もっと動詞に近くなると、品詞としては
11 形容動詞となります。
12 きれいだ、静かだ、積極的だ、穏やかだ、かすかだ、さわやかだなどです。

13 次は、⑤名詞です。簡単に言えば名前で、たくさんあります。
14 トマト、鶏、富士山、太郎君、本、一冊など、あふれていますね。

15 名詞は文章の主語になったり、文章の中で目的となる言葉になります。
「私は、朝ご飯を食べる。」といえば、「私」と「朝ご飯」が名詞で、「私」という主語が、
16 「朝ご飯」という目的語のことを「食べる」という述語を行うことになります。

Page.144 に続く

# Language Rules

## Parts of Speech

Teacher

1 Let's start with the parts of speech. First, let's look at ① “particles”.

太郎君 / は / 毎朝 / お父さん / と / 一緒に / 自宅 / の / 回り / を / 走っ / て / います。

2 In this sentence, the words は, と, の, を, て are particles.

A particle is never used by itself. They are always used with other parts of speech. However, there are times when the meaning would not be clear without the particle. A particle is used together with other parts of speech to form phrases and sentences. 3

The next is ② "Verbs". Verbs are used as the subject of a sentence and as the predicate part of a sentence. 4

5 Examples include “run, write, see, get up, open, close, come, do, and study”.

They have a very important role in expressions. In Japanese, we sometimes omit the subject when it is obvious, right? 6

For example, in 私は走る, 私は is often omitted, or you often omit あなたは in あなたは食べる？ However, don’t you think verbs-predicates such as "run" and "eat" are rarely omitted? 7

8 Then there are ③ "adjectives" and ④ "adjectival verbs".

9 Adjectives express conditions and modify nouns.

Words like “Beautiful, pleasant, refreshing, red, tall, deep, dark, round, etc.”, can also be the predicate of a sentence when expressing a condition. 10

For example, we say “This flower is beautiful”. When an adjective becomes more like a verb, it forms a new part of speech called an adjectival verb. 11

12 Like “It is clean, quiet, positive, calm, faint, refreshing, etc.”.

13 Next is ⑤ “nouns”. Simply put, they are names of things, and there are many of them.

For example, “Tomatoes, chickens, Mt. Fuji, Taro-kun, books, one book, etc.”, there are so many around us. 14

15 A noun can be the subject of a sentence or the object of a sentence.

When we say “I eat breakfast.”, “I” and “breakfast” are nouns, and the predicate of “eating” is performed by the subject “I” on the object “breakfast”. 16

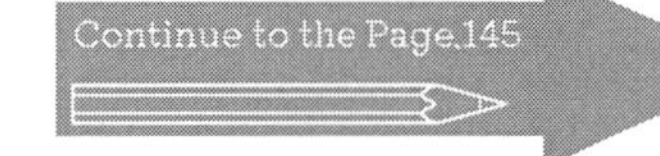
Continue to the Page.145

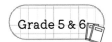

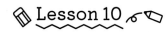

高学年

## 言葉のきまり

品詞

先生

それと、⑥副詞です。ゆっくり、たっぷり、とても、ちょっと、ざーざーと、きらきら、
17 まったくなどです。
18 副詞は、修飾語として、動詞、形容詞、形容動詞を修飾します。

そして、⑦接続詞です。接続詞は、文と文、語と語をつなげます。そして、しかし、そのうえ、
19 むしろ、それとも、ところでなどです。
20 それと、⑧感動詞です。
はい、うわっ、きゃあ、ねえ、もしもし、いよっ、おいなど、皆さんが、発表するときに最初に
21 言っている「はい」は品詞として、区分すると感動詞です。

先生

1 品詞が分かってくると、お話や文章の表現に広がりが出てきます。

2 話す、文章にするというのは、何かを聞いている人や読んでいる人に伝えるためですね。
表現が広がっていくと、それだけ、聞いている人、読んでいる人が具体的にイメージできる
3 ようになり、より詳しくそして正確に伝えることができるようになります。

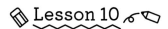

Grade 5 & 6

# Language Rules

## Parts of Speech

Teacher

And, ⑥ there are also “adverbs” such as “slowly, plentifully, absolutely, slightly, heavily,
17 glitteringly, utterly ”, etc.
18 Adverbs, act as modifiers and modify verbs, adjectives, and adjectival verbs.

And then, ⑦ there are “conjunctions”. Conjunctions connect sentences to sentences and words
19 to words. Some examples include “however, moreover, rather, or, by the way, etc.”,
20 ⑧“interjection” are words such as “Yes, wow, eek, hey, hello? alright, yo, etc”.
21 The "yes" that you say at the beginning of your presentation can be classified as interjections.

Teacher

1 Once you understand the parts of speech, you will be able to express yourself more in your sentences and stories.
2 The purpose of speaking or writing is to convey something to people who are listening or reading. The more you expand your expression, the more specific the listener or reader will be able to
3 visualize it, and the more detailed and accurate you will be able to convey it.

高学年

# 方言

先生

1 日本には各地方で方言があります。
今はTV が普及し、東京弁が全国に伝わり、次第に方言を話す人も少なくなってきましたが、
2 それでも、方言がまだまだ全国にあります。

方言は、日本語に限らず、どこの国でも多くの言語であり、その多くは、地理的な問題から
3 地域外の人とのコミュニケーションが疎通になったことによります。

4 しかし、日本の方言は意図的に作られています。
6年生になると、社会で歴史を習いますが、日本は、400 年前江戸時代という時代があり、
長く平和が続きました。江戸時代というのは、「江戸」今の東京に幕府という政府があって、
藩という今の都道府県の数の倍以上の地方に分かれていて、それぞれを「国」と呼んで
5 いました。
その藩は、江戸幕府に逆らうような動きがあるとすぐに「おとりつぶし」といって、潰されて
しまいました。その不穏な動きがないかを探るために、幕府は、各藩に、隠密というスパイを
6 送り込んでいました。どの藩もスパイ探しに追われていました。

スパイといっても、同じ日本人ですから、見た目だけではわかりません。そこで、その藩だけ
の言葉を使いだします。つまり、その藩の言葉でない言葉を使っている人、は他国の人です
7 から、スパイと分かるわけです。こうして、全国には様々な方言が生まれます。

例えば、青森県は昔、津軽藩と南部藩 2 つの藩がありました。壁があるわけでも、大きな川
があって交流ができないような地理でもないのに、津軽藩領と南部藩領では、かなり言葉
が違っていました。今も各地で生まれた方言が使われていますが、昔と違って、今は、
8 その方言が各地の郷土文化の一つの特色となっています。

日本中で同じ教科書で勉強して、同じテレビ番組を見ていますから、全国同じ言葉になる
9 ように思えますがそうはなりません。
それは、私たちの言葉の基礎が 3 歳くらいまでに出来上がり、そのころまでに聞いて覚えた
10 言葉やそのリズムを使うことになるからです。

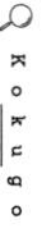

Grade 5 & 6

# Dialect

Teacher

1 As you know, each region in Japan has its own dialect.
Nowadays, with the spread of TV and the Tokyo dialect being introduced throughout Japan,
2 there are fewer and fewer people who speak dialects, but there are still dialects throughout Japan.

Dialects are not limited to Japanese, but are also found in many languages everywhere. These
3 dialects are often formed due to geographical reasons, in that places were remote from one another.

4 However, Japanese dialects were deliberately created.
In sixth grade, you will learn the history in social studies. Japan had a long period of peace during the Edo period 400 years ago. In the Edo period, the government was divided into clans, which were divided into regions more than twice the number of prefectures, and each region was
5 called a country.
As soon as a clan made a move that went against the Edo Shogunate, it was destroyed and that was called "おとりつぶし "(otoritubusi). In order to find out if there were any such plans the Shogunate sent spies, called 隠密 (secret agents), to each clan. So every clan was always on the
6 lookout for spies.

Even though they were spies, they were all Japanese people, so it was hard to tell just by their appearance. Therefore, clans started using a language that is unique to their own clan. In other words, anyone who uses a language that is not the language of that clan is from another country, so they can be easily identified as spies. That's why, a variety of dialects were born
7 throughout the country.
For example, Aomori Prefecture used to have two domains, the Tsugaru domain and the Nanbu domain. Although geographically, there wasn't a wall or a big river that separated them, the language was quite different between the Tsugaru and Nanbu domain territories. Even today, the dialects born in each region are still used, and unlike in the past, these dialects are now one
8 of the characteristics of the local culture of each region.
Since all Japanese study the same textbooks and watches the same TV programs, it would seem
9 that the language would be the same throughout the country, right? However that is not the case.
This is because the foundation of our language is formed by the age of about three, and we use
10 the words and rhythm we have learnt by that time.

高学年

# 歴史的仮名遣い

先生

1 今日からはタイムスリップして、昔の言葉を学習します。
服装や住まいがどんどん変わるように、言葉も変化していきます。もっといえば、同じ文字
2 なのに、時代とともに発音が変わってきています。

例えば、「花」は同じ文字ですが、1300 年以前は 「パナ」、それから 「ファナ」、そして
3 400 年前ころから 「ハナ」と、発音が変化しました。
川は、ひらがなで表わすと、「かは」と書いて、カバ→カファ→カワと発音が変わりましたが、
4 ひらがなは、ずーと、「かは」でした。
文字の表記が発音通りになるのは、第二次世界大戦後に、現代の発音に基づいた
5 現代仮名遣いが公布され、実際の発音通りの仮名遣いがなされるようになってからです。
つまり、第 2 次世界大戦終了前、70 年以前の書物は全て、文字と発音が違うところがある
6 ということです。
これを歴史的仮名遣いといい、日本語の書物がある約 1300 年前から 70 年前までの書物
7 を読んだり、理解するには、歴史的な仮名遣いを学習する必要があります。
ただ、歴史的仮名使いの学習といっても、小学校だと、それまで多く使われていたハ行、
はひふへほ、と 50 音表でマスに文字がないワ行のゐとゑ （カナのヱ）で書かれた
8 言葉の読み方の学習ですから、それほど難しくありません。

歴史的仮名遣いは、70 年前以前に書かれた書物を読むために学習しますが、皆さんが
9 文章を書くときは、これまで習っている発音通りの仮名遣いをしてください。
歴史的仮名遣いつまり、文字と発音が違うのは、「くっつき」の 「は、へ、を」や、接続詞の
「あるいは、または、もしくは、では、それでは、とはいえ」、その他に、
「いずは、さては、恐らくは、願わくは、こんにちは、こんばんは、これはこれは」 など限られ
10 ています。

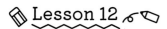

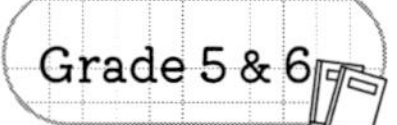


# Historical Kana Orthography

Teacher

1 Just as our clothes and housing are changing rapidly, our language is also changing.
2 More specifically, the pronunciation has changed over time, even though the letters are the same.

For example, the Kanji for flowers 花 is the same character, but its pronunciation changed from
3 "pana" before 1300, then "fana", and finally "hana" around 400 years ago.
The word 川 in hiragana was written as "ka-ha," and the pronunciation changed from “kaba” to
4 “kafa” and finally to “kawa”, but in hiragana, it was always "ka-ha.
It was not until after World War II, when pronunciation was standardized using kana, that
5 the characters were written as actually pronounced.
This means that all books written before the end of World War II, before 1970, have areas where
6 the kanji characters and pronunciations doesn’t match.
This is called historical kana , and learning historical kana is necessary to read and understand
7 books written in Japanese from about 1,300 to 70 years ago.
However, learning historical kana usage is not that difficult in elementary school, since it involves
learning only how to read words written in the ハ行 alphabet はひふへほ, which had been
8 widely used until then, and in the ワ行 alphabet ゐとゑ( ヱ), which has no letters in the 50 音cells.

Historical kana usage is useful to read books written before 70 years ago, but when you write,
9 please use the kana as you have learned to pronounce it so far.
Historical kana usage, in other words, word where thee pronunciation differs from the Japanese
is only limited to " は、へ、を" and the conjunction “あるいは、または、もしくは、では、
それでは、と はいえ ” or “いずれは、さては、恐らくは、願わくは、こんにちは、こんばんは、
10 これはこれは ”.

## Story of MOMOTARO

Once upon a time, there lived an old man and an old woman.
The old man would go into the mountains to collect firewood
and the old woman would go to the river to do the washing.
One day, while the old woman was doing the washing,
a giant peach came floating down the river.

高学年

## 古文

先生

1 言葉は時代とともにどんどん発音が変化していくことを学習しました。
2 言葉は、発音だけでなく、意味や使い方もどんどん変化していきます。

3 例えば、「切れる」という言葉があります。黒板に書いてみますね。
この「切れる」というのは、包丁やはさみが切れるという意味で使う以外に、どういうときに使うかわかりますか。
この「切れる」という言葉は、少し前までは、荒木さんが言ってくれたように頭のいい
4 人のことを指していました。
ところが、最近は、小野さんが言ってくれたように、「短気で怒りっぽい人」とか
5 「突然怒り出ている状態」を指して使うようになりました。
6 同じ切れるという表現ですが、短気で怒りっぽいという意味で使うのは、もともとは、「堪忍袋の緒が切れる」という慣用句が短縮されたものですが、もともと使っていた「切れる」よりも頻繁に使われるようになって、今ではこちらの意味で使うことが多く
7 なってきたわけです。

このように、言葉は、時代とともに意味や使い方が変化したり、使われなくなったり、
8 または新たに生まれてきたりします。
だから、歴史的仮名遣いの学習とともに、昔使われていた言葉の意味を知っておかない
9 と、日本の昔の書物が読めないことが出てきます。

### BOOK 一寸法師

一寸法師は、鬼に呑まれては、目より
出て飛び歩きければ、鬼のおぢをおののきて、
「これはただ者ならず、ただ地獄に乱こそ
出で来たれ。ただ逃げよ」と言ふままに、
打出の小槌、杖、しもつ、何に至るまで
打ち捨てて、極楽浄土の乾の、いかにも
暗き所へ、やうやう逃げにけり。

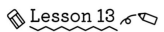

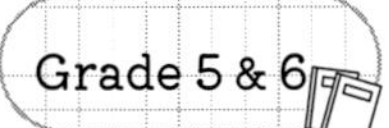


# Classical Japanese

Teacher

1 We learned that the pronunciation of words differed over time.
Words are constantly changing, not only in terms of pronunciation, but also in terms of
2 meaning and usage.
3 For example, let's look at the the word 切れる. I'll write it on the blackboard.
Do you know when this word 切れる is used other than to cutting with a knife or scissors?
4 The word 切れる used to refer to a smart person, until recently.

However, we have begun to use the term to mean "short-tempered and angry person" or "in
5 a state of sudden outburst of anger".
6 The reason for the change is the idiom 堪忍袋の緒が切れる which means I've lost my temper.
We have shortened this idiom to the expression 切れる and because of this, the angry meaning
7 of 切れる, is used more frequently today.

As you can see, language changes over time which means words may change, newly created,
8 or disappear completely.
So, along with learning historical kana you will have to know the meanings of words used in
9 the past to be able to read old Japanese books.

## Issun boushi

Issun boushi wa oni ni nomaretewa me yori Idetetobiarukereba, onimo ojiwononokite, 「koreha tadamononarzu,tada tigoku ni rankoso idekitare. tada nigeyo」 to iumamani, utide no koduti, tue, simotu, nani ni itarumade, uchisutete, gokurakujoudo no inui no ikanimo kurakitokoro e youyounigenikeri.

高学年

# 慣用句

先生

今日からは、昔からの戒めや教えという点からの学習をしていきましょう。
「三つ子の魂百まで」という言葉を知っていますか？幼い頃の性格は、年齢を重ねても
変わらないという意味です。このように，生きていく上での知恵や教えを，短い言葉で
1 たくみに言い表したものが「ことわざ」です。
2 カルタによく取り上げられているので、知っていることわざもあるかと思います。

ことわざには、昔からの人たちの多くの知恵や教訓が詰まっています。ぜひ、一つでも
3 多くのことわざを学習したいものですね。
ことわざに似ていますが、ことわざと区別する言葉があります。
それが慣用句です。毎日使っている言葉の中に、二つ以上のことば（単語）が組み合わ
さって、もとの言葉とは全く違った特別の意味で、習慣として長い間広く使われてき
4 た、ひとまとまりの言葉・文句や言い回しのことです。
5 例えば、

足が棒になる - 長く立ったり歩いたりして疲れ果て、足の筋肉がこわばる。
当てが外れる - 期待していたことが実現しない。
甘く見る - 物事をたいしたことがないと、軽く見なす
因縁を付ける - 相手を困らせるために言いがかりをつける。
首を長くする - 期待して待ち焦がれる。
様になる - それらしいようすになる。格好がつく。

6 などです。
7 スズメの涙とか猫の額といった言葉も慣用句です。
慣用句は、習慣として使われるひとまとまりの言葉や文句、言い回わしですから、ことわざ
8 のように教訓や教えは入っていません。
9 ただ、使い方や意味は、ことわざと同じように正確に理解して使えるようになることが
必要です。
ことわざと違って、慣用句はかなりたくさんあります。早めに多くの慣用句に触れて、
10 意味と使い方を知ることが、国語力を高めることにつながります。

To stretch your neck

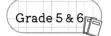

Grade 5 & 6

# Proverbs Idioms

Teacher

Do you know the saying, "The soul of a triplet lasts until it is a hundred years old"? It means that
the character of a child does not change with age. In this way, “proverbs” are short phrases that
1 cleverly express wisdom and teachings for living.

You may know some proverbs because they are often featured in karuta. Can you share any
2 proverbs you know along with their meanings?
Proverbs are filled with wisdoms and lessons from people of the past. I would very much like
3 you to learn as many proverbs as possible.
There is a phrase that is similar to a proverb but has some key differences
This is called an idiom. Idioms are used from our everyday language and it takes two or more
words ( 単語) and combine them in a way that is quite different from the original meaning.
4 Through wide use over a long period of time, these words become customary.
5 Let’s look at some examples,

足が棒になる - To have stiff legs. This means you are tired after standing or walking for long periods of time.

当てが外れる - To be contrary to one’s expectations. This means that the results weren’t the ones you were hoping for.

甘くみる - Underestimate the importance of things, and take things lightly.

因縁をつける - Pick a fight-this means to make an accusation unjustly just to annoy others.

首を長くする - To stretch your neck which means you to wait impatiently in anticipation.

様になる - To look good. Becomes more stylish.

6 etc.
7 Words such as "sparrow's tears" and "cat's forehead" are also idiomatic.
Idiomatic phrases are a collection of words, phrases, and expressions used as a matter of habit,
8 so they do not contain any moral lesson or teaching as proverbs do.
9 However, the usage and meaning, just like proverbs, must be understood and used accurately.

Unlike proverbs, there are quite a few idioms. Exposure to many idioms early on and knowing
10 their meanings and usage will help you improve your Japanese language skills.

To have stiff legs

高学年

# 四字熟語

先生

ことわざや慣用句と同じように、いくつかの漢字をひとまとめにして意味を表す言葉を
1 熟語といいます。
2 漢字の数によって、二字熟語から五字熟語などありますが、主に学習しておく必要があるのが四字熟語です。
例えば、「三寒四温」という四字熟語は、春にかけて、寒い日が三日、暖かい日が四日という
3 ように、寒暖を繰り返して温かくなる様子を四つの漢字で表現しています。

4 四字熟語の特色は、四字とも漢字であること、四字とも音読みであることです。

四字熟語は、「呉越同舟」のように中国の故事が基になっているもの、「諸行無常」のように仏教の教えからきているもの、「一騎当千」のように中世の日本の武家社会からきている
5 ものなどがあります。

欧米の各国の諸語の学術用語・ことわざなどの日本語訳から来ている四字熟語もかなり
6 あります。
「一石二鳥」はイギリスのことわざである"Kill two birds with one stone" を日本語訳
7 したもの、「三位一体」はキリスト教の根本教義を日本語訳したものです。

Grade 5 & 6

# Four-Character Idioms

Teacher

As with proverbs and idioms, kanji compound idioms are words that express a meaning by
1 combining several kanji characters together.

Depending on the number of kanji, there are different types of idioms, ranging from two to
2 five kanji idioms, but the main type you need to learn are the four-character idioms.

For example, let's look at the four-character phrase "three cold days and four warm days" which uses four kanjis to describe the repetition of three cold days and four warm days that takes
3 place over the course of spring,

4

Some of the four-character idioms are based on Chinese historical events, such as "Wu Yue Dong Ju" ( 呉越同舟), some are derived from Buddhist teachings, such as "Shogyou Mujou" ( 諸行無常), and some are derived from medieval Japanese warrior society,
5 such as "Ikki Tousen" ( 一騎当千).

There are also quite a few four-character compounds that come from Japanese translations of academic terms and proverbs from Western languages.

6 The phrase 一石二鳥 is a Japanese translation of the English proverb "Kill two birds with one stone," while 三位一体 is a Japanese translation of a fundamental
7 Christian doctrine of the trinity.

俳句は、季語を通して自然と親しむことができる文化であり、特に子供たちに自然の大切さを教えるのに 適しています。それもあって、アメリカの多くの小学校では俳句が教えられています。俳句の国際大会な ども頻繁に開催されており、私たちの想像以上に俳句は世界中で愛されています。
外国の人と話す機会が多くなるほどに、日本の文化について伝える機会も増えてきます。その時になっ て自国の文化に対する理解の無さを痛感することが少なくありません。俳句という言葉の芸術もまた、私 たち日本人と世界をつなぐ素晴らしいツールなのです。

Old pond / Frogs jumped in / Sound of water.

翻訳：小泉八雲 (Lafcadio Hearn)
日本の俳句を初めて明治時代に翻訳した人物。

これは、かの有名な俳句の

『古池や　蛙飛び込む　水の音』

松尾芭蕉

英訳です。



数々の英語訳が存在しており、海外でも "Frog Poem" として有名です。
日本の文化である俳句は , 世界最短の定型詩として世界中で人気を博しています。
その過程で日本の名句も翻訳されているのですが、訳者によって選び抜かれる言葉は様々で、それぞれの感性や個性が色濃く反映されています。そしてそれを知ることは、日本語、日本文化を客観的に知ること につながります。
The old pond, Aye!/ And the sound of a frog / leaping into the water (Basil Hall Chamberlain)
The ancient pond / A frog leaps in / The sound of the water. (Donald Keene)
「古池や」は、訳者によって "old" を使ったり "ancient" を使ったりしています。"ancient" という言葉には「古来の、由緒ある」という歴史をより感じさせる意味が含まれます。Chamberlain さんが用いた "Aye" とは驚きを表現する間投詞です。
「英語で俳句を作りたい !」という方のために基本的なルールをご紹介します。
そもそも俳句には主に二つのルールがあります。
1 五七五であること 2 季語を入れること
まず五七五ですが、英語俳句の場合では基本的に音節で数えます。音節とは、母音の数です。たとえば、"simple" ならば /'sɪm·pəl/ の中の母音は /ɪ/ と /ə/ の 2 つですので 2 と数えます。しかし、日本の俳句でも字余りや定型を無視した俳句があるように、英語俳句もそこまでこれにこだわりません。3 文で真ん中が長ければ何となくよしとされています。
季語についてですが、当然ながら国によって季節は異なり季節を感じさせるものも違ってきます。です から季語の挿入は必ずしもルールには含まれておらず、季節感がなんとなく出ていればいいといった感 じです。



出典 DMM 英会話ブログ編集部 抜粋

# 理科

subject 3

## Science

低学年

## 植物

お花を知ろう

先生

1 私たちの周りには、いろんな花が咲いていますね。

2 花には土の下に根があり、そこから茎が生えていて、葉っぱがあり、花が咲いています。

さくら

あさがお

コスモス

スイセン

3 こうなるまでの成長をみてみましょうね。

4 まず、花の種を植えます。

5 種から芽がでて、芽から葉が出て、成長して花のつぼみができて、花が咲きます。

6 花は、暖かくなりだしたら咲く花、暑い時に咲く花、涼しくなりだしたら咲く花があります。

低学年

## 植物

花を育てよう

先生

1 2年生になったので、私たちがお花を育ててみましょう。

2 班ごとに5鉢の鉢を準備しています。

3 去年の2年生も、この鉢でアサガオを育てました。

4 では、種をまく前に、植物の成長について学習しましょう。
種を蒔くところからお花が咲くまでを、順番に考えていきます。
ここに鉢があります。まず土を入れます。指が少し入るくらいの穴を掘って、その穴に
5 種を蒔いて、土をかぶせます。

6 そして、ジョウロで水をかけます。そして肥料をかけます。

7 黒板にも書きましたが、肥料をかけますというのはとても大事です。
土の中には、植物を育てる栄養分があり、水をかけてあげれば、育つことが多いのですが、
土の中の栄養分が不足することもあります。このため、肥料をかけるのですが、肥料という
8 のは、落ち葉や枯草を集めて作ったものです。

9 そうして、種をまいて5,6日すると、芽がでます。
は双葉といって2枚の葉っぱです。それからしばらくすると、本葉が出て、ぐんぐんと、
10 茎が伸びてきます。
茎は細くて弱いので、茎が掴まる棒が必要になります。棒をさすと、茎が棒に巻き付いて
11 どんどん伸びてきます。芽がでてからもずーっと、水を撒いてあげます。

11 棒は、皆さんの背の高さくらいのものを刺します。

12 花は、朝早く咲いて、午後には、しぼんでしまいます。

13 朝咲くので、アサガオといいます。

Grade 1 & 2

## Plants

### Let's Study Flowers

Teacher

1 There are many different kinds of flowers around us.
The roots of a flower are under the soil. From there, a stem grows up, then there are leaves and
2 flowers blossom.
3 Let's look at how flowers grow.

Cherry blossoms

Morning glory

Cosmos

Narcissus

4 First, we plant the seed of a flower.
From there a sprout comes out and then leaves come out. As it grows, a flower bud forms.
5 Then, a flower blooms.
There are flowers that start blooming when it gets warm, those which only bloom when it's hot
6 and others that bloom when it gets cooler.

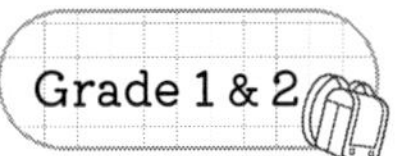

## Plants

### Growing Plants

Teacher

1 Since we are 2nd grade students now, let's try to grow plants by ourselves.
2 I have prepared five vases; one for each group.
3 2nd-graders from last year also used these to grow plants.
4 But before planting the seeds, I want us all to actually learn about the growing process.
Let's think from the beginning. We have a pot here.
First, we add the soil. Then make a little hole in the soil using your hand and put the seed
5 into that hole. After that, cover the seed up with dirt.

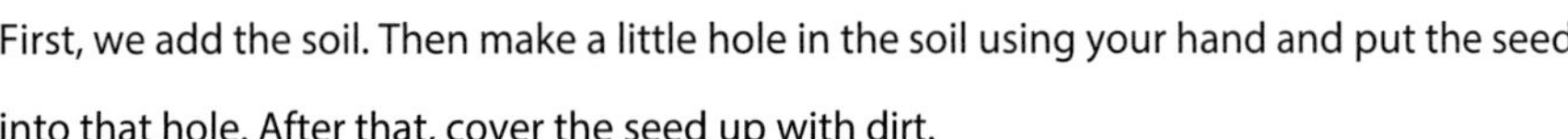

6 Finally, water them and give them fertilizer.
7 I already wrote it on the blackboard but it is very important that you use a fertilizer.
There are already some minerals in the soil but sometimes they are not enough. That's why
8 we need a fertilizer. Fertilizer is made from fallen leaves and grasses.

9 Also, in five to six days after planting the seed, you will see a bud come out of the soil.
Well, the bud that you will see is called a sprout. After that, the first leaves will come out.
10 The stem will grow then.
But in the beginning, the stems are very weak, so you should make sure the soil is solid enough.
If you use a stick, the stem will wind around it. I just want to add that you must water them
11 regularly and also, after the sprout comes out, OK?
11 And the stick should be around the same height as you.
12 And, they are going to blossom in the morning and retract in the afternoon.
13 That's why it's called morning glory!

低学年

## 植物

先生

1 今から、もっと詳しく、植物を学習していきましょう。

今回の学習は、いろんな植物の中で、被子植物で双子葉類という種類の学習が中心に
2 なります。被子植物以外には裸子植物があり、双子葉類以外には単子葉類があります。

3 被子植物で双子葉類を先に習うのは、地球の植物の多くが被子植物で双子葉類だからです。

4 地球上に植物は 27 万種類あって、その 25 万種類が被子植物でその約 8 割が双子葉類です。

種は、待っていてもそのままでは発芽しません。発芽には一定の条件がそろう必要が
5 あります。水と空気と温度です。

先生

1 胚乳がある植物を有胚乳種子、胚乳が無い種子を無胚乳種子といいます。

2 イネ、柿は有胚乳種子で、インゲン豆、アサガオやヘチマは無胚乳種子です。

3 有胚乳種子では栄養が胚乳に蓄えられ、無配乳種子は栄養が子葉に直接蓄えられます。

種子の中には胚があり、胚の中に幼芽、はいじく、幼根と子葉があります。この胚が、発芽
4 した時に、幼芽は本葉になり、胚軸は茎になり、幼根は根になります。

有胚乳種子では、胚乳と胚が種子の中にあり、無胚乳種子では種子の大部分は子葉が占めて
5 いて、種皮以外の部分がぜんぶ胚に含まれることになります。

6 子葉は発芽をした時に、最初にでる葉のことです。

子葉の枚数は、植物の種類によって違いますがインゲンマメの子葉は２枚です。

子葉は栄養を蓄えているところで、本葉が育ちだすと枯れてしまいます。

栄養分は でんぷん（澱粉）といいます。でんぷんは、ヨウ素液をくわえると、むらさき色に
7 かわります。これをヨウ素デンプン反応といいます。

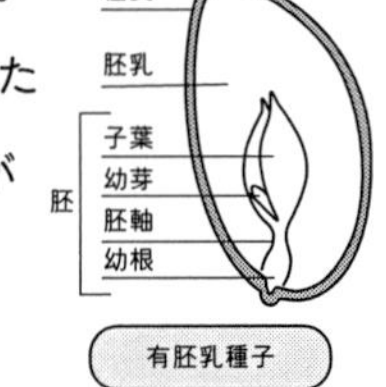


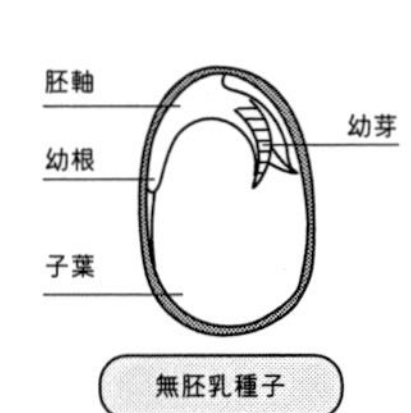


ヨウ素液に、種を輪切りにしたものと発芽後にかれた子葉を浸してみると、その紫色の濃淡で、でんぷんが含まれていたことと、それが使われたことがわかり
8 ます。

植物は、光を受けて、成長に必要な養分を作り出しています。
9 これを光合成と言います。

# Plants 3

**Teacher**

1 Now let's learn about plants in more detail.
The focus of our study will be on dicotyledonous plants, which are the most important variety
of plants. Plants are divided into two types -angiosperms and gymnosperms. Angiosperms
2 are further divided into two categories – the monocotyledons and dicotyledons.
The reason we learn about dicotyledons (a sub category of angiosperms) first is that most of
3 the plants on earth fall into this category.
There are 270,000 species of plants on earth, of which 250,000 are angiosperms and
4 about 80% of those are dicotyledons.
Seeds do not germinate if you just leave them alone. Certain conditions must be met for
5 germination. What are the conditions? Water, air, and temperature.

**Teacher**

A plant with an endosperm is called an albuminous or endospermic seed, and a seed without
1 endosperm is called an exalbuminous or non-endospermic seed.
Rice and persimmon are examples of plants with endospermic seeds, while kidney beans,
2 morning glories and loofahs are examples of plants with non-endospermic ones.
For albuminous seeds, nutrients are stored in the endosperm, while for albuminous seeds,
3 nutrients are stored directly in the cotyledons or seed leaves.
Within the seed is an embryo, and this embryo contains primary roots, embryonic leaves
and a cotyledon. When this embryo germinates, the embryonic leaf becomes a true leaf,
4 the cotyledon becomes a stem, and the primary roots becomes a root.
In an endospermic seed, the endosperm and embryo are contained within the seed, here as in
a non-endospermic seed, the cotyledons make up the bulk of the seed, and all but the seed
5 coat is contained within the embryo.
6 The cotyledon is the first part that emerges when germination occurs.
The number of cotyledons varies depending on the type of plant, for kidney beans there are two.
The cotyledons are where nutrients are stored and will wither when the true leaves begin to grow.
Plant nutrient is called starch. When iodine solution is added to starch, it turns purple. This is
7 called the iodine-starch reaction.
When the cotyledon sprouts after germination,
if you slice the seed and immerse it in iodine
solution, you can see a purple shade in the
8 starchy areas.

Seed coat
Endosperm
Embryo
Cotyledon
Embryonic leaf
Hypocotyl
Radicle
Endospermic seed

Hypocotyl
Radicle
Cotyledon
Embryonic leaf
Non-endospermic seed

Plants produce the nutrients they need for growth by primarily receiving light.
9 This process is called photosynthesis.

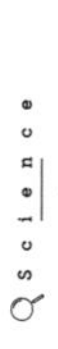

低学年

## 植物 3

先生

1 本葉がでると、太陽の光を浴びて、植物は光合成をしながら成長して花をつけます。

2 花には、種類によって、雄花と雌花といって男子と女子に分かれて花が咲くものと、一つの花の中にめしべとおしべがあるものがありますが、どちらも受粉が必要です。

3 直物はそのものでは自力で受粉ができないので、他の力を借りて受粉しますが、ハチやチョウなどの昆虫の力を借りる花が多く、昆虫が集まるように蜜をだし、それを吸いに来た昆虫の体に花粉がついてめしべに運んで受粉します。

4 受粉すると花は枯れて種を作ります。

5 花の色がきれいなのは、昆虫が飛びながら発見しやすいようにです。

6 付け加えると、成長には肥料が欠かせません。

7 肥料として ちっ素 (ちっそ)とリンとカリウムが 肥料の３要素、「肥料の三大要素」などといいます。

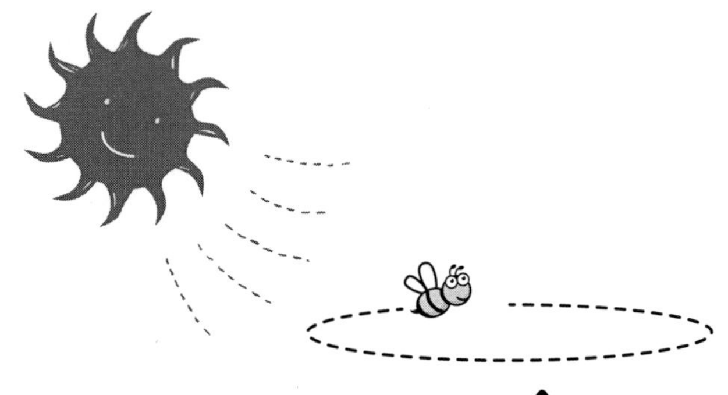

## Plants

Teacher

When the plant's real leaves emerge, they are exposed to sunlight and undergoes
1 photosynthesis, eventually producing flowers.
Depending on the type these flowers can either be classified as male or female flowers or
2 they can be both, or with a stamens and stamens, both of which require pollination.

Plants cannot self-pollinate so many flowers are pollinated with the help of insects such as bees and butterflies. Plants produce nectar to attract insects, and during their honey-making procedures, these insects will gather up the flower's pollen. The pollen attaches to the bodies
3 of the insect and is brought to another flower for pollination.

4 Once pollinated, the flowers wither and produce seeds.
5 The flowers often have beautiful colors so that insects can easily spot them while flying.
6 The only thing I want to add is that fertilizer is also essential for growth.
The three elements of nitrogen, phosphorus, and potassium, are the three major elements
7 of fertilizer.

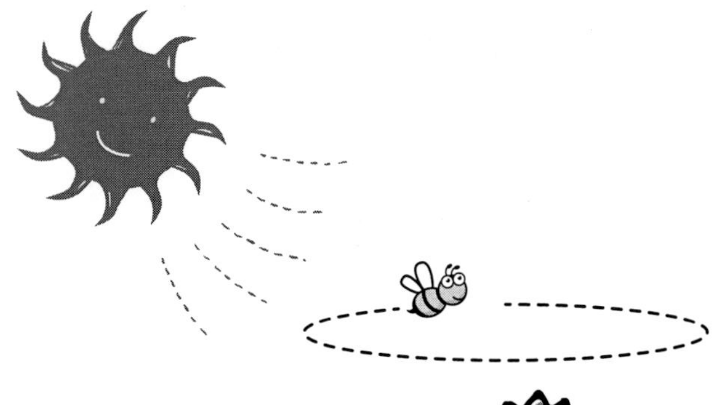

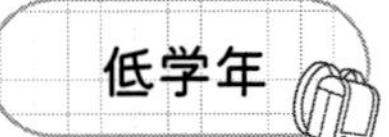


# 天気

天気を知ろう

先生

1 天気予報って知ってますか。
テレビのニュースの前にやっていたり、画面の上の方に表示がでたりしますね。
2 天気にはどんな種類があるか、あげてみましょう。
3 晴れ、曇り、雨、雪が基本ですね。
黒板に、名前とそれぞれのマークを描きます。このマークは、テレビでよく見ていると
4 思います。
朝から晩まで一日中、ずっと晴れていたり、ずっと雨だったりすることは少なくて、
5 時間によっては、晴れたり、曇ったりしますね。
6 これをお天気といって、それが変わり方によって、言い方があります。
7 晴れていたのに、曇りに天気が変わることを、晴れのち曇りといいます。
8 晴れているのに、時々曇ったりすることを、晴れ時々曇りといいます。
9 同じように、曇りのち雨、雨のち晴れ、曇り時々雨、雨時々曇りというように言います。

10 そして、晴れ時々曇りというときは、マークの間に斜め線をひいて表します。

11 晴れのち曇りというときは、マークの間に矢印を書いて天気の変化を表します。

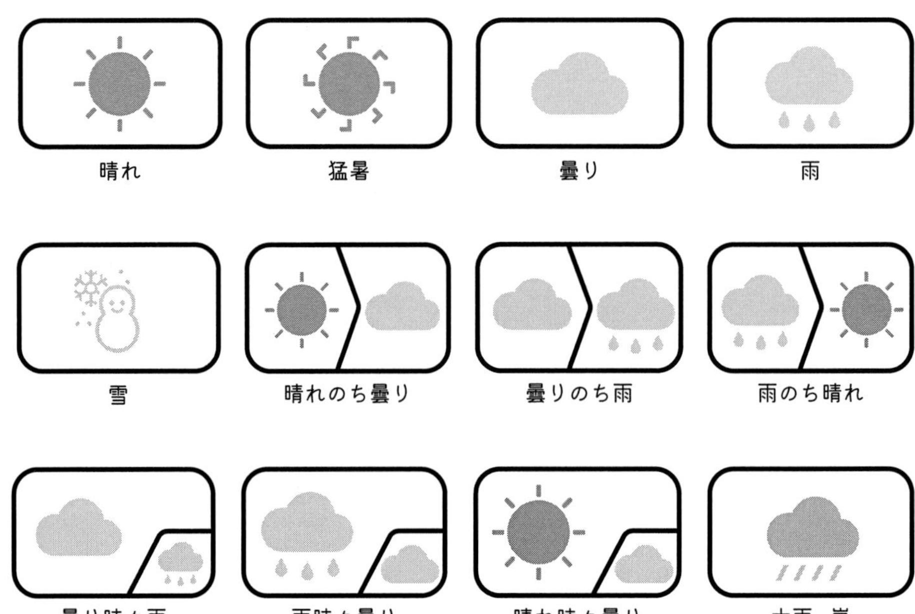

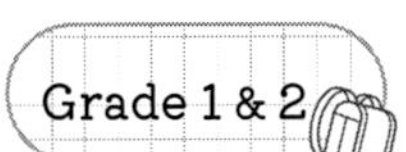


# Weather

## Let's Learn about the Weather

**Teacher**

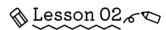

1 Do you know what a weather forecast is?
Sometimes they do it on TV before a news program or you may also see it on the top part of
2 the screen of your television. Let’s list different kinds of weather.
3 Mostly we use sunny, cloudy, rainy, and snowy.
I will write symbols for each kind weather on the blackboard. I'm sure you often see them on
4 television.
You can also see that there are not many days that are sunny or rainy all day. Depending on the
5 time of a day it gets sunny and cloudy.
6 This is called weather and depending on the way it changes; we have different ways of saying it.
7 We say sunny with clouds later when it's sunny then it changes to cloudy weather afterwards.
8 We say sunny and partly cloudy when it's sunny but gets cloudy occasionally.
Similarly, we can say cloudy with rain later, rainy with sun later, cloudy with occasional shower,
9 and rainy with partly cloudy.

For instance, when we say sunny with partly cloudy then we show it by putting a slash between
10 the symbols.
11 When we say sunny with clouds later, then we use an arrow to show the weather will changes.

Sunny

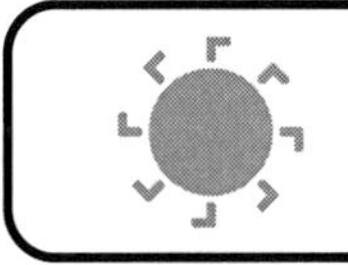
Brutal heat

Cloudy

Rainy

Snowy

Sunny, clouds later

Cloudy, rain later

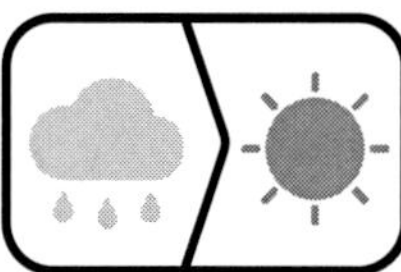
Rainy, sun later

Cloudy, occasional shower

Rainy, partly cloudy

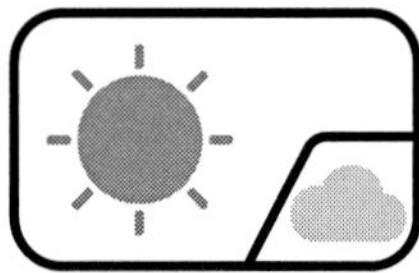
Sunny, partly cloudy

Raining heavily・Stormy

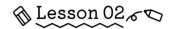

低学年

## 天気

天気を知ろう

先生

温度計って、皆さん、知っていますか。
皆さんの体にも体温があって、大体 36 度くらいです。
風邪をひいて熱がでると、38 度から 40 度くらいの高い熱に上がることがあります。
皆さんの体温を測るのが体温計といって、脇に挟んだり、耳の中にいれたりして測ります。

天気と気温は大変関係が深いです。例えば、雪の日は、寒いので気温が５度以下になります。
温度計とは温度を測る道具です。
このような棒状になって、温度の上がり下がりで、中の液が上下するものが普通です。
今は、時計と一緒に数字で表示されているものや、よく、ビルの壁に数字で表示されていることが多いので、すぐに知ることが出来ます。

中学年

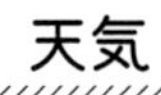

## 天気

天気と気温

先生

暑さや寒さは、主に空気の温度によって決まります。
この空気の温度を気温といいます。
気温は、測る高さで違っています。

気温は測る高さによって違うので、気象台でおこなう気象観測では世界中を通して1つの約束をしています。
それが地面よりの高さ 1.5 メートルくらいのところの気温を測るということです。

外で気温をはかるには、つぎの３つに注意します。
①太陽の光が、温度計に直接あたらないようにする。
②風通しのよいところに温度計をおき、風かよくあたるようにする。
③雨や雪がかからないようにする。
これら①②③の条件を備えた特別の箱の中で気温をはかります。
この箱を百葉箱とよびます。

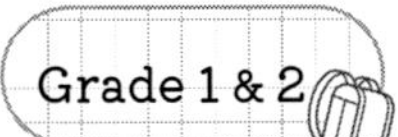


## Weather

Let's Learn about the Weather

Teacher

1 Does everybody know what a thermometer is?

2 Your body has a temperature which is normally around 36℃.

3 When you catch a cold and have a fever, you might get a high fever like 38℃ or 40℃.

We measure our body temperature with a thermometer which we use by putting it under our
4 armpit or inside your ear.

Temperature and weather are actually closely linked. For example, on a snowy day, it's very cold
5 and the temperature goes down below 5℃.

6 A thermometer is a tool used to measure temperature.

7 It looks like a stick and a liquid inside goes up and down to show the change in temperature.

Nowadays, we have ones with a display that shows numbers and time. You often see them
8 displayed on the outside of a big building, that way, we can easily know the temperature.

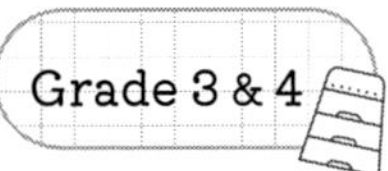


## Weather

Weather and Temperature

Teacher

1 Hot and cold are determined primarily by the temperature of the air.

2 The temperature of the air is called the air temperature.

3 The air temperature is different at different heights where it is measured.

Because temperatures vary depending on the height at which they are measured, the weather
4 observations made by weather stations around the world have one universal rule.

5 That is to measure the temperature at a height of about 1.5 meters above the ground.

6 To measure the temperature outside, pay attention to the following three points.

7 (1) Sunlight should not shine directly on the thermometer.

8 (2) Place the thermometer in a well-ventilated place so that it is well exposed to the wind.

9 (3) Don't let the thermometer be covered with rain and snow.

10 The temperature is measured in a special box equipped with these conditions (1), (2), and (3).

11 This box is called a hyakubako (Stevenson Screen).

高学年

# 天気

## 大気

先生

1 私たちがすむ地球はとても不思議な星です。
2 生物が生きていくには、酸素が必要です。
3 地球にはその酸素があります。
4 しかも、壁がないのに、地球からその酸素は宇宙に放出してなくなることがないです。

5 まるで、目に見えないバリアで覆われて星なのです。
6 このバリアを大気といいます。

地球はこうした大気のおかげで何億年、何十億年も前から命がつながってきて
7 いるんですね。
地球は太陽の周りを回っていること、地球が自転していることで受ける
8 太陽の光の量がいつも変化します。

9 大気は、太陽からの熱を受けると、いろいろな方向に動きます。
10 これが風です。

11 大気中には、水蒸気や雲や雨雲など、さまざまなものがあります。
それらが、この風の働きで、地球のまわりを動き回り、その動いたところで、
12 雨をふらせたり、雪をふらせたりしています。
そのために、天気は、毎日晴れたり、くもったり、雨がふったりと、いろいろに変化すると
13 いうわけです。

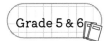

# Weather

## Atmosphere

Teacher

1 The earth we live on is a very mysterious planet.

2 Oxygen is necessary for living things to survive.

3 The Earth has oxygen.

And even though there is no wall, the oxygen is not released from the earth into space and
4 never runs out.

5 It is as if the planet is covered by an invisible barrier.

6 This barrier is called the atmosphere.

7 Life on has existed for billions and billions of years thanks to this.

The earth revolves around the sun and the amount of sunlight it receives changes all the time
8 due to the earth's rotation.

9 When the atmosphere receives heat from the sun, it moves in various directions.

10 This is wind.

11 In the atmosphere, there are various things such as water vapor, clouds, and rain clouds.

These things move around the earth by the action of the wind, and where they go, they make it
12 rain or snow.

13 This is why the weather changes and why we have sunny, cloudy, and rainy days.

高学年

# 天気 4

## 雲

先生

1 「晴れ」とか、「くもり」とかはどうやって決めているのでしょうか。

2 まず、空をおおう雲の量を雲量といいます。

雲量が9割以上の場合をくもりといい、雲量が1割以下の状態で、雨や雪などの降ってない状態を快晴、雲量が2割から8割のときを,晴れといいます。

4 雲はその形と現れる高さによって10種類の雲形に分類されています。

5 そのうち、高い巻雲、中くらいの乱層雲、低い積乱雲をまず覚えてください。

＜巻雲＞は、すじ雲といわれ、絹のような光沢をもち、刷毛ではいたような雲、あるいは毛のような繊維組織状の雲です。[6]

光線の屈折の具合で太陽や月の周りに「かさ」が見えることがあります。[7]

8 氷の結晶が集まってできています。

＜乱層雲＞は、雨雲で、暗灰色の層状の雲で、太陽や月を完全に隠す厚い雲です。[9]

通常連続性の降水を伴います。雨や雪を降らせる代表的な雲です。[10]

＜積乱雲＞は、雷雲、入道雲と呼ばれています。積雲に比べ鉛直方向に著しく発達した雲です。[11]

雲の高さは10kmを超えることもあり、時には成層圏まで達します。[12]

13 塔状、カリフラワー状、ドーム状となっています。

14 落雷、突風、短時間の強い雨やひょうを伴います。

強い上昇気流、下降気流により竜巻やダウンバースト(※)などの激しい気象現象をもたらします。[15]

※ ダウンバースト…積乱雲から下向きに吹き出す強い風。

16 航空機の着陸時等に事故を引き起こすことがあります。

Page.172 に続く

Grade 5 & 6

# Weather



## Clouds

Teacher

1 How do you decide if it is "sunny" or "cloudy"?
2 First, the amount of clouds covering the sky is called the cloud cover.
When the cloud cover is 90% or more, it is cloudy. When the cloud cover is 10% or less and
3 there is no rain or snow, it is clear, and when the cloud cover is 20% to 80%, it is sunny.
Clouds are classified into ten different cloud formations according to their shape and
4 the height at which they appear.
Among them, it is important to remember the high-level cirrus clouds, medium-height
5 nimbostratus clouds, and low-level cumulonimbus clouds.

<A cirrus cloud> is called a suji cloud, and has a silky sheen
6 and a brush-like or hair-like fibrous structure.
Due to the refraction of light rays,
7 they may create a halo effect around the sun or moon.
8 They are made up of ice crystals.

<A nimbostratus> is rain clouds, with dark gray stratocumulus,
9 thick clouds that completely hide the sun and moon.
It is usually accompanied by continuous rainfall.
10 These are typical clouds that bring rain and snow.

<Cumulonimbus cloud> is also called thundercloud or
towering cumulus cloud. It is a cloud that is significantly more
11 vertically developed than cumulus clouds.
Cloud heights can exceed 10 km, and sometimes reach
12 the stratosphere.
13 They may be tower, cauliflower, or dome-shaped.
14 It is accompanied by lightning strikes, gusty winds, and brief periods of heavy rain or hail.
Along with string updrafts, downdrafts cause severe weather phenomena such as tornadoes
15 and downbursts (*).
*Downburst: Strong winds blowing downward from a cumulonimbus cloud.
16 It may cause accidents during aircraft landing, etc.

Continue to the Page.173

高学年

## 天気 4

### 雲

先生

17 地球上の雲は、気象衛星という、人工衛星によって撮影されています。

18 日本では気象衛星は、「ひまわり」という気象衛星が（2016 年の時点）運用されています。
日本での天気予報は、気象衛星からの情報も参考にしますが、それだけではなく、日本各地
19 の地上からの観測所からの情報も元にして、決められています。

日本には、アメダスという気象観測のシステムがあり、観測装置が日本国内各地の
20 約 1300 ヶ所の気象観測所にあります。
気象観測の情報には、気象衛星やアメダスのほか、気象レーダーや海洋・海上気象観測や、
21 などの情報があります。
これらの、情報を元にして、気象庁は天気図や予報天気図を作成し、気象庁は天気予報を
22 発表します。

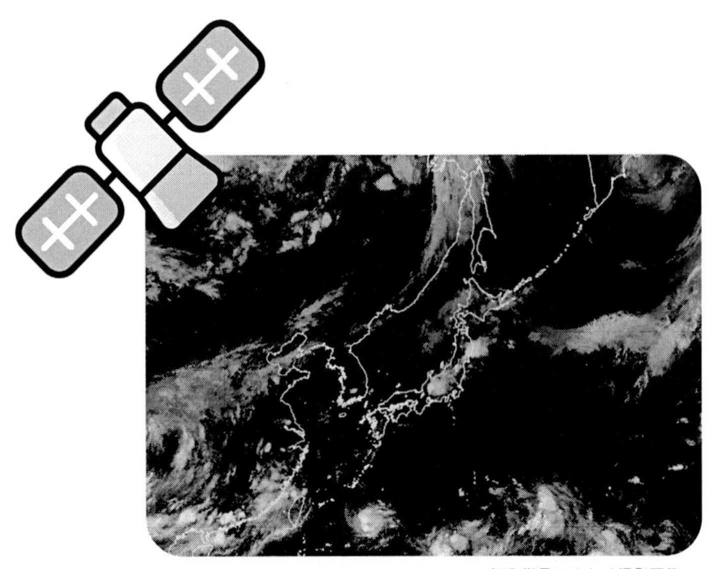

気象衛星ひまわり撮影画像

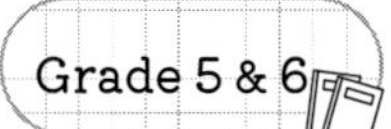

Grade 5 & 6

# Weather

## 4

Clouds

Teacher

17 Clouds above the earth are photographed by artificial satellites, called meteorological satellites.

18 In Japan, the meteorological satellite called Himawari, has been in operation since 2016.

19 Weather forecasts in Japan are determined based not only on information from weather satellites, but also from ground-based stations around Japan.

20 Japan has a weather observation system called AMEDAS, with observation equipment located at approximately 1,300 weather stations throughout Japan.

21 In addition to meteorological satellites and AMEDAS, there is information from meteorological radar, oceanographic and maritime meteorological observations, and other sources.

22 Based on this information, the Japan Meteorological Agency (JMA) produces weather maps and forecast weather maps, and the JMA issues weather forecasts.

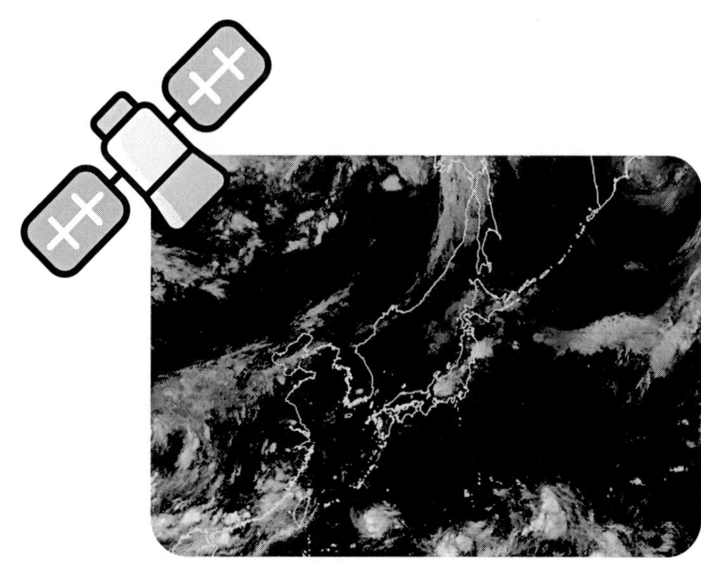

気象衛星ひまわり撮影画像

高学年

## 天気 5

### 風

先生

1 日本の付近では、天気は、西から東へと変わっていきます。

気象衛星の画像を見ると雲のうごきは、南北方向の雲の動きについては季節などによって違いますが、東西方向の動きについては、ほぼ、西から東の方へと、雲は移動します。
2 日本の上空では、偏西風という西から東への、西風吹いています。

3 風について学習しましょう。
4 まず、大気にも重さがあります。
5 だから大気中のものにも重さが高気圧にかかります。

6 この空気の重さがかかる力を 大気圧 といい、押しつぶす方向の力を気圧といいます。

高

高圧で押されているところ（高気圧）と、
7 気圧の圧力が低いところ（低気圧）ができます。
8 高気圧の場所からは、風が右回り（時計回り）で吹き出します。
9 上空から地表へと風が流れる 下降気流 が発生します。
10 上から下への流れの為、雲ができにくく、天気は晴れることが多いです。vv

まっすぐ吹き出すのではなく、渦をまいて吹き出す理由は、地球が自転していることであり、詳しくは上の学年で習いますが転向力という力により、圧力の傾きに対して右側に
11 風がそれます。

低

12 低気圧の場所では、風が吹き込みます。風向きは、
13 左回りの反時計回りで吹きこみます。

低気圧の中心近くでは、地表から上空へと風が流れる上昇気流のため雲ができやすく、
14 天気は悪い、雨が降っているわけです。

夏の終わりごろ、太平洋の洋上で、強い日差しのため、大量の水蒸気が蒸発し、積乱雲などを
15 ともなう熱帯低気圧が太平洋上で発達します。

この夏の終わりごろの、南方からおとずれる熱帯低気圧が、強い風雨を発生させることが
16 多く、この強い風雨を台風といいます。
17 台風は、風速が秒速で 17.2m/ 秒 をこえる風を発生させます。

台風は低気圧なので、ほかの低気圧と同様に、衛星から見た場合の風の向きは、
18 反時計回りであり、雲は渦（うず）をまいています。

# Weather 5

## Wind

Teacher

Across Japan, the weather changes from west to east.
1 Satellite images show that cloud movement in the north-south vectors varies with the season
and other factors, but in the east-west direction, clouds always move from west to east.
2 This is because over Japan, there is a strong westerly wind blowing from west to east, which is
called the westerlies.
3 Let's learn more about wind.
4 First of all, the atmosphere has weight.
5 Therefore, anything within the atmosphere receives pressure from it.

The force exerted by the weight of the air is called atmospheric pressure, and the force in
6 the direction of crushing is called barometric pressure.
A high-pressure area (high pressure) and a low-pressure area (low pressure)
7 are created.
8 From high pressure areas, the wind blows to the right.
9 As a result, a downdraft occurs when wind flows from the sky to the ground.
10 Because of the top-to-bottom flow, it is difficult for clouds to form and the weather is often clear.
The reason why the wind blows in a whirlpool instead of blowing straight out is that the earth
rotates on its axis, and as you will learn in the upper grades, a force called the Coriolis force
11 causes the wind to shift to the right of pressure gradients.

12 In low-pressure areas, winds blow in.
13 The wind direction blows to the left in a counterclockwise direction.
Near the center of the low-pressure area, the wind flows upward from the surface to the sky
14 due to the updrafts, so clouds tend to form, causing rain and bad weather.
In late summer, strong sunlight over the Pacific Ocean causes a large amount of water vapor to
15 evaporate, and a tropical cyclone with cumulonimbus clouds develops over the Pacific Ocean.

These tropical cyclones that come from the south often produce strong winds and rains, which
16 are called typhoons.
17 Typhoons are categorized as clouds that generate wind speeds exceeding 17.2 m/sec.
Since typhoons are low-pressure systems, like other low-pressure systems, the direction of
18 the wind is counterclockwise when viewed from a satellite, and the clouds form a whirlpool.

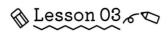

中学年

# 太陽

1 昼間、太陽が出ているとき明るいですね。これは、太陽が光を放っているからです。
2 太陽の光は目には見えませんが、四方八方にまっすぐに飛んでいます。
3 その光を遮るものがなければ、花壇では花に太陽の光が届きます。
4 しかし、お水をやるために私たちがお花の前に立ったら、私たちの体で、太陽の光を遮って
5 しまいます。
6 そうすると、太陽の光を遮ったところだけ暗くなります。これが影です。
7 だから、太陽と反対側に影はできます。
8 太陽のように光を放つもとを光源といいます。
9 光源から放つ光は一直線です。
だから、移動すると、遮るものがなくなった場所は光が戻って明るくなり、移動することで
10 遮られた場所は影ができます。

先生

1 海の先から太陽が昇ってくる状況を日の出といいます。
2 そして、それが夕刻に沈んで行って暗くなることを日の入りといいます。

1 太陽は、東から出て、南を回って西に沈みます。
そして、東から昇って、だんだん高さが高くなり12時頃に一番高いところに達して、それ
2 から西に向かって次第に低くなっていきます。
3 この一番高いところに来ることを南中と言います。
前の授業でも言いましたが、光はまっすぐ進みます。だから、東の昇るときや西に沈むとき
は斜め横から光が来ますから、影が長くなり、南にある時は上から光が来ますから影が
4 短くなります。
5 今、背中に太陽の光が当たっていますね。ポカポカしますね。
太陽の光が当たるところ、これを日なたといいますが、日なたは、明るいだけでなく温かく
6 なります。どれくらい差があるか知りたいですよね。こういう時に使うのが温度計です。

皆さんが、風邪をひいたとき熱を測るのは体温計ですが、温度計は同じ仲間で、
7 体温計と違い、0度から100度まで測れるようになっています。温度計は、先の丸く膨らん
だところに水銀という液体が入っていて、この液体は温度によって、上の管を上下するよう
8 になっています。

1 鏡を使ってまっすぐ進む光の角度を変えることを反射といいます。
2 また、レンズやガラスの厚みの違いによって光の角度をかえることを屈折といいます。

# The Sun

Teacher

1 During the day, when the sun is out, it is bright. This is because the sun is shining.
2 The sun's light is invisible to the eye, but it is flying straight in all directions.
3 If there is nothing to block that light, the sun's rays will reach the flowers in the flower beds.
4 But when we stand in front of the flowers to water them, we block the sun's rays with our bodies.
5 Then it becomes dark only where we blocked the sun's rays.
6 This is called our shadow.
7 So the shadow will be on the opposite side of the sun.
8 A source of light like the sun is called a light source.
9 The light emitted from the light source is a straight line.
So, when you move, light returns to brighten the areas that are no longer obstructed, and
10 shadows form in the areas that are obstructed by the movement.

Teacher

1 The situation where the sun rises from beyond the sea is called sunrise.
2 The setting of the sun at dusk is called sunset.

Teacher

1 The sun rises in the east, turns south, and sets in the west.
It rises from the east, gradually increasing in height until it reaches its highest point
2 around 12:00 p.m., and then gradually decreases toward the west.
3 This highest point is called the southernmost point of the sky.
As I said in the previous lesson, light travels in a straight line. So, when it rises in the east or sets
in the west, the light comes from diagonally across, so the shadows are longer, and when it is in
4 the south, the light comes from above, so the shadows are shorter.
5 You have the sun on your back right now. It feels warm, doesn't it?
Where the sun shines, is called the sunlit area, the sunlit area is not only bright but also warm.
If you would like to know how much difference in temperature there is, a thermometer is used
6 in these situations.
Thermometers are used to measure fever when you catch a cold, but temperature gauges are
7 in the same family, and unlike thermometers, they can measure from 0 to 100 degrees Celsius.
The temperature gauge has a round bulge at the end filled with a liquid called mercury, which
8 moves up and down the upper tube depending on the temperature.

Teacher

1 Changing the angle of light that travels straight ahead using a mirror is called reflection.
Also refraction is the process of changing the angle of light by varying the thickness of the
2 lens or glass.

中学年

## 星と月

1

### 星

先生

1 私たちは地球という星に住んでいます。

2 地球の形を知っていますか。

3 地球儀を見たことがありますか。

4 地球はボールのように球になっています。

5 地球は宇宙という空間の中にある星のひとつです。

そして宇宙には、たくさんの星があります。昼間は太陽の光で見えませんが、

6 夜空に無数の星が輝いています、

7 星は、どれも同じ明るさではありません。

星の大きさや地球からの距離によって、明るさが違います。

8 また光の色も違います。

9 太陽のような星は温度が高い星で、青白く光っています。

10 温度が低くなるにつれて赤くなっていきます。

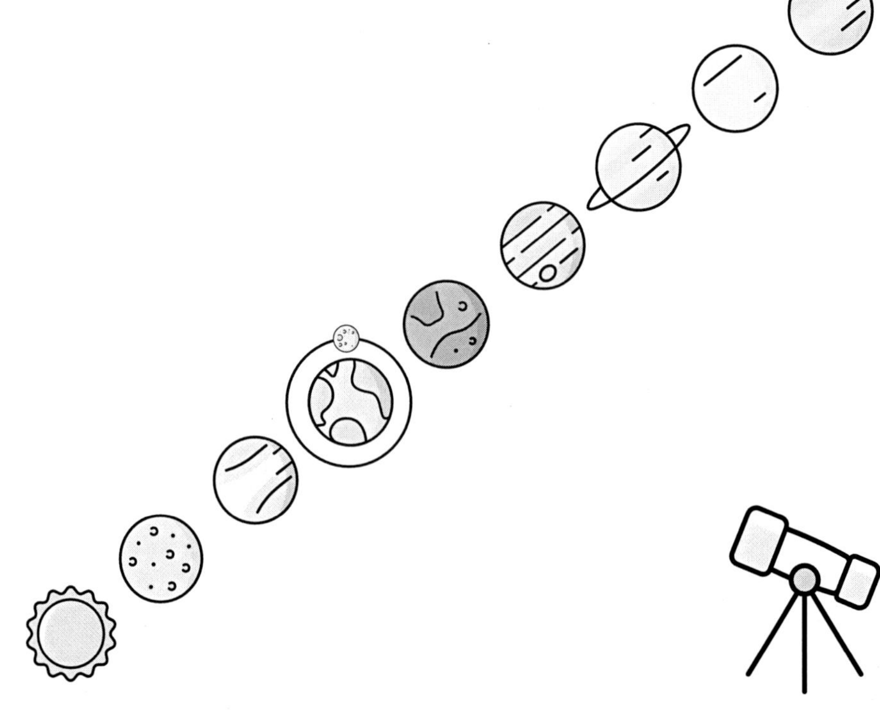

Grade 3 & 4

# Stars and Moon

1

## Stars

Teacher

1 We live on a planet called Earth.

2 Do you know the shape of the earth?

3 Have you ever seen a globe?

4 The earth is a sphere like a ball.

5 Earth is one of the stars in the space called the universe.

And there are many stars in space. We cannot see them in the daytime because of the light of
6 the sun, but countless stars shine in the night sky.

7 Stars do not all have the same brightness.

The brightness varies depending on the size of the star and its distance from the earth. The
8 color of the light also differs.

9 Stars like the sun are hotter and glow bluish-white.

10 They become redder as their temperature decreases.

# 星と月

## 星

先生

昔の人は、その中でもとくに明るい星に注目して、その集まりをいろいろな人や動物、
1 道具に見立てて名前をつけていました。これを 星座（せいざ）といいます。
2 先ほどの誕生月の 12 星座もその一部です。
3 七夕の物語のように星や星座にはいろいろな神話やお話があります。
4 星座は全部で 88 個です。日本からは、およそ 50 個の星座を見ることができます。
5 私たちが見える星座は、季節によって違います。なぜだかわかりますか。
6 私たちが住んでいる地球は、1 年をかけて太陽の周りを回っています。
7 さらに、地球は北極と南極を軸にして自転しているからです。
8 ちょうど、四角部屋の中で真ん中に立って体を一回転したのと同じで、季節によって見て
いる壁が違うのと同じです。だから、春に見える星座、夏に見える星座、秋に見える星座、
9 冬に見える星座が違う上に、星座が時間によって移動しているように見えるのです。

10 ただ、1 年中見ることができる星があります。それが北極星です。
11 北極星は、2 等星なので、探しづらいかもしれません。
かわりに、北斗七星やカシオペヤ座を利用して、北極星を探すことが多いです。
北斗七星は、星座ではなく、おおぐま座の一部です。北極星は、星座ではなく、こぐま座の
12 一部です。こぐま座の、しっぽの先が北極星になっています。
北極星は、一年中、見えるのですから、こぐま座もしっぽの先と、その近くは、一年中、
見えるのです。北極星という北の空にある星と、そのまわりにある北の空の星座は、一年中、
13 みることができますが、南、東、西の空の星座は、季節によってかわります。

日本は、地球の北がわの北半球（きたはんきゅう）にあるので、日本からは北極の方角に
14 ある空が見えます。南極のほうの空は、日本からは地面にかくれて見えません。
15 だから南の春の星座は秋には見えません。南の夏の星座は冬には見えません。

16 逆に南の秋の星座は春には見えませんし、南の冬の星座は夏には見えません。

南半球の人たちが星座を見たら、南半球では、南の空にある星座は一年中、同じで、
17 北の星座が、季節によってかわります。

北の空では、だいたい 1 時間に 15 度くらい、北極星のまわりを、北極星を中心とした円に
18 そって、回っています。向きは、時計の針（はり）とは反対向きです。
19 星座早見表は、何月何日何時のどちらの空に指定して、見える星座を確認できる大変便利です。

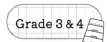

Grade 3 & 4

# Stars and Moon

1

## Stars

Teacher

In ancient times, people paid attention to the brightest stars among them and named them
1 after people, animals, and tools. These are called constellations.
2 The 12 constellations of the birth month mentioned earlier are also part of these.
3 There are many myths and stories about the stars and constellations.
4 There are 88 constellations in total. From Japan, we can see about 50 constellations.
5 The constellations we can see are different depending on the season. Do you know why?
6 The earth on which we live revolves around the sun over the course of a year.
7 Furthermore, this is because the earth rotates on its axis around the north and south poles.
8 It is just like standing in the middle of a square room and turning your body one way or the other.
Each time you turn you see a different wall. Just like the walls, every time the earth rotates you
see a different season. That is why the constellations visible in spring, summer, fall, and winter
9 are different, and in addition, the constellations appear to move with time.
10 However, there is one star that can be seen all year round. It is Polaris.
11 Polaris is a second magnitude star, so it may be difficult to find.
Instead, we can use the Big Dipper and Cassiopeia to find it. The Big Dipper is not a constellation,
but part of Ursa Major. Polaris is not a constellation, but part of Ursa Minor.
12 Polaris is at the tip of the tail of Ursa Minor.
Since Polaris is visible all year round, the tip of its tail and its vicinity in Ursa Minor are visible
all year round. The star in the northern sky called Polaris and the constellations in the northern
sky around it can be seen all year round, but the constellations in the southern, eastern, and
13 western skies change with the seasons.
Japan is located in the northern hemisphere of the earth, so the sky in the direction of
14 the North Pole is visible from Japan. The sky toward the South Pole is obscured by the ground.
So the spring constellations in the south are not visible in the fall. The southern summer
15 constellations are not visible in winter.
Conversely, the southern autumn constellations are not visible in the spring, and the southern
16 winter constellations are not visible in the summer.
When people in the Southern Hemisphere look at the constellations, the constellations in the
17 southern sky are the same all year round, while those in the north change with the seasons.

In the northern sky, it rotates about 15 degrees per hour around Polaris in a circle with Polaris
18 at its center. The direction of rotation is opposite to that of the hands of a clock.
The constellation quick guide is very useful to check the visible constellations by specifying
19 which sky, on which day of the month, and at which time of day.

中学年

## 星と月 2

月

先生

1 月は身近な星というほかに、私たちの生活にも大変影響をしています。
潮干狩りをしたことがありませんか。海に行くと、潮に満潮と干潮があって、潮の満ち引き
2 は月に引っ張られて起きています。
毎日見る太陽はいつも同じですが、月は三日月になったり、満月になったりと形が
3 変わります。
これは、月は自分で光を発するのではなく、太陽の光で光っていて、太陽の光が当たる
4 部分が、日によって違う角度から見えるからです。

5 満月→下弦の月→26 日の月→新月→上弦の月→次の満月と、変っていきます。

6 だいたい約 30 日で、はじめの満月から次の満月までを、繰り返します。

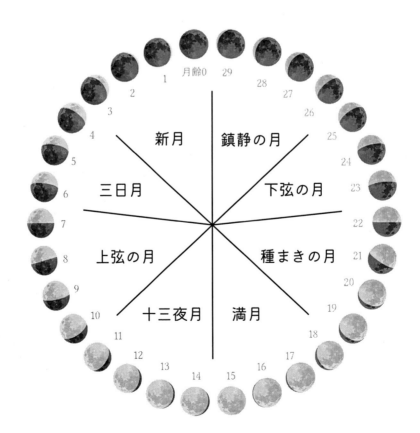

月齢0 1 2 3 4 5 6 7 8 9 10 11 12 13 14 15 16 17 18 19 20 21 22 23 24 25 26 27 28 29

新月
鎮静の月
三日月
下弦の月
上弦の月
種まきの月
十三夜月
満月

Grade 3 & 4

## Stars and Moon

### Moon

**Teacher**

1 Besides being a familiar star, the Moon is also very influential in our lives.
Have you ever been tidal fishing? When you go to the ocean, there are high and low tides,
2 and the ebb and flow of the tide is pulled by the moon.
The sun we see every day is always the same, but the moon changes its shape, becoming
3 a crescent moon or a full moon.
This is because the moon does not emit light by itself, but is illuminated by the sun's light, and the part of the moon that is illuminated by the sun is seen from different angles on
4 different days.
It changes from full moon to lower sine moon to 26th moon to new moon to upper sine
5 moon to next full moon.
6 It takes about 30 days from the first full moon to the next full moon and back again.

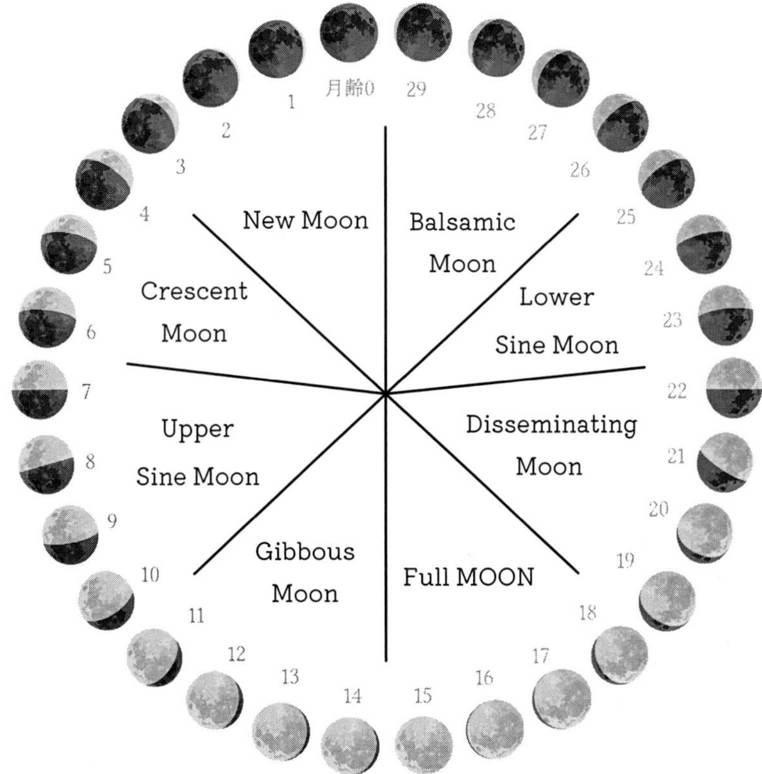

高学年

## 植物の成長と日光の関わり

先生

1 植物が光合成を行って作り出す栄養分はデンプンといいます。
デンプンは、エネルギーの元になる栄養で、水と空気中の二酸化炭素から作られた
2 ブドウ糖分子がいくつもつながったものです。
3 植物がデンプンをつくるには、日光と二酸化炭素と水が必要です。
4 デンプンというのは、漢字で、澱粉と書きます。
もともとはジャガイモをすって水にさらした時に水の底にたまった沈殿した粉なので
5 澱粉（デンプン）という名がつきました。
6 光合成は、植物の葉で作られますから、デンプンはすべての植物で作られます。
光合成は、葉の裏側に気孔という呼吸のできる鼻みたいなところがあり、そこから
7 二酸化炭素を取り入れます。
この気孔の周りにある孔辺細胞に葉緑体という
8 組織があり、そこで光合成を行います。
この図を見て下さい。唇のように見えるのが
9 孔辺細胞で、孔辺細胞の隙間が「気孔」です。

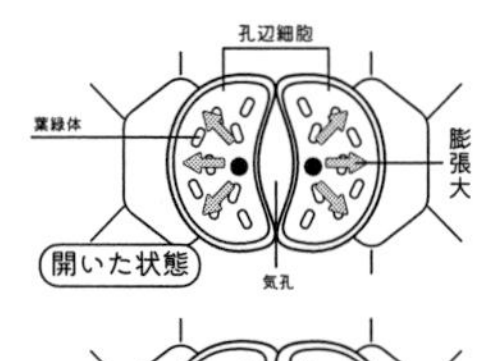


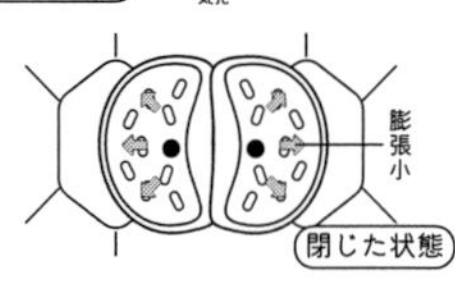


10 葉緑体で光合成が行われていることと光が必要であることを確認してみましょう。
11 ふいりの葉・アルコール・ヨウ素液・アルミニウムはくを用意します。
12 光の当たらない部分を作るため、葉の一部をアルミニウムはくで覆います。
13 葉に十分な光を当てたのち、速やかに摘み取ります。夜になるとでんぷんが分解され、
14 根・茎に送られてしまうためです。
葉をあたためたアルコールで脱色します。ヨウ素液に浸して確認すると、緑色の部分かつ
15 光の当たった部分のみ青紫色になります。
16 では、次に、光合成に二酸化炭素が必要であることを確認してみましょう。
17 使うのは水草です。少量の水酸化ナトリウムを溶かした水溶液に、BTB 液を入れます。

18 水溶液はうすい青色になります。
19 ここに息を吹き込むと、二酸化炭素が入ることで、うすい黄色に変化します。
黄色になった溶液に水草を入れ、光を当てると、溶液の色が黄色から緑、青に変化します。
次に、光合成で酸素が発生することを確認してみましょう。水草に光を当て、発生する
20 気泡を試験管などで集めます。

21 集めた気体に火のついた線香を入れてみますよー。ほら、線香が激しく燃えました。
22 燃えるということは酸素があるからですね。
23 これで、光合成は二酸化炭素＋水（＋光）→デンプン＋酸素となることが確認できました。

# Relationship between plant growth and sunlight

Teacher

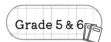

1 The nutrient produced by plants through photosynthesis is called starch.

Starch is a nutritional source of energy and is composed of a number of connected glucose
2 molecules made from water and carbon dioxide in the air.

3 Plants need sunlight, carbon dioxide, and water to produce starch.

4 The word "starch" is written in Chinese characters as " 澱粉".

Originally, the name "starch" came from the precipitated powder that accumulated at
5 the bottom of the water when potatoes were grounded and exposed to water.

6 Photosynthesis is produced in the leaves of plants, so starch is produced in all plants.

Photosynthesis is carried out by taking in carbon dioxide through the pores on the underside
7 of leaves, which are like nasal passages for respiration.

The pore cells around these pores contain chloroplasts,
8 and this is where photosynthesis takes place.

Look at this diagram. You can see something that
looks like lips. These 'lips' are pore cells
9 and the gaps between the pore cells are called stoma.

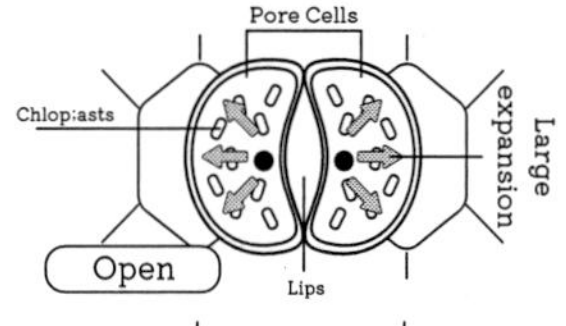


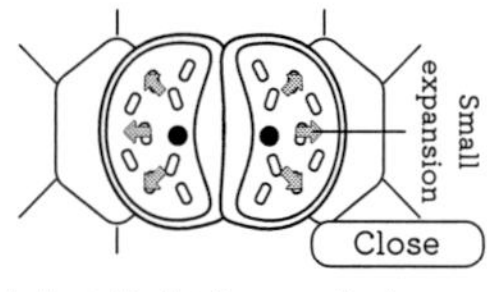


10 Let's confirm that photosynthesis is taking place in chloroplasts and that light is needed.

11 I have prepared variegated leaves, alcohol, iodine solution, and aluminum foil for you.

12 To create areas that are not exposed to light, cover parts of the leaves with aluminum foil.

13 Promptly pluck the leaves after they have been exposed to sufficient light.

14 This is because starch is broken down at night and sent to the roots/stems.

Then we bleach the leaves with warm alcohol. When immersed in iodine solution, only
15 the green areas and the areas exposed to light turn bluish-purple.

16 Now let's move on to confirm if carbon dioxide is necessary for photosynthesis.

For this, we will use water grass. Add BTB (Bromothymol blue) solution to an aqueous solution
17 in which a small amount of sodium hydroxide has been dissolved.

18 The resulting solution is light blue.

19 If you blow into the solution, carbon dioxide will enter the solution and it will turn light yellow.

When the water grass is placed in the yellow solution and exposed to light, the color of
the solution changes from yellow to green to blue. Next, let's check to see if photosynthesis
produces oxygen. Shine light on the water grass and collect the bubbles generated in a test
20 tube or something similar.

21 Now, I'll put a lit incense stick in the collected gas. See, the incense burns intensely.

22 If it burns, it is because there is oxygen.

23 This confirms that photosynthesis is carbon dioxide + water (+ light) → starch + oxygen.

中学年

## 昆虫の生態

先生

1 私たちの周りには、色んな生き物がいて、春は、気温も上がり、生き物たちの活動が始まる
季節です。
昔は、身近に多くの昆虫がいて、チョウの卵や幼虫もすぐに見つけることが出来ましたが、
2 今はなかなか見つけられなくなりました。

3 チョウは、卵から幼虫、さなぎとなり、成虫と成長していきます。
4 卵はキャベツの葉っぱに産み落とされます。
5 チョウは卵から孵ると葉を餌とします。
キャベツはアブラナ科という直物の一つで、とても辛い成分が含まれていて、ほかの昆虫
は餌としません。ライバルが少なければ、餌に困りませんから、モンシロチョウはキャベツ
6 に卵を産み付けます。
7 同じチョウでも、アゲハチョウはミカンの葉に卵を産み付けます。

チョウは、飛びながら植物の色や形、においをたよりに植物に近づき、その植物に触って、
8 その葉の味を調べて、幼虫が食べることのできる植物がどうかを見分けます。
前足の脚先で味を調べて、その植物が子供の食べ物になることがわかってはじめて
9 卵を産みます。
モンシロチョウの卵も孵化した幼虫も黄色ですが、キャベツを食べているので、
10 緑色になっていきます。
11 また、幼虫の皮は体の大きさに合わせて伸びないため、4回脱皮をします。
12 その後、さなぎになり、その後にモンシロチョウの成虫になります。
13 このさなぎという過程を完全変態といいます。
14 カマキリやセミは幼虫から脱皮を繰り返してそのまま成虫になり、不完全変態といいます。

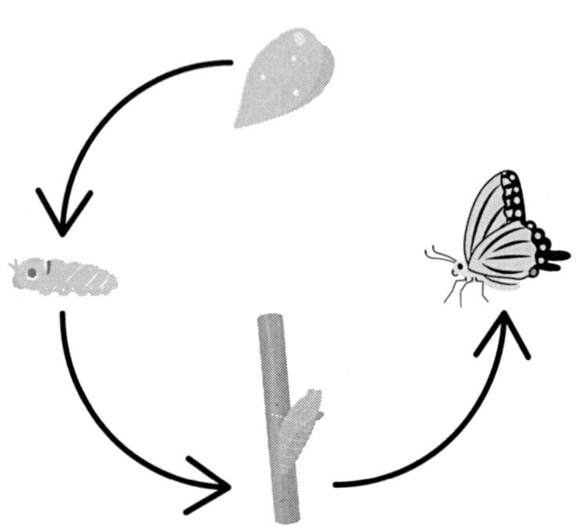

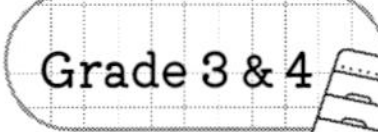


# Life Cycles of Insects

Teacher

1 Spring is the season when the temperature rises and creatures begin their activities.

In the past, there were many insects around us and we could easily find butterfly eggs and
2 larvae, but now it is not so easy to find them.

3 Butterflies grow from egg then become larva to chrysalis then adult butterflies.
4 The eggs are laid on cabbage leaves.
5 When the butterflies hatch from their eggs, they feed on the cabbage leaves.
Cabbage is a member of the Brassicaceae family, which is a direct species that contains a very
pungent ingredient that other insects do not feed on. If there are few rivals, there is no need to
6 worry about food, so the butterfly lays its eggs on cabbage.
7 In the same butterfly family, the swallowtail butterfly, lays its eggs on tangerine leaves.

As they fly, butterflies approach plants based on their color, shape, and smell, then touch them
8 and examine the taste of their leaves to determine if the plant is suitable for their larvae to eat.
They examine the taste with the toes of their front feet and lay eggs only when they know that
9 the plant will be food for their young.
Both the eggs and the hatched larvae of the white-bellied butterfly are yellow, but since they
10 feed on cabbage, they turn green.
11 In addition, the skin of the larvae does not stretch as it grows so it sheds its skin four times.
12 It then becomes a chrysalis, after which it becomes a white adult.
13 We call this final stage a complete metamorphosis.
In contrast, insects like mantis and cicadas do not change their body shape but just bigger.
14 This is called incomplete metamorphosis.

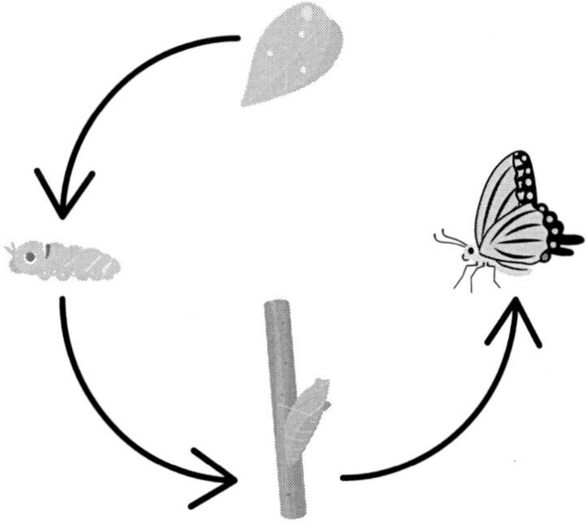

中学年

# 昆虫の生態

先生

1 昆虫に限らず、生き物は、何代にもわたって、命をつないでいきます。
何億年という昔からそれぞれの命をつないでいます。
2 ただ、その何億年もの命をつないでいく中で、どの生き物も、生き残るに適した進化と
いうのをしていきます。
チョウやカブトムシは、卵から生まれた時から成虫と同じ形でなく、幼虫の時は、
栄養を蓄え、大きく育つために適した形をとり、十分に育てるときになったら、さなぎと
いうカプセルの中で、幼虫時代の形から、成虫の形に変身することで命をつなぐ進化を
3 しました。
だから、さなぎのときは、幼虫時代の形もなく、成虫の形を作っている状態ですから、
4 液状になっています。それがチョウの進化です。

5 モンシロチョウの成虫の体のつくりを学習します。
6 モンシロチョウの体は、頭、胸、腹の三つの部分からなっていて、頭に触覚があり、羽が４枚、
足が６本あります。
7 頭には触角と目と口が、胸に羽と足がついています。
8 触角は人間の鼻の役割をしていてにおいを感じます。
9 仲間も、臭いで確認しています。
口は、ストローのような形をしています。1本ではなく、左右２本のくだが合わさったもの
10 で普段はくるくると巻かれています。
11 蜜を吸うときには、この口を伸ばして花の中に差し込んでいるのです。

12 モンシロチョウの寿命は、産卵の時期によって大きく違います。

夏に産卵された場合は、卵から成虫となって寿命が尽きるまで1か月以内ですが、
12 秋に産卵された場合は、越冬するため５か月位が寿命です。
なお、チョウは、一匹でなく、一頭と数えますが、これは明治初期に西欧文化を導入した際、
13 昆虫を「head」の単位で数えることを誤訳したことが原因です。

本来、日本では人間や馬より同等あるいは大きい場合は頭、小さい場合は匹と数えて
14 いました。

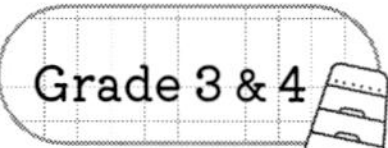


理科

Science

Grade 3 & 4

# Life Cycles of Insects

Teacher

1 Not only insects, but all living creatures pass their species on from generation to generation.
However, in the course of their hundreds of millions of years of life, all living things evolve in
2 a way that is suitable for their survival.

Butterflies and beetles do not look like adult insects after they hatch. As larvae, they take a form
suitable for storing nutrients and growing large, and when it is time to fully nurture them, they
transform from their larval form to their adult form in a capsule called a chrysalis, thus evolving
3 to sustain life.
So, when it is a chrysalis, it is in a liquid state because it has no shape from its larval stage and
4 is in the process of becoming an adult. That is the evolution of the butterfly.

5 Now we will learn about the body structure of the adult cabbage white butterflies.
6 The body of the cabbage white butterfly consists of three parts: head, breast, and abdomen.

7 The head has an antenna, four wings, and six legs.
8 The antennae act as the human nose and sense smell.
9 They also identify their mates by smell.
The mouth is shaped like a straw, not a single straw, but two straws, one on each side, which
10 are usually coiled around each other.
11 When they suck nectar, they extend and insert it into the flower.

The lifespan of the cabbage white butterfly varies greatly depending on the time of year when
12 they lay eggs.
If the eggs are laid in summer, the life span from egg to adult is less than one month, but if the
12 eggs are laid in fall, the life span is about five months as they hibernate over winter.
Meanwhile, we count butterfly in Japan as “itto” instead of “ippiki”. This is due to the fact that
when Western culture was introduced in the early Meiji period (1868-1912), the word ‘insect’
13 was mistakenly translated as ‘head’ in Japanese.
Normally, if an animal is about the same size or more than a human or a horse, we count them
14 as ‘tou’ while smaller ones are counted as ‘hiki’.

高学年

# 魚 1

メダカの生態

先生

1 今日からは魚（さかな）について学習します。

2 今、さかなといいましたが、漢字では魚と書き、音読みではギョと読みます。

3 訓読みではウオとも読みますね。平安時代はウオと読んでいました。

4 江戸時代になって、さかなという呼び方が普及していました。
今は、さかなと呼ぶのが一般的で、ウオは、魚市場とか限られています。

5

6 まず、魚の生態を知るところから教科書は始まります。

7 教科書では、メダカの生態を知ろうということで取り上げられています。

8 メダカは、目が大きく、頭部の上端から飛び出していることが名前の由来です。
もともと、日本のどこにでもいる淡水魚で、昔から教科書に登場する魚でしたが、
水質汚染が進み、2003年5月に環境省が発表したレッドデータブックに絶滅危惧種と
9 して指定された希少な魚です。

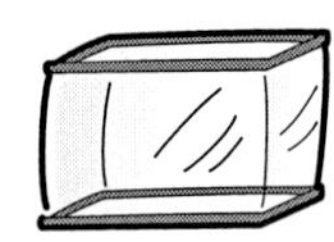

10 では、メダカの飼い方です。

11 まず、水槽に水道水を用いる場合は、一日以上、放置した汲み置きの水が必要です。

12 出した直後の水道水をそのまま、使ってはいけません。

13 水道水には、消毒用の薬品が入ってるので、直接あたえると、メダカを死なせてしまいます。
次に、水を交換する時は、一度に全部を交換せず、3分の一もしくは半分づつ、汲み置きの
14 水と交換します。

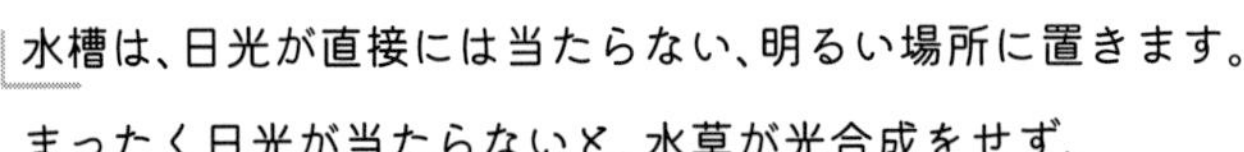

15 水槽の底には、水でよく洗った石や砂を、しきつめておきます。

16 マツモやキンギョモなどの水草を入れます。

17 メダカはオス、メス3匹くらいずつ入れます。

18 水槽は、日光が直接には当たらない、明るい場所に置きます。
まったく日光が当たらないと、水草が光合成をせず、
19 水中の酸素が作られないのでダメです。

20 しかし、日光が直接当たると、水温が高くなり過ぎてしまいます。
エサは、1日1回か2回、余らないようにあげます。

21 水温を知るため、温度計が必要です。

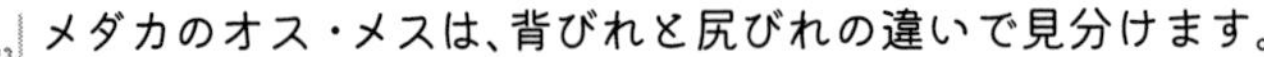

22 メダカのオス・メスは、背びれと尻びれの違いで見分けます。

23 オスは背びれに切り込みあり、メスは切り込みがありません。
メスの尻びれは、尾に近づくほど細くなる三角形のような形ですが、オスは平行四辺形の
24 ような形です。

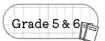

# Fish

## Life Cycles of Killifish

Teacher

1 From today, we will learn about fish (sakana).

2 I just said "sakana," but in kanji it is written " 魚" and read phonetically as "gyo".

3 In kun-yomi, it is also read as "uo". In the Heian period, it was read as "uo".

4 However, since the Edo period, the term "Sakana" has become widespread.

Nowadays, it is more common to call it "sakana", and "uo" is limited to those who work in
5 fish markets.

6 The textbook begins with an introduction to fish ecology.

7 The goal is to cover the ecology of killifish.

8 The killifish gets its name from its very large eyes, which protrude from the top of its head.

Originally the killifish was a freshwater fish that could be found anywhere in Japan and had
appeared in textbooks for a long time. However, due to water pollution, it was classified as a rare
9 and endangered in the Red Data Book released by the Ministry of the Environment in May 2003.

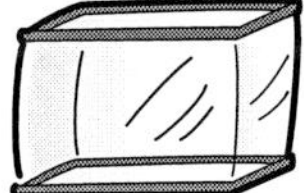

10 Now, let's talk about how to raise killifish.

11 First, if tap water is used for the aquarium, it must be left for at least one day.

12 Do not use water straight from the tap.

13 Tap water contains disinfectant chemicals that will kill killifish if you put them in it immediately.

Next, when changing the water, do not replace all the water at once, but instead replace it
14 one-third or half at a time with freshly pumped water.

15 The bottom of the tank should be lined with well-washed stones or sand.

16 Add water plants such as hornwort into the tank.

17 Place about 3 male and 3 female killifish.

18 Place the aquarium in a well-lit area that is not directly exposed to sunlight.

If there isn't enough sunlight, the plants will not undergo photosynthesis and oxygen will not
19 be produced in the water.

20 However, direct sunlight will cause the water temperature to rise too much.

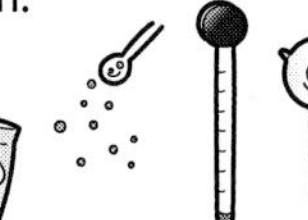

Feed the killifish once or twice a day, but not too much
21 You also need a thermometer to determine the water temperature.

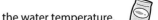

22 You can tell the gender of a killifish by the difference between their dorsal and anal fins.

23 Males have an incised dorsal fin, while females do not.

The female's tail fin is triangular in shape, tapering toward the tail, while the male's fin is like
24 a parallelogram.

高学年

# 魚

メダカの産卵

先生

1 先生　メダカのメスは水温が20℃～25℃くらいになると、産卵します。
メダカのたまごは透明で無色で、たまごの一個あたりの大きさは、だいたい直径が1.0mm
2 から1.5mmくらいです。
3 一回の産卵で、たまごを5個から10個くらい、産みます。
オスがメスに並んで泳ぎ、寄り添い、メスのたまごに、精子(せいし)というものを
4 含くんだ液をかけると、たまごに子供がやどります。これを受精といいます。
5 産卵が終わったら、メスは、たまごを水草にくっつけます。
メダカのたまごには、長い毛が、たまごの一部から、数本出ていて、
6 この毛は 付着毛（ふちゃくもう）と呼ばれます。
生まれたばかりのときは、多くのあわのような粒が、全体的に散らばっ ていますが、
7 数時間後するとあわの粒が一方に集まり、いくつかの大きな丸い物になります。
また、つぶの集まった側に対する反対側が、盛り上がってきます。
8 卵の中には、小さな泡のようなものがたくさん見られます。この泡は油滴です。
9 受精卵は、油滴と反対側を中心にしてメダカの体が作られます。
10 3日後ぐらいで、大きな丸いものがより粒が少なくなり、くっきりとしてきます。
11 たくさんあった油滴がくっつきあって3個になりました。
12 数は減りましたが一つ一つの油滴は大きくなりました。
13 眼がはっきりとしてきました。
14 8日後ぐらいになると、心臓のようなものが動き始めるのが見えます。
15 頭に近い腹部で血液が流れていきます。
16 血液が送り出されている心臓も確認できます。
17 11日後ぐらいで、子メダカが、たまごからかえります。
18 これをふ化といいます。
産んで間もないメダカの卵は、固くてなかなか破れませんが、ふ化の直前には、
19 メダカのひたいからふ化酵素が出され、卵の膜が溶かされ柔らかくなります。

20 これが、メダカの誕生です。

数時間

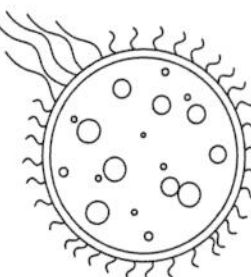

2～3日目

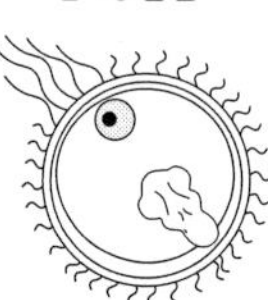

4～6日目

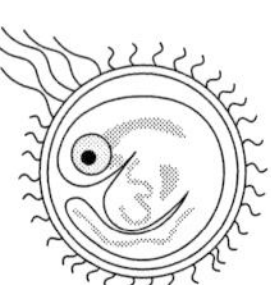

10～12日目

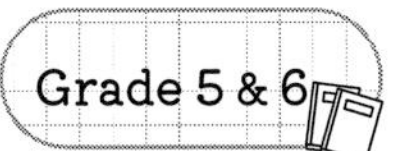

## Fish

2

### Spawning of killifish

Teacher

1 Female killifish start reproduction when the water temperature reaches about 20-25°C.
The egg of a killifish is transparent and colorless, and each egg is roughly 1.0 mm to
2 1.5 mm in diameter.
3 They lay 5 to 10 eggs in a single reproduction cycle.
While the male swims alongside the female, it splatters a sperm-filled fluid over the female's egg,
4 and the egg is fertilized. This is called fertilization.
5 Once reproduction is complete, the female attaches the eggs to the water plants.
6 The egg of a killifish has several long hairs protruding from it, called attaching filaments.

After laying, the eggs appear to have many large foamy grains scattered about, but after
7 a few hours, the grains of foam gather to one side and become several large round objects.
Also, the opposite side to where these gather, the eggs seem to swell. Inside the egg, you will
8 see many small bubbles.
9 These bubbles are oil droplets and the killifish embryo will develop around them.
10 After about 3 days, the large round bodies become less grainy and more distinct.
11 The oil droplets start to stick together to form three large ones.
12 The number of oil drops decrease, but each drop is now larger.
13 The eyes have become clearer.
14 After about 8 days, you can see the heart starting to beat.
15 You can also see blood flowing near the stomach and head.
16 The heart, which is pumping blood, can also be seen.
17 About 11 days later, the killifish will emerge from the egg.
18 This is called hatching.
The eggs of a newly laid killifish are hard to break, but just before hatching, special hatching
enzymes are released from the killifish's body, softening the egg membrane and helping to
19 melt it.
20 This is the birth cycle of the killifish.

a few hours

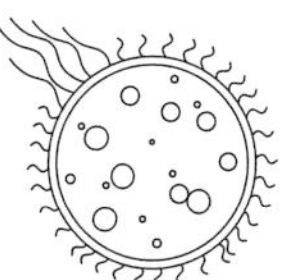

2~3 days

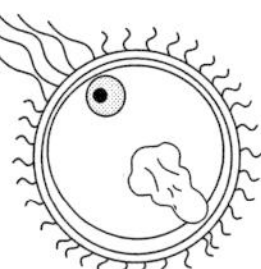

4~6 days

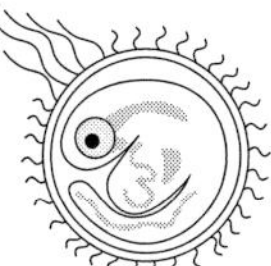

10~12 days

高学年

# 魚

## プランクトン

先生

1 メダカの食べ物は、水中の植物性プランクトンや蚊の幼虫のボウフラです。

2 プランクトンというのは、小さすぎて人間の目には見えない水中を漂って生活する
3 生物をいい、光合成を行える植物性プランクトンと行えない動物性プランクトンがいます。

メダカが食べているプランクトンは、目では見えないので顕微鏡を使わないとみることが
4 できません。

5 実際にプランクトンを見てみましょう。

ミジンコ, マルミジンコ, カイミジンコ, アブラミミズ, ボウフラ, カゲロウの幼虫、
6 ゾウリムシ, ミドリムシ, アオミドロ, ハリケイソウ

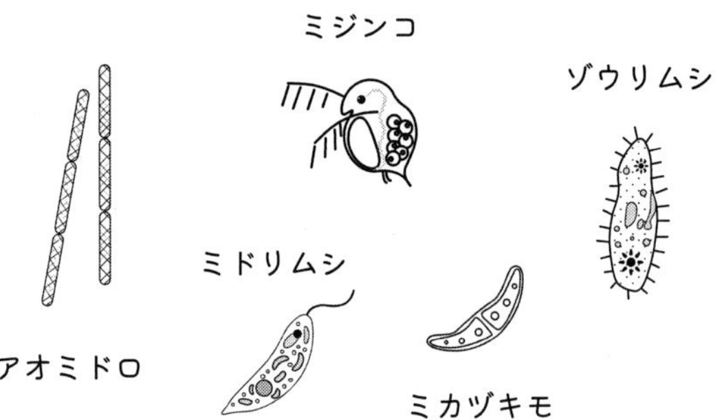


その中で、メダカのえさとなっている植物性プラントンはアオミドロ、ミカヅキモ、
7 ミドリムシですね。ミジンコ、ゾウリムシなどが動物性プランクトンです。

このプランクトンがいて、これを食べる小魚や魚がいて、その魚を食べる大きな魚がいて、
8 その魚を私たちは食べて、生きています。

9 これを食物連鎖といいます。

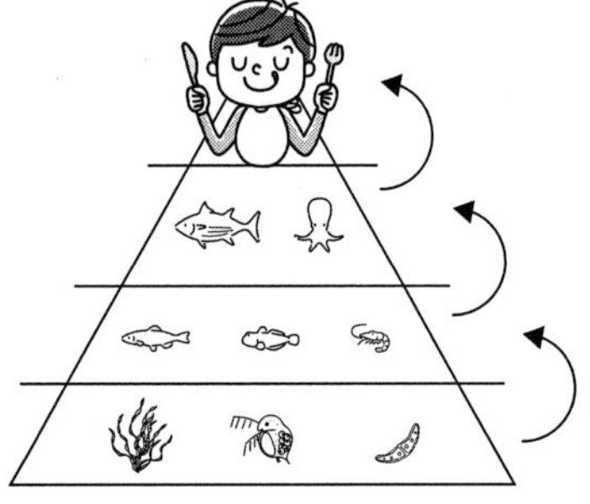

食物連鎖については、上の学年いくと詳しく学びますが、生き物が生きていくためには
12 「食べる」ことが欠かせません。

こんな目に見えないプランクトンが絶滅したら、小魚も、それを食べる魚も絶滅してしまい、
13 私たちも食べるものがなくって生きることができません。

14 命がつながっていることを覚えておきましょうね。

Grade 5 & 6

# Fish 3

## Plankton

Teacher

1 The killifish's food is plant phytoplankton and mosquito larvae in water

2 Plankton are organisms that live in the water, and are too small to be seen by the human eye.

There are phytoplankton (plant plankton) that can perform photosynthesis and
3 zooplankton (animal plankton) that cannot.

The plankton that the killifish eats is invisible to the human eye and can only be seen with
4 a microscope.

5 Let's take a look at a real plankton.

Daphnia magna, Daphnia magna(Chydoridae), Daphnia magna(Ostracod),mosquito larva,
6 paramecium, euglena, spirogyra and synedra

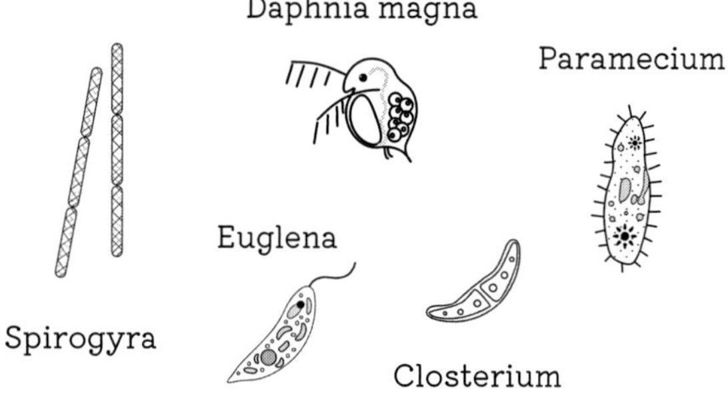


Among them, the phytoplankton that are used as food for killifish are spirogyra, Closterium,
7 and euglena. Daphnia magna, paramecium and slipper animalcule are zooplankton.

There is plankton, and there are small fishes that eat it. There are bigger fish that eat those
8 small fish, and we eat those fish to live.

9 This is called the food chain.

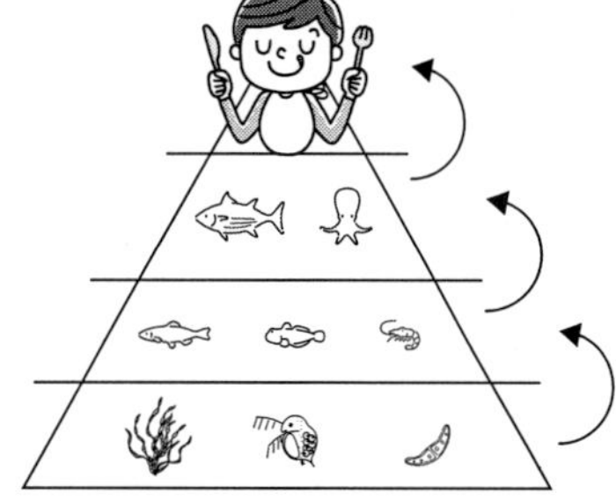

You will learn more about the food chain in the upper grades though.

12 "Eating" is essential for living creatures to survive.

If these invisible plankton were to become extinct, small fish and the fish that eat them would
13 also become extinct, and we would have nothing to eat and will not be able to live.

14 Let's remember that all living things are connected.

高学年

## 体のつくりと働き

### 呼吸

先生

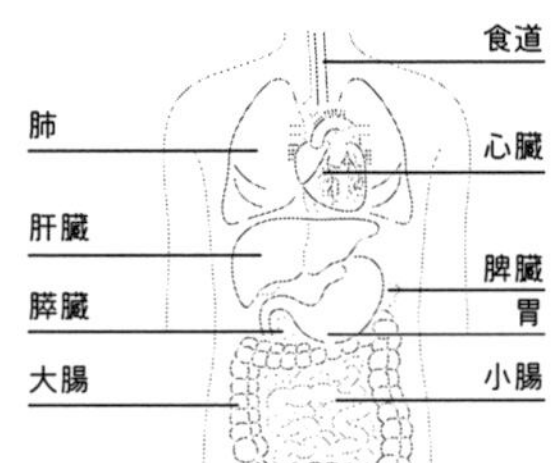


1 今日から、体のつくりと働きを学習してきます。
2 まずは、呼吸です。
空気を吸って、空気のなかの酸素を取れて、
3 二酸化炭素の多い空気を吐き出します。

二酸化炭素がふくまれていることは、ふくろの中に石灰水を入れたふくろに、
4 息を吹き込めば、石灰水が白く、にごることで確認できます。
肺は、左右に１個ずつ、あります。
5 空気は、のど や鼻から、肺へと向かって吸い込まれます。
のどや鼻を通って、気管を通り、気管の先が２本に分かれていて、この気管が２本に
6 分かれている部分を気管支といいます。
肺の中には、気管支が小さな細気管支に枝分かれしていて、その先に 肺胞という
7 小さな袋 があり、毛細血管がついていて酸素と二酸化炭素の交換を行います。
なお、肺の大きさですが、心臓が左に寄っている為に、左肺は右肺より小さく、形も２葉です。
8 右肺は３葉に分かれている構造を持ちます。

9 人間だけでなく、犬も牛も肺で呼吸しています。
10 水中の生き物は多くがエラ呼吸です。魚には、肺はありません。
魚は、口から水を吸い込み、その口の中の水をエラに通して、エラで水から酸素を取り込み、
11 二酸化炭素を排出します。
12 エラの内部には、毛細血管がたくさんあります。

13 動物等の哺乳類、鳥類やトカゲや蛇などの爬虫類は呼吸です。
14 ですから、クジラとイルカは海に住んでいますが、ほ乳類ですので肺で呼吸しています。

15 植物も呼吸をします。
16 光合成を行う一方で酸素を取り入れて、二酸化炭素を吐き出しています。

Grade 5 & 6

# Body Formation and Function 1

## Respiration

Teacher

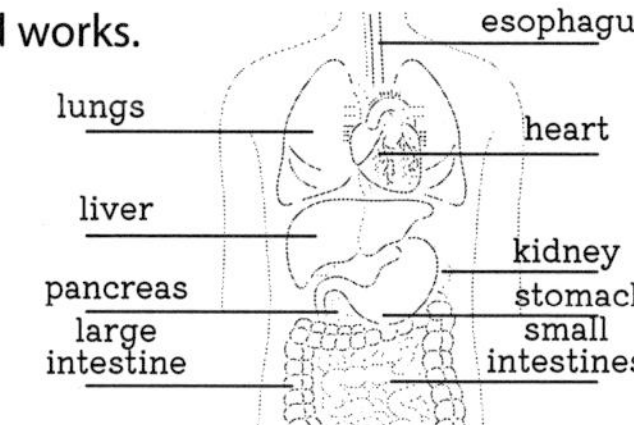


1 Today, you will start learning about how the body is built and works.

2 First, breathing.

We breathe in air, which removes oxygen from the air,

3 and exhale air with a high carbon dioxide content.

The presence of carbon dioxide can be confirmed by blowing into a pouch filled with

4 limewater. The carbon dioxide turns lime water white and cloudy.

There is one lung each on the left and on the right.

5 Air is drawn into the lungs through the throat and nose.

Through the throat and nose, air passes through the trachea, which is divided into two at

6 the end, and the part where the trachea is divided into two is called the bronchus.

In the lungs, bronchi branch off into small bronchioles, which end in small sacks called alveoli,

7 which contain capillaries for the exchange of oxygen and carbon dioxide.

The left lung is smaller than the right lung because the heart is located on the left side, and it

8 has two lobes. The right lung has a three-lobed structure.

9 Not only humans, but also dogs and cows breathe through their lungs.

10 Most underwater creatures breathe through their gills. Fish do not have lungs.

As they suck in water into their mouths, it passes through the gills. The gills remove oxygen

11 from the water and expel carbon dioxide.

12 There are many capillaries in the gills.

13 Animals such as mammals, birds and reptiles such as lizards and snakes all breathe.

Whales and dolphins live in the ocean, but they also breathe through their lungs because they

14 are mammals.

15 Plants also breathe.

16 During photosynthesis, they take in oxygen and release carbon dioxide.

高学年

# 体のつくりと働き

食べ物

先生

1 口から入った食べ物は、食道という管を通って、胃に入ります。
2 それから、小腸に入って大腸に向かいます。そして最後に肛門から出ていきます。
3 口から肛門まで、食べ物の通り道は一本の管になっています。
4 食道から袋のようになった胃。そして小腸、大腸と長い管になっています。

5 これを消化管といい、吸収しやすいように食べ物を体内で変えること消化といいます。

6 消化管は、伸ばすと長さはおよそ９ｍで、人の身長の５倍から６倍になります。

7 食べ物はこの管をおよそ１日かけて通り抜け、便になります。
8 消化というのは、分解されて体内で必要な栄養分として吸収されることですね。
9 口の中は「つば」という液体でしめっていますね。唾液といいます。
食べ物を口入れて、歯で噛み砕き、唾液と混ぜると、食べ物の中のデンプンは、
10 麦芽糖という糖に変化します。
11 胃では、胃液で食物のタンパク質を消化して、ペプトンに分解します。
12 小腸では、消化とともに栄養を吸収し、血液によって肝臓に送られます。
13 小腸の内側には、1ミリぐらい飛出したじゅう毛が、数えきれないほどあります。
消化によってできたアミノ酸・ぶどう糖・脂肪酸・グリセリン灰分・水分などの栄養素は、
14 じゅう毛の表面から吸収されます。
15 大腸では消化は行われず、水分が吸収され、残ったものが便として排出されます。

胃と小腸で栄養素を吸収しますが、小腸で消化するのに必要な消化液は小腸では作られ
16 ません。小腸の消化液はすい臓から送り込まれます。

17 胃から小腸につながるところを十二指腸といいます。
18 そこに、すい臓から送り込まれるすい液が小腸の消化液です。
19 肝臓からもたん汁という胆液が送り込まれます。

消化器では、炭水化物はブドウ糖、タンパク質はアミノ酸、脂肪は脂肪酸とグリセリンまで
20 分解されます。

Page.200 に続く

Grade 5 & 6

# Body Formation and Function 2

## Food

Teacher

1 Food travels from the mouth through a tube called the esophagus and enters the stomach.
2 It then enters the small intestine and travels to the large intestine. Finally, it leaves our body
3 through the anus. From the mouth to the anus, food travels in a single path.
From the esophagus, the stomach is like a pouch while the small and large intestines are
4 like long tubes.
This is called the gastrointestinal tract, and the process of changing food in the body so that
5 it can be easily absorbed is called digestion.
The digestive tract, when extended, is approximately 9 meters long, five to six times
6 the height of a person.
7 Food passes through this tube for approximately one day and then becomes stool.
8 Digestion means that the food is broken down and absorbed by the body as necessary nutrients.
9 Your mouth is moistened with a liquid called "spit". This is called saliva.
When you put food in your mouth, chew it with your teeth, and mix it with saliva, the starch
10 in the food changes into a sugar called maltose.
11 In the stomach, gastric juice digests food proteins and breaks them down into peptones.
12 In the small intestine, nutrients are absorbed and sent by the blood to the liver.
13 On the inside of the small intestine, there are countless hairs about 1mm long!
Nutrients such as amino acids, glucose, fatty acids, glycerin ash, and moisture produced
14 by digestion are absorbed from the surface of the hairs.
Digestion does not take place in the large intestine; instead, water is absorbed and what
15 remains is expelled as stool.
The stomach and small intestine absorb nutrients, but interestingly the digestive juices needed
for digestion in the small intestine are not actually produced in the small intestine. The digestive
16 juices in the small intestine are delivered from the pancreas.
17 The connection between the stomach and the small intestine is called the duodenum.
18 Here, digestive fluid from the pancreas, along with bile juices from the liver, are mixed with the
19 food.

20 In the digestive tract, carbohydrates are broken down to glucose, proteins to amino acids,

高学年

# 体のつくりと働き 2

食べ物

先生

1 肝臓は、小腸で吸収したブドウ糖をグリコーゲンに変えます。
グリコーゲンになることで、体内で保存がしやすくなり、体のエネルギーが不足する時は、
2 糖に分解され、体の各部におくられて、エネルギー源になります。
3 タンパク質やアミノ酸が分解されるとアンモニアという有毒な物質ができてしまいます。
4 ほ乳類では、このアンモニアを、肝臓で毒性の低い尿素という物質に変えます。
5 尿素は、水に溶けるので、尿とともに体外へ排出されますが、ここは腎臓が行います。
6 腎臓は、血液から不要な物をこしとって、血液をきれいにする働きをしています。
7 尿素も、じん臓でこしとられ、余分な水分と一緒にぼうこうへ送られ対外に排出されます。

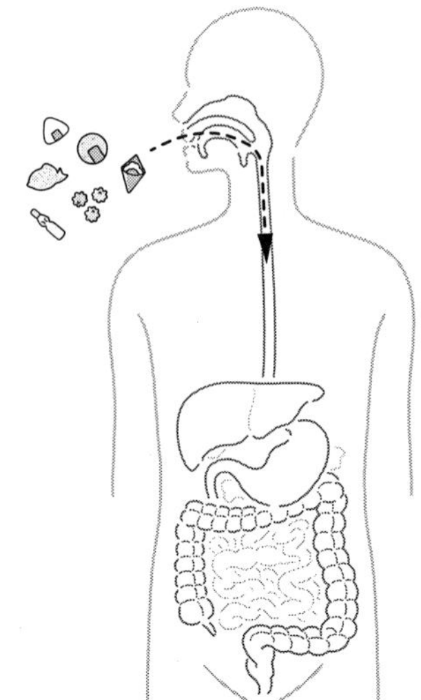

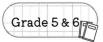

Grade 5 & 6

# Body Formation and Function 2

Food

Teacher

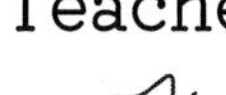

1 The liver converts the glucose absorbed in the small intestine into glycogen.
When the body lacks energy, the glycogen is broken down into sugar, which is then delivered
2 to various parts of the body to be used as an energy source.
3 When proteins and amino acids are broken down, a toxic substance called ammonia is formed.
4 In mammals, ammonia is converted to a less toxic substance called urea in the liver.
5 Urea is soluble in water, it is excreted out of the body in urine, by the kidneys.
6 The kidneys work to cleanse the blood by filtering out unwanted substances from the blood.
Urea is also removed by the kidneys and sent with excess water to the bladder, where it is
7 expelled from the body.

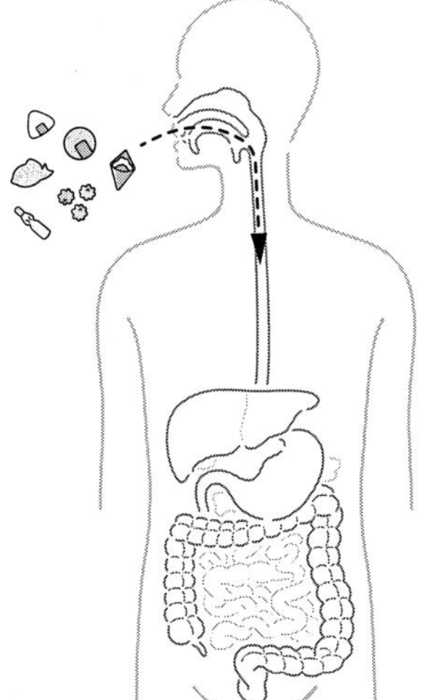

高学年

# 体のつくりと働き 3

## 血液

先生

1 体に血が流れていることは皆さん知っていますね。血液はいくつか種類があります。

2 血液型はA型、B型、O型、AB型があります。

人間の血液型もまだ発見されて100年くらいですから、他の生き物の血液型については今まだ研究中ですが、テナガザルはA型とB型、チンパンジーはA型とO型、

3 ゴリラはB型しかないことまでは分かっているようです。

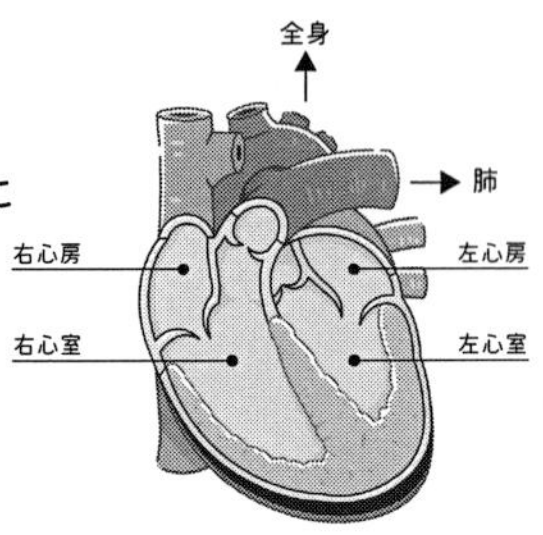


血液は血管を通して、心臓から全身に送られ、血管を通して、全身から心臓にもどってきます。指先の隅々まで運ぶために

4 毛細血管が網目のように張り巡られています。

5 心臓から送られる血液は酸素や栄養分を含みます。

6 血管を大動脈といいます。

7 心臓に戻ってくる血液は二酸化炭素や老廃物が含まれ、血管を大静脈といいます。

心臓は, 厚い筋肉でできていて, 周期的に収縮して血液に圧力をかけ, 血液を全身に

8 送りだすポンプのはたらきをします。

9 これによって全身に血液中の酸素と栄養分を送り届けることができます。

10 心臓には左心房, 左心室, 右心房, 右心室の4つの部屋があります。

左心室の壁の筋肉は全身に血液を送り届けるのに強い力が必要なために, 特に分厚い

11 筋肉でできています。

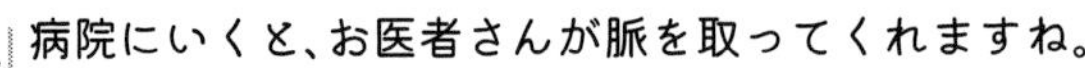

12 病院にいくと、お医者さんが脈を取ってくれますね。

左手をだして、手のひらを上にして、手首に見えている血管の上を右手

13 の人差し指と中指で軽く押さえてください。

ドクッドクッとなっているのがわかりますか。これが脈拍です。この脈拍のリズムは

14 心臓の収縮のリズムと同一です。今、脈拍が感じていますね。

15 心臓から全身に送り出されている大動脈のリズムです。

16 大動脈は、壁が厚く、弾力があります。

17 一方で大静脈は壁が薄く、ところどころに逆流を防ぐ弁があります。

心臓から肺に繋がる動脈は肺動脈といい、二酸化炭素の濃度が高く、逆に肺から心臓に

18 繋がる肺静脈は、酸素が酸素の濃度が高くなっています。

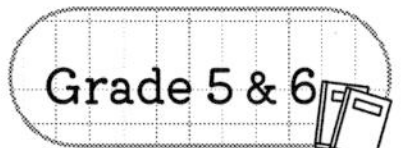

Grade 5 & 6

# Body Formation and Function 3

## Blood

Teacher

1 We all know that blood flows through the body. We also know that there are several blood types.
2 There are four blood types A, B, O, and AB.
Human blood types have only been discovered about 100 years ago, so the blood types of other creatures are still being studied. But we do know that gibbons have only type A and type B,
3 chimpanzees have type A and type O, and gorillas have only type B.

Blood is sent from the heart to the entire body through blood vessels, and from the entire body back to the heart through blood vessels. Capillaries are arranged like a mesh to carry blood to
4 every corner of the body down to the fingertips.
5 Blood sent from the heart contains oxygen and nutrients.
6 The blood vessel that carries blood away from the heart is called the aorta.
Blood returning to the heart contains carbon dioxide and waste products, and the blood vessel
7 that carries it is called a vein
The heart is made up of thick muscles that periodically contract to exert pressure on the blood
8 and pump blood throughout the body.
9 This allows oxygen and nutrients in the blood to be delivered throughout the body.
10 The heart has four chambers: the left atrium, left ventricle, right atrium, and right ventricle.
The wall muscles of the left ventricle are especially thick because they need to be strong to
11 deliver blood throughout the body.

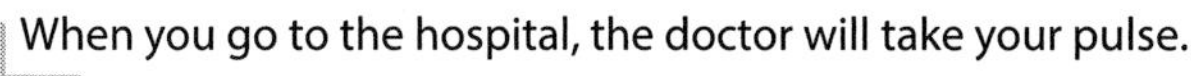

12 When you go to the hospital, the doctor will take your pulse.
Take your left hand, palm up, and lightly press down with the index and middle fingers of your
13 right hand on the blood vessel visible at your wrist.
Do you hear a thumping sound? This is the pulse. The rhythm of this pulse is identical to the
14 rhythm of the heart's contraction. You are now feeling your pulse.
15 It is the rhythm of the aorta, which pumping blood out from the heart to the rest of the body.
16 The aorta has thick and elastic walls.
17 The veins on the other hand, have thin walls and valves in some places to prevent backflow.
He arteries leading from the heart to the lungs are called pulmonary arteries and have a high concentration of carbon dioxide, while the pulmonary veins leading from the lungs to the heart
18 have a high concentration of oxygen.

中学年

## 電気

1

### 電池の働き

先生

1 これは乾電池といいます。乾電池を見てください。

2 おへそが出ている面と平らな面がありますね。

3 おへその出ている面を「+」、平らな面を「−」といいます。

4 電気の通り道が一つの輪になっているとき豆電球にあかりがつき、電気の通り道を回路といいます。

5 なぜ、乾電池の出っ張っている「+」面と「−」面に、どう線が繋がっているときだけ、電気が流れるのでしょう。

6 それは、乾電池はその物が電気の入れ物になっているのでなく、乾電池の中に２種類の化学物質が入れてあって、「+」と「−」が繋がった時だけ、電気が発生するようになっているからです。

7 「+」面と「−」面以外は単なる筒でしかないからです。導線が繋がっていると電球が付きます。

先生

1 電池には「+」と「−」があって、豆電球の赤いコード、青いコードを乾電池の+と−につなぐと豆電球は光りました。

2 電池を二つ縦につなぎます。

3 この時、必ず+側に−側を連結します。

4 同じ側をつけても電流は流れません。

5 一回一回、電池を付けたり、はずしたりするのは大変ですから、コードにスイッチをつけましょう。

6 スイッチは、くっつけたら電流が流れ、離したら電流が流れません。

7 電池が二つ連結すると流れる電流が２倍になりました。

8 では、今度は、電池を横に並べてみましょう。羽根の回転は同じです。
電池を連結するつなぎ方を直列つなぎ、横に並べるつなぎ方を並列つなぎといい、
直列つなぎでは電流が２倍流れますが、並列なぎでは電流の量は変わりませんが、
２倍の時間になります。

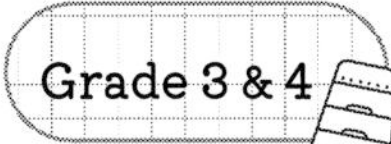

Grade 3 & 4

# Electricity

## The Function of Batteries

Teacher

1 This is called a dry cell battery. Let's look at dry cell batteries.
2 A battery has a protruding side and a flat side, right?
3 The protruding side of the battery is called "+" and the flat side is called "-".
When the path of electricity is in a single loop, the bean bulb lights up, and the path of
4 electricity is called a circuit.
Why does electricity flow only when wires are connected to the protruding "+" and "-" sides
5 of the dry cell?
That is because a dry cell battery is not an electrical container in itself, but rather two different
chemicals are placed inside the dry cell battery, and electricity is generated only when the "+"
6 and "-" are connected.
Everything other than the "+" and "-" sides is just a tube so a light bulb comes on when
7 the conductors are connected.

Teacher

Batteries have "+" and "-" cords, and when the red and blue cords of the bean bulb are
1 connected to the + and of the dry cell battery, the bean bulb glowed.
2 You should connect two batteries vertically.
3 At this time, always be sure to connect the + side to the - side.
4 No current will flow if the same side is attached.
5 Since it is difficult to put in and take out the batteries one by one, let's put a switch on the cord.
The switch allows current to flow when they are attached and does not allow current to flow
6 when they are disconnected.
7 When two batteries are connected, the current flowing through them doubles.
The method of connecting batteries together is called series connection, and the method of
connecting them side by side is called parallel connection. In series connection, the current
flows twice as much, but in parallel connection, the amount of current remains the same, but
8 the time required to complete the operation is twice as long.

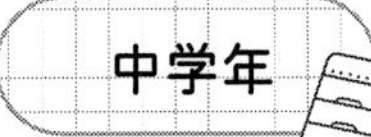

中学年

# 電気

2

## 電池の働き

先生

1 電流とは電気の流れです。

今、石油や石炭に頼らない、きれいなエネルギーの開発に取り組まれていて、太陽の光を
2 利用したエネルギーが実用化してきました。

3 光電池　呼び方は、『ひかりでんち』でなく、『こうでんち』で、光を電気に変える機械です。

4 太陽電池（たいようでんち）ともいいます。

5 光電池にも、プラス極とマイナス極があります。

6 光電池でも、豆電球をつけたり、モーターをまわせたりします。

7 光電池での、電気を流す強さは、電池にあてた光が強いほど強くなります。

8 光電池は、落としたりして壊さなければずっと、使えます。

光電池のことを、英語で、「ソウラ・セル」(SOLAR CELL)というのですが、そのため、
9 光電池をつかった品物の名前が「ソーラー〇〇」というふうな名前がつくことが多いです。

10 光電池の形は、平たい板のような形をしています。

板のような形をしたものをパネルということがあるので、板のような光電池を
11 ソーラーパネル(SOLAR PANEL)ということもあります。

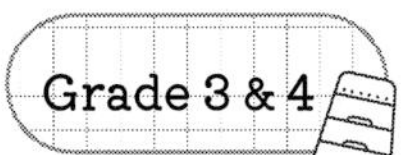


# Electricity

## How Batteries Work

Teacher

1 Current is the flow of electricity.
Efforts are now being made to develop clean energy sources that do not rely on oil or coal,
2 and energy from the sun's rays is becoming more practical.
Photovoltaic cells are not called "Hikaridenchi" but "Koudenchi," and are machines that convert
3 light into electricity.
4 They are also called solar cells (taiyo-denshi).
5 Photovoltaic cells also have positive and negative poles.
6 Photovoltaic cells can also be used to turn on a miniature light bulb or to power a motor.
The stronger the light shining on the battery, the stronger the electricity flowing through
7 the photovoltaic cell.
8 Photovoltaic cells can be used for a long time as long as they are not broken.
A photovoltaic cell is called a "solar cell" in English, which is why products using photovoltaic
9 cells are often named "solar cells"

10 The photocell is shaped like a flat plate.
A photovoltaic cell that looks like a board is sometimes called a solar panel
11 because a panel is sometimes shaped like a board.

高学年

# 電磁石

先生

1 磁石と電流を別々に学習しましたね。
2 ところが、実は、電流が流れると、コードが磁石にもなっているのです。
3 これを電磁石といいます。
4 コードは、中が電流を通す銅線でその周りを感電しないように絶縁にしてあります。

5 銅線を近づけても磁石にくっつきません。
6 いいですか、先生がやってみますから、見ていてください。
7 ほら、くっつきませんね。コードは磁石ではありません。
8 ところが、方位磁石の上で、コードに電流を通すと、ほら、方位磁石が動きましたね。
9 方位磁石が動いたということは、コードが磁石になったということです。
10 前の学習を思い出してください。
11 磁石で鉄のはさみの先をこすると、はさみがそのあともずーと磁力を持っていましたね。

12 電磁石では、電流を止めると、鉄くぎはただのくぎで、磁力がありません。

13 実際に実験を通じて確認してみましょう。「百聞は一見にしかず」です。
14 班ごとに机を寄せてください。
各班の班長は、教壇に、ポリエチレン管と、エナメル線、釘、乾電池、スイッチ、クリップ、
15 紙やすりを取りに来てください。
16 では、最初はどの班も同じように作ります。
17 エナメル線を 20 回、ポリエチレン管にまきつけてください。
18 これをコイルといいます。
エナメル線の両端を紙やすりで削ってエナメルをはがして、電球に電流を流した時と
19 同じようにスイッチを乾電池に繋いでください。

20 はい、スイッチを入れて、クリップをエナメル線に近づけてください。
21 くっつきますか？少しだけしかつきませんね。
22 では、スイッチを切って、コイルの中にくぎを入れてください。
では、もう一度、スイッチを入れて、クリップをコイルから
23 はみでている釘の先端に近づけてください。
24 はい、スイッチを切ってください。
25 クリップが離れましたね。
26 これが電磁石です。

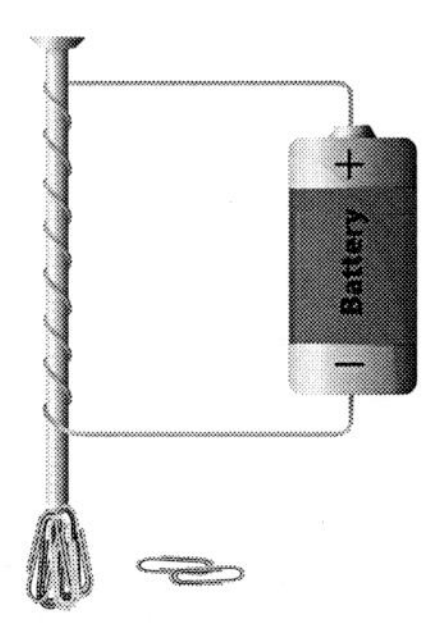

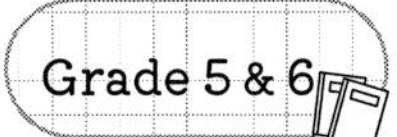

# Lesson 10 理科 Science

Grade 5 & 6

## Electromagnetism

**Teacher**

1 We learned about magnets and electric current separately.

2 However, in fact, when an electric current flows through cords they also become a magnet.

3 This is called electromagnetism.

4 The electrical cord has a copper wire inside that conducts electric current and is insulated around it to prevent anyone from getting an electric shock.

5 The copper wire will not stick to the magnet when it is close to it.

6 Okay, let's see if I can do that.

7 See, it doesn't stick. The cord is not a magnet.

8 But if you pass an electric current through the cord, the compass moves.

9 The fact that the compass moved means that the cord became a magnet.

10 Please remember the previous lesson.

11 If you rub the tip of a pair of iron scissors with a magnet, the scissors remain magnetic for a long time after that.

12 With an electromagnet, when the current is stopped, the iron nails are just nails and have no magnetic force.

13 Let's actually confirm this with an experiment. “Seeing is believing”.

14 Please pull your desks together into groups.

15 The leader of each group should come to the podium to get a polyethylene tube, enameled wire, nail, dry cell battery, switch, paper clips, and sandpaper.

16 Now, at first, each group will make the same thing.

17 Wrap the enameled wire around the polyethylene tube 20 times.

18 This is called a coil.

19 Then, shave both ends of the enameled wire with sandpaper, peel off the ends of the enamel, and connect them to the dry cell battery in the same way as you did during your lightbulb experiment.

20 Yes, now turn on the switch and bring the clip close to the enamel wire.

21 Does it stick? It sticks only a little.

22 Now, turn off the switch and put the nail in the coil.

23 Now, turn it on again and move the clip closer to the tip of the nail that is protruding from the coil.

24 Now please turn off the switch.

25 The clips have come apart, haven't they?

26 This is electromagnetism

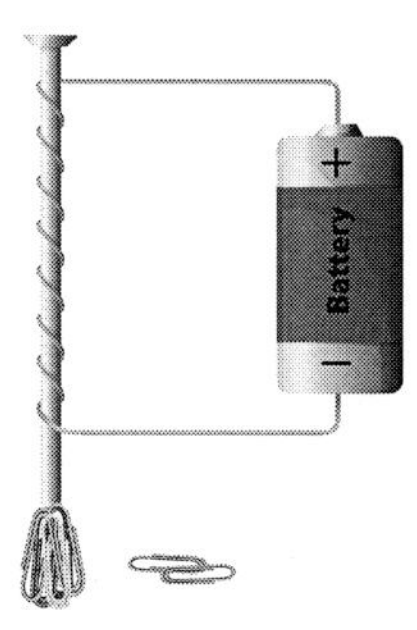

高学年

## 電磁石

先生

1 電流を流すと、コードが磁力を帯びます。

2 そのコードをまいたコイルの回りには磁力の世界ができます。

3 これを磁界と言います。

4 磁力の強さを決めるのは、コイルにまくコードの量と流す電流の量です。

だから何重にもまいたり、同じ巻き数なら乾電池を一個より２個にしたりした方が、

5 磁力が増します。

そのコードが太いものと細いものではどうだと思いますか。

6 細い方が磁力が強くなります。

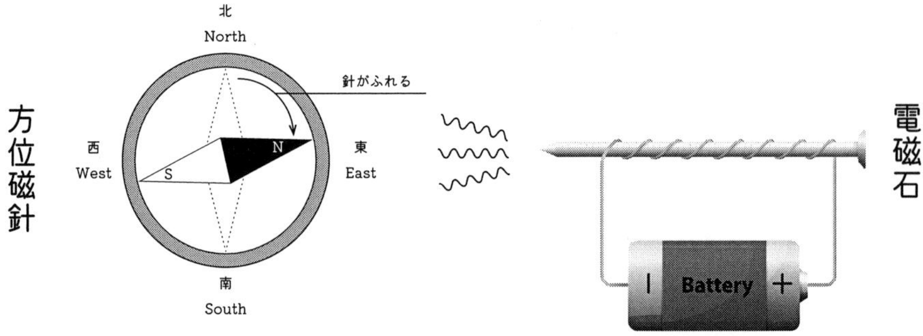

Grade 5 & 6

# Electromagnetism

Teacher

1 When an electric current is applied to the cord, it becomes magnetized.

2 The magnetic force generated by a simple cord wrapped in a coil can really power the world.

3 This is called a magnetic field.

4 The strength of the magnetic force generated depends on the amount of coiled cord and the amount of current that flows through it.

5 Therefore, it is better to use two batteries than one for the same number of coils, or to use multiple coils, to increase the magnetic force.

6 What do you think is the difference between using a thicker cord and a thinner cord? The thinner the wire , the stronger the magnetic force.

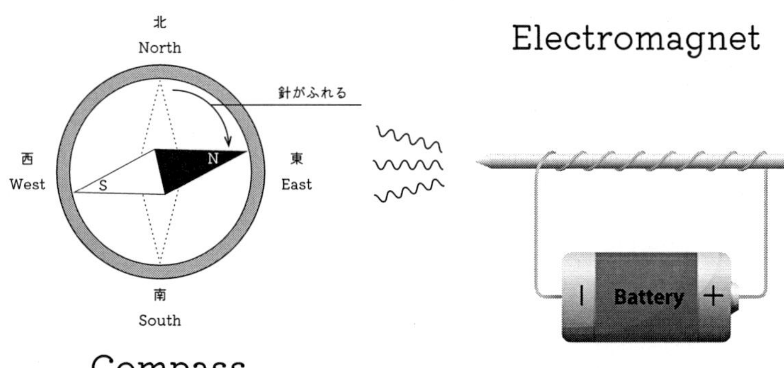


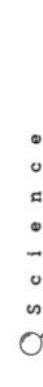

中学年

# 閉じ込めた空気と水

先生

1 ゴムです。
2 ゴムは伸ばすと、元に戻ろうとして勢いよく縮ますね。
3 その逆がこの空気の圧縮です。
ペットボトルの大きさを埋める体積分の空気を、ペットボトルよりはるかに小さい
4 のにギュッと押さえつけたら、元の体積に戻ろうと反発します。
筒の中で押し棒に押されて同じ状態が起きて、元の体積に戻ろうとして一番弱いところ
5 として筒の前にあった弾を飛ばしたわけです。

6 空気はこのように体積を圧縮することができます。

先生

1 水はどうでしょうか。
空気と水の体積の圧縮の差をこの注射器で実験してみましょう。
2 注射器のピストンを押してみてください。
3 はい、ピストンから手を離して下さい。
4 ほら、ピストンが押し戻されましたね。
5 では次に注射器の中を水で一杯にして、もう一度ピストンを押します。
6 水は体積を変化することが無いことがわかります。
7 これは、空気が気体という物質で、水が液体という物質だからです。
イスやテーブルは大変固くて、液体以上に体積を変化できません。イスやテーブルを
8 固体といいます。
同じ大きさに入っている気体は、圧縮して体積を縮めることができますが、液体は体積を
9 縮めることができません。
気体は体積を縮めることはできますが、もとの体制に戻ろうとする力が働くことが
10 わかりました。逆に言えば、気体は体積を大きくすることもできます。
11 液体は体積を変えることが出来ません。
12 しかし、液体が液体でなくなったらどうでしょう。
13 皆さん、氷を見たことがありますね。
14 熱い飲み物から湯気が出ているのを見たことがありますね。
15 氷が解けるとどうなりますか。
16 水ですね。熱い飲み物が冷えたら湯気はでませんね。
17 つまり、液体は氷という固体にも、空中に浮かぶほど軽い粒にもなることができるのです。
18 さらには、湯気を通りこして気体になることもできます。そうしたらどうなりますか。
液体だったときの体積は気体になるとすごく大きな体積になって、液体だった時に入って
19 いた入れ物には収まらなくなって、空気鉄砲と同じようにポーンと飛び出すことになります。

Grade 3 & 4

# Air and Water Compression

Teacher

1 This is rubber.
2 When rubber is stretched, it shrinks vigorously as it tries to get back to its original shape.
3 The opposite of this is what happens during the compression of air.
If a volume of air that fills the size of a plastic bottle is squeezed into something much smaller
4 than the bottle, it will rebound to return to its original volume.
The same situation occurs when a push stick is pushed inside the cylinder of the air gun,
the bullet in front of the cylinder is sent flying as it is the only way that the air pressure could be
5 released in its attempt to return to its original volume.
6 Air can thus be compressed in volume.

Teacher

1 However, what about water?
Let's experiment with this syringe to see the difference in compression between air and water
2 volumes. Please push the piston of the syringe.
3 Now, please take your hand off the piston.
4 See, the piston has been pushed back.
5 Now fill the syringe with water and push the piston again.
6 We can see that water does not change volume.
7 This is because air is a substance called gas and water is a substance called liquid.
Chairs and tables are called solids. Solids are very hard and it is even more difficult to change
8 their volume than liquids.
Gases of the same size can be compressed and shrink in volume, but we cannot reduce
9 the volume of a liquid.
In addition, though the volume of a gas can be reduced, there is a force that tries to return
10 them to their original state. Conversely, gases can also increase in volume.
11 A liquid cannot change its volume.
12 But what if a liquid ceases to be a liquid?
13 You have all seen ice.
14 You have seen steam coming out of a hot drink.
15 What happens when the ice melts?
16 Water. When a hot drink cools down, there is no steam, right?
17 In other words, a liquid can become either a solid, ice, or a particle so light that it floats in the air.
18 Furthermore, it can pass through steam and become gas. What happens then?
The volume of the liquid becomes so large that it can no longer be contained in the container
19 it was in when it was a liquid, and just like an air gun, it will pop out

高学年

## ものの燃え方と空気

先生

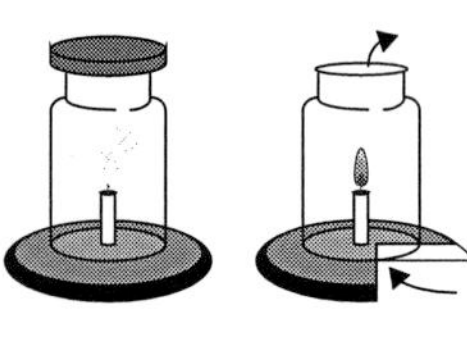

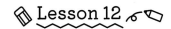

1 今日の実験にはガラス瓶に火のついたろうそくを入れて行います。
説明通りにやっていれば安全ですが、火を使うのは大変危険ですし、
2 もしかするとガラス瓶が破裂するかもしれません。
3 ふざけたり、よそ見をしたりしながらの実験は絶対にしないでください。
先ず、瓶の口にふたをしたり、ほとんど閉めてしまったりするとすぐに火が消えましたら、
4 瓶の中の空気に火が燃え続けられない変化があったことが分かります。

次に、底に隙間を作ると、ろうそくが燃え続けて、隙間に近づけた線香の煙が瓶の口に
向かって流れることから、空気に流れがあると燃え続けることと、瓶の中の空気は口から
5 上に抜けていくことが分かります。

先生

1 ものが燃えるには空気が必要です。というより、空気の中に含まれる酸素が必要です。
2 しかし、酸素があれば、なんでも燃えるわけではありません。
3 燃えるのは、炭素を含んだ物と、火のような高い熱が必要です。
4 燃えたから、酸素が使われて、二酸化炭素ができたんですよ。
5 光合成で空気中の二酸化炭素を吸収して、酸素を出しますと習いましたね。
7 その二酸化炭素の炭素とはこの燃える物質と酸素がくっついた気体という意味だったんです。
8 私たちの地球は空気に包まれていて、その空気の中に酸素があるから呼吸ができます。
9 魚が水の中で生きているのは、水の中の酸素を体内に取り入れているからです。
ろうそくの火がついたり、消えたりするのは空気の中の酸素と二酸化炭素が関係します
というと、空気は酸素と二酸化炭素から構成されているように思えますが、実は、空気の中
10 にある二酸化炭素は1%以下、酸素は21%としかありません。
11 大部分は窒素です。
12 窒素は物が燃えることにも、呼吸をすることにも関係ありません。
まず、なぜ空気中に酸素や二酸化炭素が少ないのかというと、酸素は炭素等他の物質と
13 くっつきやすいこと、二酸化炭素は酸素や窒素に比べると水に溶けやすいからです。

人間に限らず生き物には窒素が必要です。しかし、必要な窒素を作り出すことができません。
14 かといって、気体の窒素は体にとりいれることができません。
空気中の窒素を固形にできるのは、豆類にあるバクテリアだけです。
だから、私たちの体に必要な窒素は豆類を食べて補給したり、豆類を食べて体内に窒素を
15 取り入れた動物の肉を食べて取り入れたりしています。
16 ちなみに呼吸をして窒素を吸ってもそのまま吐き出して酸素だけを取りいれています

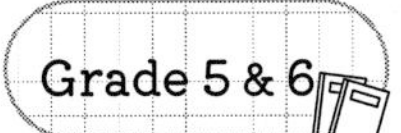

Grade 5 & 6

# How Things Burn and Air

**Teacher**

1 Today's experiment will involve placing a lit candle in a glass jar.
It is safe if you follow the instructions, but using fire is very dangerous and
2 may possibly cause the glass bottle to explode.
3 Never experiment while fooling around or looking away.
First, if the fire goes out as soon as you close or almost close the lid on the mouth of the bottle,
you know that there was a change in the air inside the bottle that prevented the fire from
4 continuing to burn.
Next, if we make a gap at the bottom, the candle will continue to burn and the smoke from
incense sticks placed close to the gap will flow toward the mouth of the bottle. This shows that
air flows and this flow will keep the candle and that the air in the bottle will escape up through
5 the mouth.

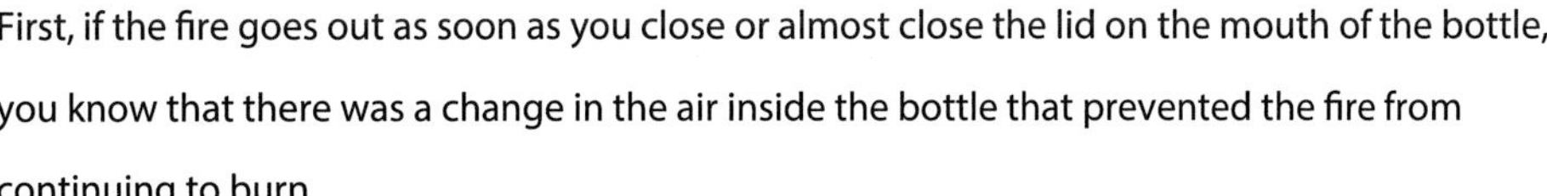

**Teacher**

1 Air is needed for things to burn. Rather, it needs the oxygen contained in the air.
2 However, oxygen is not enough to burn everything.
3 Burning requires carbon-containing materials and high heat, such as fire.
4 Oxygen was used and carbon dioxide was created because it burned.
5 You learned that photosynthesis absorbs carbon dioxide from the air and gives off oxygen.
7 When burning, the oxygen in the air combines with the carbon in what is being burnt.
8 Our earth is surrounded by air, and the oxygen in that air allows us to breathe.
9 Fish live in water because they can use the oxygen from the water
When we say that the lighting and extinguishing of a candle is related to the oxygen and
carbon dioxide in the air, it seems that air is composed of oxygen and carbon dioxide, right?
10 But in fact, there is less than 1% carbon dioxide and only 21% oxygen in the air.
11 The vast majority of air is made up of nitrogen.
12 Nitrogen has nothing to do with burning things or breathing.
First, the reason why there is so little oxygen and carbon dioxide in the air is because oxygen
easily attaches itself to other substances such as carbon, and carbon dioxide is more soluble
13 in water than oxygen and nitrogen.
Nitrogen is necessary for all living things, not just humans. However, we cannot produce
14 the nitrogen we need, nor can we absorb it from the atmosphere.
Only bacteria found in legumes can solidify nitrogen from the air.
Therefore, our bodies are supplied with the nitrogen it needs by eating legumes, or by eating
15 meat from animals that have nitrogen into their bodies.
16 Interestingly, when we breathe in nitrogen, we breathe it out and take in only oxygen.

高学年

## ものの燃え方と空気

先生

1 ろうそくを燃やすと、瓶の中の中野酸素が使われて、二酸化炭素が増えます。
だから、空気の入れ替えができないと、燃え続けるために必要な酸素が不足するので火が
2 消える。
3 ここまでは、実験と説明で理解できました。
4 でも、実際に酸素が減った？二酸化炭素はどれくらい増えた？を調べたいですよね。

5 これを調べるには、ろうそくを燃やす前の瓶とろうそくを燃やした後の瓶にそれぞれ
6 石灰水を入れて、ふると分かります。
石灰水は、水酸化カルシウムを水にとかした水溶液です。
7 石灰水は、アルカリ性の溶液で、二酸化炭素のように、水にとけると、酸性の溶液になる
気体をよく溶かします。
二酸化炭素が石灰水にとけると、中で化学変化が起きて、二酸化炭素と石灰水の一部が
8 結びつき、水にとけない、白い炭酸カルシウム という物に変わります。
9 そのため、溶液中に白い粉ができてきて、白くにごります。

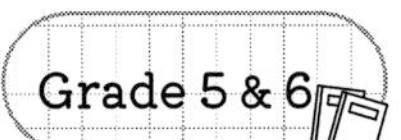

Grade 5 & 6

## How Things Burn and Air 2

Teacher

1 When a candle burns, the oxygen in the bottle is used and carbon dioxide increases.
So, if the air cannot be replaced, the fire will go out because there is not enough oxygen to
2 keep it burning.
3 So far, the experiments and explanations have helped us understand that.
But did oxygen actually decrease? How much did carbon dioxide increase?
4 We want to find out, don't we?
5 To find this out, fill a jar before and after burning a candle with lime water and shake each jar.
6 Lime water is an aqueous solution of calcium hydroxide dissolved in water.
Limewater is an alkaline solution and when it comes into contact with carbon dioxide,
7 it will absorb the gas and become acidic.
When carbon dioxide is dissolved in limewater, a chemical change occurs within the solution,
and a portion of the carbon dioxide and limewater combine to form white calcium carbonate,
8 which is not soluble in water.
9 As a result, a white powder is formed in the solution and it turns the solution white and cloudy.

高学年

## ものの燃え方と空気

先生

1 では、空気を構成する酸素を集める実験をします。

空気の中から酸素だけを取りだすことは難しいので、オキシドールという液を分解して
2 酸素を発生させます。

3 発生させた酸素を集めるには酸素の特性を生かします。

酸素という気体は、物質を燃やす働きがあるという特性以外に水に溶けにくい、無色、
4 無臭という特性をもち ます。

5 水溶けにくいという気体の集め方は水上置換です。

6 次にオキシドールは知っていますか。身近な薬品の一つです。

7 けがをしたときに最初に脱脂綿に濡らしたりして傷口に掛けて消毒をする液です。

オキシドール
酸素
水
二酸化マンガン

8 オキシドールは、過酸化水素といいます。

9 漢字で書くとこうなります。

10 つまり、酸素が過、多いという意味です。

酸素はすぐにいろんな物質にくっついてしまうので、空気中の酸素の割合が少ないと
11 説明しましたね。

12 傷口に塗ると傷口を酸化して殺菌します。

13 オキシドールから酸素を取り出すには、二酸化マンガンを触媒として使います。

触媒とは、化学変化のときに自分自身が変化せずに、他の物質の反応の速さを変化させる
14 物質のことです。

うすい塩酸
二酸化炭素
水
石灰石

15 次に、二酸化炭素を集めてみます。

二酸化炭素は空気より重い、無色無臭、
そして石灰水を白く濁る、水に溶けにくいという
16 特色があります。

17 二酸化炭素は、石灰石に、うすい塩酸をくわえると作ることが出来ます。

18 薄い塩酸が、触媒です。

酸素の時は水上置換法で集めましたが、二酸化炭素は空気より重いので、
19 下方置換法も使えますし、水に溶けにくいので水上置換法も可能です。

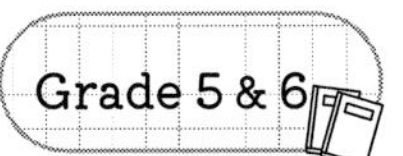

Grade 5 & 6

# How Things Burn and Air 2

Teacher

1 Now, we will conduct an experiment to collect oxygen, which is a component of air.
Since it is difficult to extract only oxygen from the air, we need to use a liquid called oxindole
2 to generate it.
3 To collect the oxygen generated, we take advantage of the properties of oxygen.
In addition to its ability to burn substances, oxygen is a gas that is insoluble in water, colorless,
4 and odorless.
The way to collect gases that are difficult to dissolve in water is by a method known as water
5 displacement.

6 Next, do you know what oxydol is? It is one of the most familiar chemicals.
When an injury occurs, this solution is first used to wet a cotton ball and applied to the wound
7 to disinfect it.

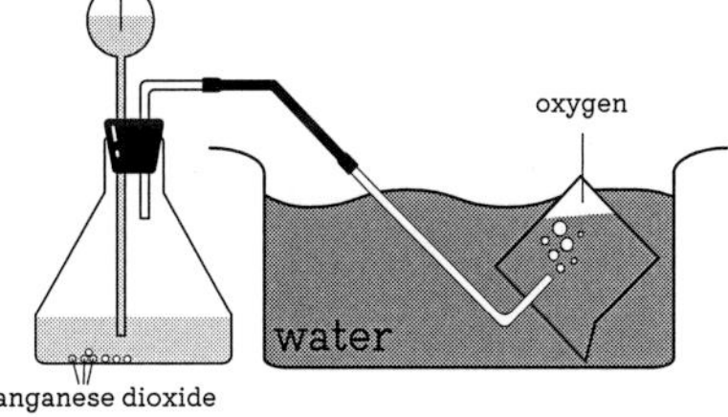


8 Oxydol is also called hydrogen peroxide.
9 Written in Chinese characters, it looks like this.
The literal meaning is that there is too much or too
10 little oxygen.
As I explained before the percentage of oxygen in the air is low because oxygen quickly
11 attaches itself to various substances.
12 When applied to a wound, it oxidizes and sterilizes the wound.
13 To extract oxygen from oxindole, manganese dioxide is used as a catalyst.
A catalyst is a substance that changes the rate of reaction of another substance during
14 a chemical change without changing itself.

light hydrochloric acid
carbon dioxide
water
limestone

15 Next, we are going to collect carbon dioxide.
Carbon dioxide is heavier than air, colorless,
odorless, and makes limewater cloudy,
16 it is characterized by its insolubility in water.
17 Carbon dioxide can be made by adding light hydrochloric acid to limestone.
18 Thin hydrochloric acid is the catalyst.
When we collected oxygen, we used the water displacement method, but carbon dioxide is
19 heavier than air, so we can use the downward displacement method

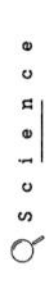

中学年

## 物の溶け方/ 水溶液

先生

1 水に物質を溶かしているものを水溶液といいます。
2 海の水がしょっぱいのは、海の水の中に塩がとけているからです。
100ｇの水の体積は 100 ㎤です。水 100g に塩 5g を溶かす、水 100g に砂糖 10ｇを
3 溶かしても、体積は 105 ㎤にも 110 ㎤になりません。なぜでしょう。
4 重さが 5g 増えても体積が 5 ㎤増えないのは、その粒の大きさにあります。

5 塩や砂糖の粒は水の粒より小さいんです。
6 ピンポン玉の入っている箱に黒ゴマを混ぜても箱から溢れませんね。
それは粒の小さな黒ゴマがピンポン玉の隙間にはいったから、黒ゴマ分重くなりますが、
7 体積は増えていません。
8 これが、水に物質が溶けるということです。
9 ただ、どれだけでも溶けるわけではありません。限界があります。
10 その限界を飽和と、どれくらいの量が溶けるのかを溶解度と言います。
11 飽和になるまでは水溶液は透明です。透き通っています。
透き通っているといっても、無色ではなく、例えばコーヒーの粉を溶かすと、
12 茶色に透き通ります。

先生

1 そこまではわかりましたか。
水溶液にどれくらいの物質が溶けているかの割合を濃度といいます。
2 飽和の限界に達するまではどこの濃度も同じです。
3 飽和を超えるとそれ以上は解けませんから、粒のまま残って底にたまります。

4 温度を上げると、溶ける量は増えます。
5 どれだけ増えるかは溶かす物質によります。
6 塩は温度が上がってもあまり溶けません。
7 小学校の実験では、ホウ酸やミョウバンを使います。
8 これらは温度によって溶ける量が大きく変化します。
調べるのは、ビーカーやメスシリンダーを使います。ビーカーやメスシリンダーには
目盛が ml でついていますので、50ml や 100ml 等区切りのいい量の水を入れ、
9 温度を変化させながら、物質ごとに溶ける量を調べます。

その結果、温度ごとに溶ける量の変化を記したグラフを溶解度曲線といいます。
高い温度の時に溶けていた量が低い温度になると溶けなくなると、結晶という粒
10 になります。

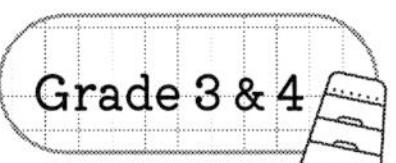



Grade 3 & 4

## Dissolving Things / Aqueous Solutions 1

Teacher

1 We call a liquid with substance dissolved in it a solution.
2 Ocean water is salty because salt is dissolved in ocean water.
The volume of 100 g of water is 100 $cm^3$. If you add 5g of salt or 10g of sugar, the volume will
3 not change to 105 $cm^3$ nor 110 $cm^3$. You must be wondering why.
The reason an increase of 5 g in weight does not increase the volume by 5 $cm^3$ is due to
4 the size of the grains.
5 Grains of salt and sugar are smaller than grains of water.
6 If you mix black sesame seeds into a box of ping pong balls, the box will not overflow.
This is because the small black sesame seeds fit into the space between the ping pong balls,
7 making them heavier, but not increasing their volume.
8 This is how a substance dissolves in water.
9 However, it is not possible to dissolve any amount. There is a limit.
10 That limit is called saturation, and how much can be dissolved is called solubility.
11 The aqueous solution is clear until it reaches saturation. It is transparent.
Transparent does not mean colorless; for example, if you dissolve coffee powder,
12 it will turn brown and transparent.

Teacher

1 Is it clear so far?
The ratio of how much of a substance is dissolved in an aqueous solution is called
2 the concentration. Every concentration is the same until the limit of saturation is reached.
Once saturation is exceeded, it will not dissolve any further, so it will remain as grains and
3 accumulate at the bottom.
4 As the temperature is increased, the amount of a substance that can be dissolved increases.
5 How much it increases depends on the substance to be dissolved.
6 Salt does not dissolve well when the temperature is raised.
7 In elementary school experiments, we use boric acid and alum.
8 The amount of these substances that dissolve varies greatly depending on the temperature.
To check this, we will us beakers and measuring cylinders. Beakers and measuring cylinders
have a scale in milliliters, so we can fill them with water in quantities of 50 ml, 100 ml,
or whatever volume we want. We can then check the amount of each substance that dissolves
9 while changing the temperature.
The resulting graph showing the change in solubility at different temperatures is called
a solubility curve. When we lower the temperature of the solution, the solubility will decrease
10 and the substance will re-solidify into a grain called a crystal.

高学年

## 物の溶け方/水溶液

先生

1 酸っぱい味のする物質の性質を酸性といいます。
一方で、草木を燃やしたあとにできる灰を水に溶かした灰汁（あく）のように、
2 苦い味のする物質の性質をアルカリ性といいます。
3 酸性の呼び名は酸っぱいを意味するacid 語源はラテン語のacere（すっぱい）という語
に由来しています。
4 また、アルカリ性の語源はアラビア語で木灰を意味するアルカリから来ています。

5 酸性・アルカリ性には、弱いとか強いとかいう度合い(強さ)があります。
この酸・アルカリの度合い（強さ）を表すのに、pH（ピーエッチ）と呼ばれる数値を
6 使います。
昔は「ペーハー」という読み方が一般的でした。
7 「ペーハー」という読み方はドイツ語での読み方です。
6 ピーエイチという読み方は、英語での読み方です。
pH は酸性からアルカリ性の間に0 ～ 14 の目盛りをつけて、酸・アルカリの度合いを
その目盛りの数字で表すもので、pH7 を中性とし、それ未満を酸性、それより大きければ
9 アルカリ性としています。
pH7 よりも値が小さければ小さいほど酸性の性質が強く、値が大きければ大きいほど
10 アルカリ性の性質が強いことになります。

11 酸性、アルカリ性を調べるのには、リトマス紙を使います。
リトマス紙は、リトマスゴケをアンモニアと水酸化ナトリウム水溶液を加えて
12 にこんだものを塗りつけたものです。
リトマス紙が、酸やアルカリに反応して色が変わるのは、リトマス紙の主な成分が
アゾリトミンという酸性の赤色の色素で、アルカリとくっついて青色の塩を作るため、
13 アルカリ性で青色になり、酸性で赤色になるという性質によるものです。
酸性は、なめるとすっぱい味（酸味）があり、マグネシウムやアルミニウム、
14 亜鉛など金属と反応して水素を発生させます。
15 アルカリは、なめるとしぶみがあり、指先につけると、ぬるぬるします。

Grade 5 & 6

## Dissolving Things / Aqueous Solutions 2

Teacher

1 The property of this sour-tasting substance is called acidity.

On the other hand, the properties of substances with a bitter taste, such as lye, which is made
2 by dissolving the ash produced after burning plants and trees in water, are called alkalinity.

3 The word acidity comes from the Latin word acer, meaning sour.

4 The word alkalinity comes from the Arabic word alkali, meaning wood ash.

5 Acidity and alkalinity have a degree of weakness or strength.

6 A numerical value called pH is used to express the degree (strength) of acidity or alkalinity.

7 In the past, "Peher", which is the German reading, was the common pronunciation.

8 The current commonly used pronunciation "P.H." is the English reading.

pH is on a scale from 0 to 14 from acidic to alkaline, and the degree of acidity or alkalinity is
9 indicated by the number on the scale.

A pH of 7 is considered neutral, less than pH7 is acidic, and greater than pH7 is alkaline.
10 The smaller the value the more acidic it is, while a larger value indicates a more alkaline property.

11 Litmus paper is used to test for acidity and alkalinity.

Litmus paper is made by coating Roccella, a fungus, with ammonia and sodium hydroxide
12 solution.

Litmus paper changes color in response to acids and alkalis because the main ingredient of
litmus paper is azolitmin, an acidic red pigment that reacts with alkalis to form blue salts,
13 making it blue in alkaline conditions and red in acidic conditions.

Acidic substances have a sour taste when licked, and reacts with metals such as magnesium,
14 aluminum, and zinc to produce hydrogen.

15 Alkali has a tingling sensation when licked, and is slimy when applied to the fingertips.

高学年

## 物の溶け方/水溶液

先生

1 リストマス紙で調べてみましょう。
赤と青のリトマス紙を白い紙の上に並べて、液をガラス棒の先に付けて、
2 まず青色リトマス紙につけます。
3 次にガラス棒をよく洗って、液を同じく先について、赤色リトマス紙につけます。

4 ところで、酸性とアルカリ性を学習するのはなぜだと思いますか。
5 例えば、土壌が酸性だと農作物の発育がよくありません。
私たちの体も酸性が高くなると、体内のカルシウムを溶かしてしまったり、
6 免疫力が落ちたりして、癌になりやすいなどの問題がおきます。
ですから、どの食品が酸性なのかアルカリ性なのかを学習して、
7 アルカリ性の食べ物を積極的にとるようにしてください。

8 リトマス紙のような試薬をPH指示薬と言います。
9 リトマス紙以外に、BTB溶液、フェノールフタレイン溶液などがあります。
10 BTB液は酸性で黄色、中性が緑、アルカリ性は青に変化します。
11 フェノールフタレイン液では、アルカリ性に反応して赤くなります。
12 植物の中にも指示薬になるものがあります。
ムラサキキャベツの葉にふくまれるアントシアニンは、紫色ですが、酸性では赤、
13 アルカリ性では緑になります。

| Battery acid | Stomach acid | Vinegar | Orange juice | Tomato | Black coffee | Urine | water | Sea water | Baking soda | Indigestion tablet | Ammonia solution | Soapy water | Bleach | Drain cleaner |
|---|---|---|---|---|---|---|---|---|---|---|---|---|---|---|
| 0 | 1 | 2 | 3 | 4 | 5 | 6 | 7 | 8 | 9 | 10 | 11 | 12 | 13 | 14 |

Acid　Neutral　Alkali

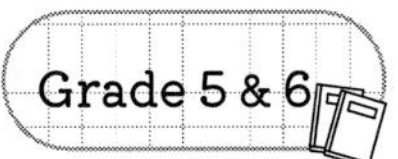


## Dissolving Things / Aqueous Solutions 3

**Teacher**

1 Let's exam them using litmus paper.
Place the red and blue litmus paper on a white sheet of paper and put the sample liquid on
2 the tip of a glass rod, and apply it first to the blue litmus paper.
Next, wash the glass rod well, put the sample liquid on the tip of the rod again,
3 and apply it to the red litmus paper.

4 By the way, why do you think we learn acidity and alkalinity?
5 For example, if the soil is acidic, crops do not grow well.
When our bodies are highly acidic, calcium in our bodies dissolve, our immunity is weakened,
6 and we are more prone to cancer and other problems.
Therefore, be sure to learn which foods are acidic or alkaline, and be sure to actively eat
7 alkaline foods.

8 A reagent that acts like litmus paper is called a PH indicator.
9 In addition to litmus paper, BTB solution and phenolphthalein solution are also available.
10 BTB solution turns yellow for acidic, green for neutral, and blue for alkaline.
11 In phenolphthalein solution, it reacts to alkalinity and turns red.
12 Some plants can also be used as indicators.
Anthocyanins in the leaves of the purple cabbage are purple, but turns red in acidic conditions
13 and green in alkaline conditions.

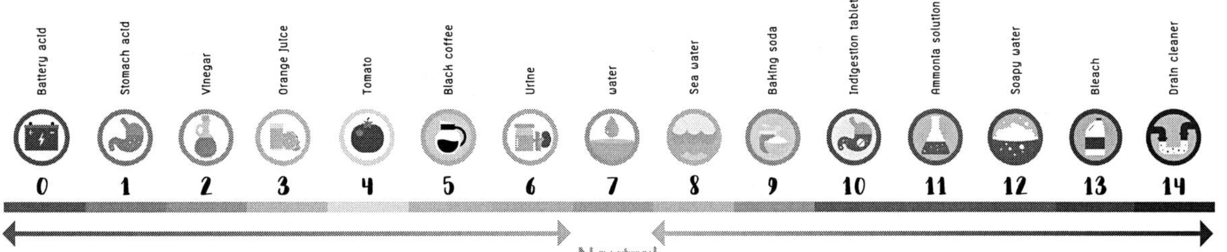

高学年

# 振り子

先生

1 皆さんは、ガリレオ・ガリレイという学者の名前を聞いたことがありますか。
2 テレビ番組ではなくてですよ。
3 17世紀、1600年代に活躍したイタリアの物理学者で天文学者です。
4 様々な理論を発見したし、その理論に基づくものを作り出しています。
ガリレオによって、発見された理論は大変貴重なものが多く、それまでの常識を
5 根底からひっくり返すものがありました。
例えば、それまで地球が宇宙の中心で、宇宙は地球の周りをまわっているという天動説を
6 間違いで、地球が太陽の周りをまわっているという地動説もそうです。

7 私たちは、理科で、ガリレオが発見したこれらの貴重な理論を学習していきます。
8 その一つが、今から学習する振り子です。
9 振り子ってみたことがありますか。
テレビの催眠術師が、眠くなーると言ってひもから垂らしたおもりを揺らしている
10 あれです。
ガリレオが発見した振り子についての理論というのは、振り子が一往復する時間は、
11 垂らしているおもりの重さでなく、ひもの長さによるというものです。
また、同じ長さなら、大きく振れている時も小さく振れている時も往復の時間は同じと
12 いうものです。
ただ大きく振れるといっても、例えば90°とか70°の角度からの振るとかかる時間が
13 変わります。
この振れる往復の時間は、重さでなく長さに関係すること、同じ長さなら、重さが違っても、
14 また振れ幅が違っても往復の時間が同じということを振り子の等時性と言います。

15 この原理を使ったものが、振り子時計です。
16 昔はどの家庭にもありましたから、振り子の説明をするときはまずこの振り子時計の話
から始められたのですが、今はどこの家にもほとんどありませんから、
本の中での紹介だけになってしまいます。
17 振り子は、地球ではいつまでも振れることはありません。
18 それは空気という抵抗があるからです。
ですから、空気がない宇宙でしたら、
19 いつまでも振れています。

Galileo Galilei

Grade 5 & 6

# Pendulums

Teacher

1 Have you ever heard of the scholar Galileo Galilei?
2 I don't mean the TV show.
3 He was an Italian physicist and astronomer active in the 17th century, 1600s.
4 He has discovered a variety of theories and he is creating things based on those theories.
Many of the theories discovered by Galileo were extremely valuable and turned conventional
5 wisdom on its head.
For example, the celestial motion theory that the earth was the center of the universe and
the universe revolved around the earth was wrong, and the geocentric theory that the earth
6 revolved around the sun was right. This also applies.
7 We will be studying these valuable theories discovered by Galileo in science.
8 One of them is the pendulum, which we are about to study.
9 Have you ever seen a pendulum?
You know, the one where the hypnotist on TV swings a weight hanging from a string to make
10 you fall asleep?
Galileo's theory of the pendulum is that the time it takes for the pendulum to make one round
11 trip depends on the length of the string, not on the weight of the weight hanging from it.
Also, if the length of the swing is the same, the round trip time is the same whether the swing
12 is large or small.
Even if it is just a large swing, for example, the time it takes to descend from a 90°angle is
13 different from the time it takes to descend from a 70°angle.
The reciprocating time of the swing is related to the length of the pendulum, not its weight,
and if the length is the same, the reciprocating time is the same even if the weight is different
14 or the amplitude of the swing is different.
15 This is called isochronism.
16 The pendulum clock is the one that uses this principle.
In the past, every home had a pendulum clock, so when explaining about pendulums,
one could start with this pendulum clock, but nowadays there are almost none in every home,
17 so the only introductions are in books.
18 A pendulum cannot swing forever on Earth.
This is because of the resistance of air.
Therefore, in space, where there is no air,
19 the pendulum will swing forever.

Galileo Galilei

高学年

# つりあいとてこ

先生

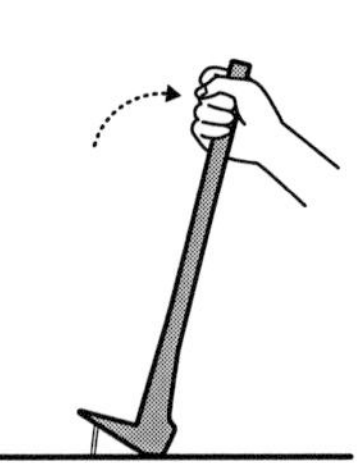

1 今日から新しい単元の学習をします。

2 てこは、小さな力で大きなものを動かす原理です。

3 この原理は、すでに 2000 年以上前にアルキメデスという学者によって発見されました。

4 てこは、棒を支える支点、棒に力を加える力点、棒が力を働かせる作用点で成り立っています。

道具箱を開いてください。

5 中からはさみを出してください。

6 はさみも、てこをつかっています。

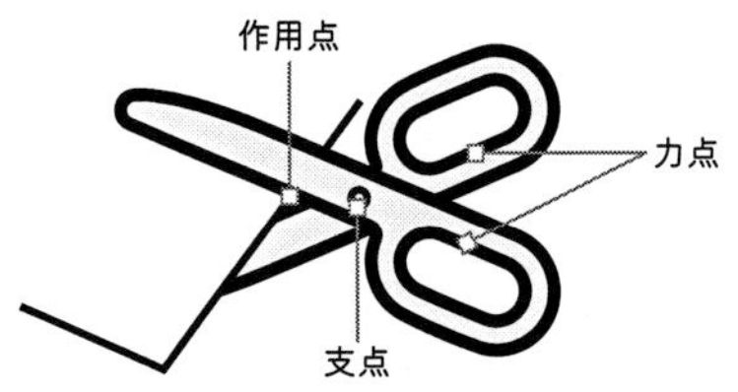


7 指を入れるところが力点、中心軸の「かしめ」の部分が支点、

8 刃の部分を作用点となっています。

9 この３つの点の位置によって、てこは３つのタイプがあります。

10 まずは、はさみのような作用点―支点―力点の順にならんでいるものです。

11 つぎに、支点―作用点―力点の順です。栓抜きです。

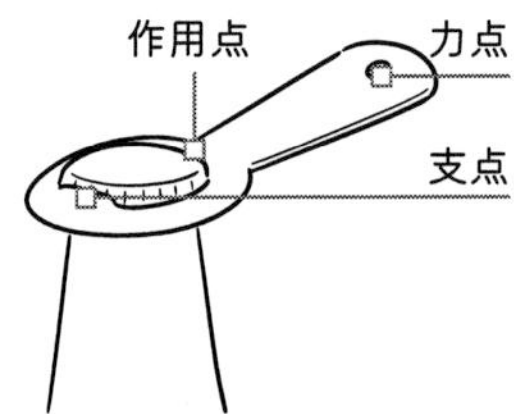


12 それから、支点―力点―作用点の順です。ピンセットです。

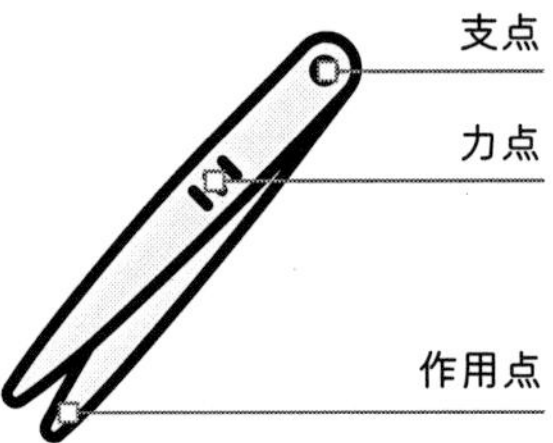


13 てこの場合、支点と力点が近くなるほど、手ごたえが大きくなります。

14 また作用点が支点に近くなるほど、手ごたえが小さくなります。

Grade 5 & 6

# Balance and Leverage

Teacher

1 Today we will start a new unit

Leverage is the principle of moving large objects with

2 a small amount of force.

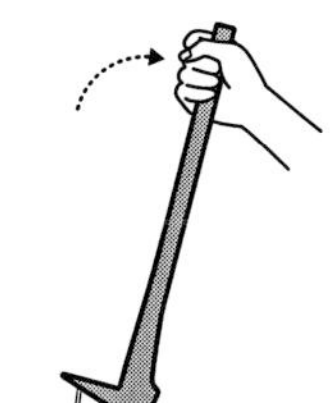

3 This principle was discovered by a scholar named Archimedes more than 2000 years ago.

A lever consists of a fulcrum that supports the bar, a point of force that applies a force to the bar,

4 and an action point where the bar exerts a force.

Please open the toolbox and

5 take out the scissors from inside.

6 Scissors also use the principle of leverage.

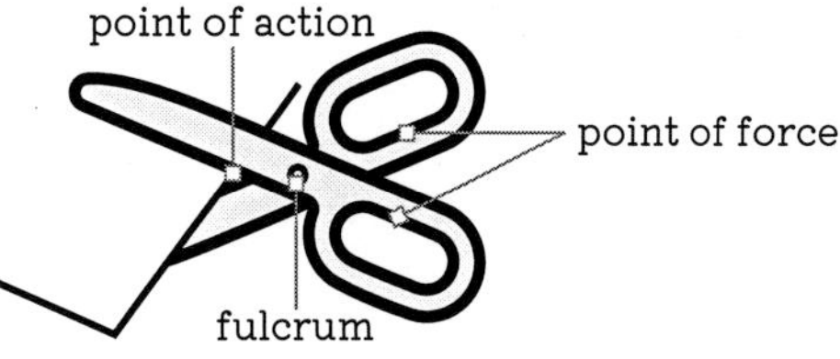


7 The point where the fingers are inserted is the point of force, and the central axis.

8 Where the two blades intersect is the fulcrum and the blade part is the point of action.

9 Depending on the position of these three points, there are three types of leverage.

10 The first is a scissors-like arrangement of action point, fulcrum, and force point, in that order.

11 Next is the fulcrum - point of action - point of force like bottle openers.

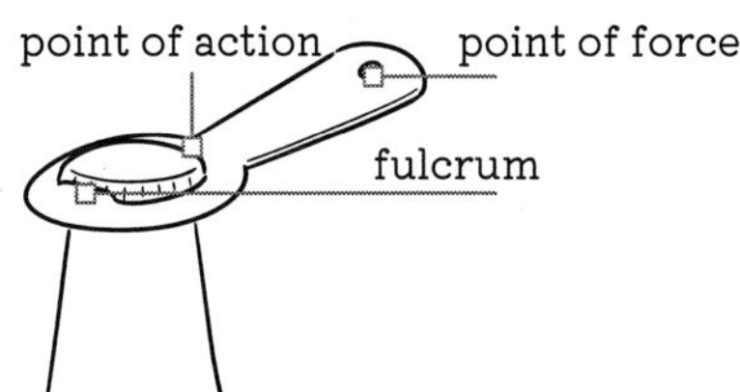


12 Then, fulcrum - force point - point of action, in that orderl like tweezers.

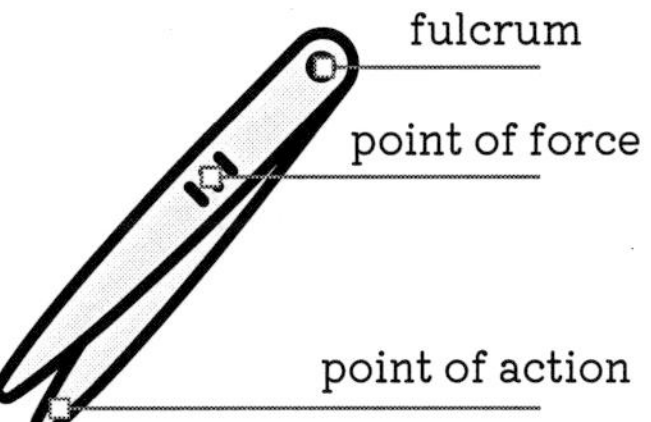


13 In the case of a lever, the closer the fulcrum and force point are, the greater the leverage.

14 Also, the closer the point of action is to the fulcrum, the less effort or power is required

高学年

# つりあいとてこ

先生

1 支点が中にあるてこは、支点を中心にして右側に傾ける働きと左側に傾ける働きがあります。

2 同じ力で傾けたら釣り合っています。

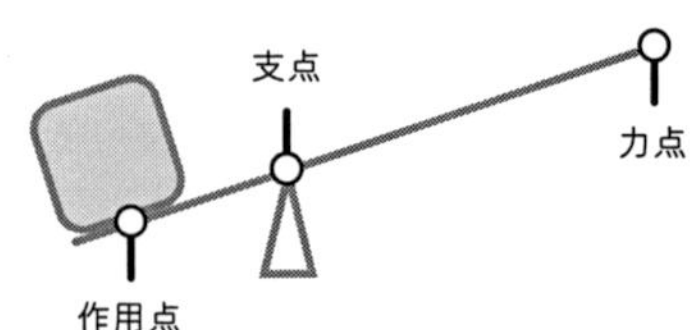


3 その働きは、支点からの距離と重さが左右同じであれば釣り合います。

つまり、重い石を動かす場合、作用点である石の支点からの距離×重さ＝力点から支点までの距離と力ですから、石から支点までの距離が短く、力点から支点までの距離が

4 長ければ、その分少ない力で重い石を動かせることにありますね。

5 (作用点)石の重さ　10 kg　支点までの距離 1m とします。

6 (力点)　支点までの距離　4m とします。

7 10 kg×1m＝□kg×4m で釣り合いが取れますから、□は 2.5 kgとなります。

8 このてこの考え方で釣り合いの問題を考えてみましょう。

9 図のてこはつり合っています。

10 (問題)おもりＡは何g ですか。棒の重さは考えないものとします。

11 おもりの重さ×支点までの距離 ＝ おもりの重さ×支点までの距離

12 A × 20 ＝ 50 × 60

13 A＝3000 ÷ 20＝150 でA は 150g と分かります。

14 図２のてこはつりあっています。

15 おもりA は何g ですか。

16 ただし、棒の重さは考えないものとします。

おもり× 支点までの距離＝おもり× 支点までの距離より、

17 30×A=10×60　　A=600÷30=20g　です。

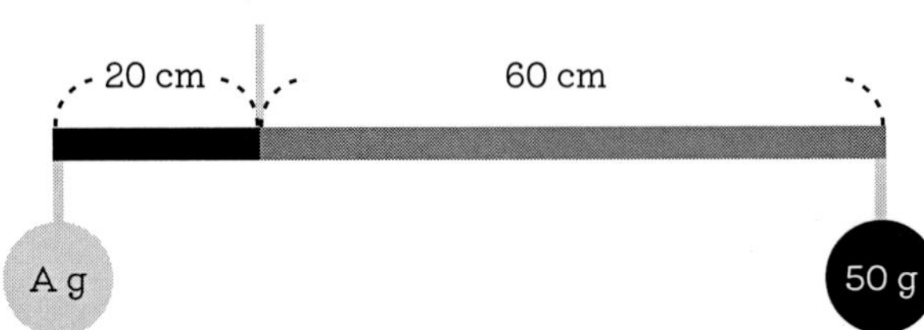

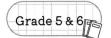

Grade 5 & 6

# Balance and Leverage

Teacher

1 A lever with a fulcrum inside has the ability to tilt to the right and to the left around the fulcrum.

2 If they tilt with the same force, they are balanced.

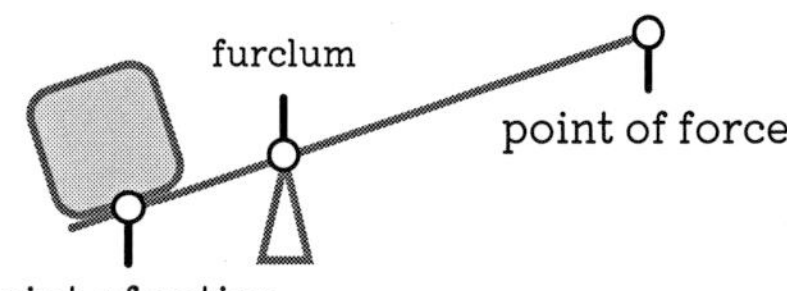


3 Its action is balanced if the distance from the fulcrum and the weight are the same on both sides.
In other words, when moving a heavy stone, the distance from the fulcrum of the stone or
4 the point of action x weight = distance from the force point to the fulcrum and force.

5 (Action point) Let's assume the weight of the stone is 10 kg and the distance to fulcrum is 1 m.

6 (force point) Assume that the distance to the fulcrum is 4m.

7 Since 10 kg x 1 m = □ kg x 4 m is balanced, □ is 2.5 kg.

8 Now let's consider the balancing problem that is connected to this leverage concept

9 In this diagram, the lever is balanced.
The question is: What is the weight of the counterweight A? Let's assume that we don't need
10 to consider the weight of the bar.

11 The formula is: Weight of weight x distance to fulcrum = Weight of weight x distance to fulcrum

12 $A \times 20 = 50 \times 60$

13 $A = 3000 \div 20 = 150$, which tells us that A is 150 g.

14 In this diagram 2, they are balanced as you can see.

15 In this case, what is the weight of A?

16 However, please remember that the weight of the bar should not be considered.
Given that weight x distance to fulcrum = weight x distance to fulcrum,
17 30 x A = 10 x 60    A = 600 / 30 = 20g

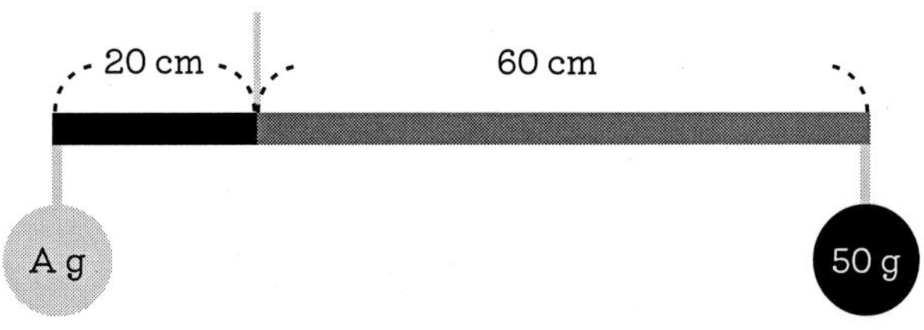

# 学習指導案

# 小学校第○学年○○科学習指導案

期　日：　令和○○年○月○日
時　間：　第○校時
対　象：　第○学年○組○○名
学校名：　○○立○○小学校
授業者：　○○　○○　印

1　単元（題材）名

「　　　　　　　　　　　　　　　　　　　　」

2　単元（題材）の目標

(1)

(2)

(3)

3　単元（題材）の評価規準

| 知識・技能 | 思考・判断・表現 | 主体的に学習に取り組む態度 |
|---|---|---|
| | | |

4　指導観

(1) 単元（題材）観

(2) 教材観

(3) 生徒観

5　年間指導計画における位置付け

| 学年 | 第○学年 | 第○学年 | 第○学年 |
|---|---|---|---|
| 単元（題材）名 | | | |
| 主な内容 | | | |

# Elementary School Grade XX Study Guidance Plan

Date: XX, 20XX
Time: XXth school period
Target: Class XX, Grade XX, XX students
Name of school: XX Elementary School
Classroom teacher: XXXX Seal

## 1 Unit (subject) name

「　　　　　　　　　　　」

## 2 Unit (subject matter) objective

(1)

(2)

(3)

## 3 Unit (subject) evaluation criteria

| Knowledge and Skills | Thinking, Judgment, Expression | Proactive attitude toward learning |
|---|---|---|
| | | |

## 4 One's philosophy of teaching

(1)Unit (subject) view

(2)View of teaching materials

(3)one's View (opinion) of students

## 5 Positioning in the annual teaching plan

| Grade | Grade | Grade | Grade |
|---|---|---|---|
| Unit (subject) name | | | |
| Main contents | | | |

## 6　単元（題材）の指導計画と評価計画（全○時間扱い）

| 時 | ★目標　○学習内容　・学習活動 | ■評価規準（評価方法） |
|---|---|---|
| 第1時 | ★ | |
| | ○<br>・<br>○<br>・ | ■ |
| 第2時 | ★ | |
| | ○<br>・<br>○<br>・ | ■ |

## 7　指導に当たって

(1)

(2)

(3)

## 8　本時（全○時間中の○時間目）

### (1) 本時の目標

### (2) 本時の展開

| 時間 | ○学習内容　・学習活動 | ・指導上の留意点 | ■評価規準（評価方法） |
|---|---|---|---|
| 導入<br>（　　分） | ○<br>・ | ・<br>・ | |
| 展開<br>（　　分） | ○<br>・<br>○<br>・ | | ■ |
| まとめ<br>（　　分） | ○<br>・<br>・ | ・<br>・ | |

### (3) 板書計画

| |
|---|
| |

## 6 Instructional and evaluation plans for the unit (subject matter) (treated for all X hours)

| Time | ★Objectives ○Learning content ・Learning activities | ■Evaluation Criteria (Evaluation Methods) |
|---|---|---|
| 1st | ★ | |
| | ○<br>・<br>○<br>・ | ■ |
| 2nd | ★ | |
| | ○<br>・<br>○<br>・ | ■ |

## 7 At the time of instruction

(1)

(2)

(3)

## 8 This hour (hour ____ of ____ hour)

(1)Goals for the period

(2)Development of this time

| Time | ○Learning content ・Learning activities | ・Guidance Notes | ■Evaluation Criteria (Evaluation Methods) |
|---|---|---|---|
| introduction ( min) | ○<br>・ | ・<br>・ | |
| development ( min) | ○<br>・<br>○<br>・ | | ■ |
| summary ( min) | ○<br>・<br>・ | ・<br>・ | |

(3)Syllabus plan

| |
|---|
| |

# 学習指導案　基本的　チェックリスト

＜目標に関すること＞

- 「2　単元の目標」「3　関連する学習指導要領における領域別目標」「7　単元の指導計画と評価計画」「9　本時」に書いた内容は一貫しているか。
（学習指導要領で定められた○○について、「この単元では○○に焦点化して指導する。そのためにこのように単元を計画し、本時では○○を行う。」というつくりになっているか。）

- 単元の目標、本時の目標は英語で表現したり伝え合ったりできるようになる内容を「～できる」の形で設定しているか。
（文法項目ではなく、その文法を使って英語で表現できるようになることを目標にしているか。）

＜評価に関すること＞

- 目標と評価の観点が合っているか。

- 単元の最後に、その単元で生徒が身に付けた内容（英語で「～できる」）を評価する計画になっているか。

- １単位時間に評価する項目が多すぎないか。
（現実的に時間内に見られる評価にしぼり、「後日ペーパーテストで」「ワークシート」など様々な手段での評価を考慮していくとよい。）

＜授業の進め方に関すること＞

- 生徒と目標（ゴール）を共有しているか。

- 対話的な言語活動を取り入れているか。

- 既習事項を踏まえた指導になっているか。

- 生徒の発話を予想して活動を考えているか。

- 生徒の反応や理解度を考えながら、教師の英語での生徒とのやり取りを考えているか。

- 目的に対応した振り返りを行っているか。

# Study Guidance Plan Basic Checklist

< Things related to goals >

- Are the contents written in "(2) Goals of the unit", "(3) Goals by area in the related Courses of Study", "(7) Instructional plan and evaluation plan of the unit", and "(9) This period" consistent?
  (Regarding ____ defined in the Courses of Study, "In this unit, we will focus on ____ and teach it. (For this reason, the unit is planned in this way and ________ will be taught in this period. (Is the unit structured in this way?)

- Are the goals of the unit and the goals of the lesson set in the form of "~can do' in order for students to be able to express themselves and communicate with each other in English?
  (Is the goal to be able to express oneself in English using the grammar rather than the grammatical items?)

< Matters related to evaluation >

- Do the goals match the perspective of evaluation?

- Is there a plan to evaluate what students have acquired in the unit ("~can do' in English) at the end of the unit?

- Are there too many items to be assessed in one credit hour?
  (It would be better to limit the evaluation items to those that can be seen within a realistic time frame, and consider various means of evaluation, such as a "paper test" or "worksheet" at a later date.)

< Matters related to how to conduct the class >

- Do you share the goals with students?

- Do you incorporate interactive language activities?

- Do you teach based on what students have already learned?

- Do you plan activities while anticipating students' speech?

- Do you consider the teacher's interaction with the students in English, taking into account the students' responses and level of understanding?

- Do you conduct reflection activities that correspond to the objectives?

# 学習指導要領「生きる力」

第１章 総則

第４指導計画の作成等に当たって配慮すべき事項

各学校においては，次の事項に配慮しながら，学校の創意工夫を生かし，全体として，調和のとれた具体的な指導計画を作成するものとする。

(1) 各教科等及び各学年相互間の関連を図り，系統的，発展的な指導ができるようにすること。

(2) 学年の目標及び内容を２学年まとめて示した教科及び外国語活動については，当該学年間を見通して，地域や学校及び児童の実態に応じ，児童の発達の段階を考慮しつつ，効果的，段階的に指導するようにすること。

(3) 各教科の各学年の指導内容については，そのまとめ方や重点の置き方に適切な工夫を加え，効果的な指導ができるようにすること。

(4) 児童の実態等を考慮し，指導の効果を高めるため，合科的・関連的な指導を進めること。

以上のほか，次の事項に配慮するものとする。

(1) 各教科等の指導に当たっては，児童の思考力，判断力，表現力等をはぐくむ観点から，基礎的・基本的な知識及び技能の活用を図る学習活動を重視するとともに，言語に対する関心や理解を深め，言語に関する能力の育成を図る上で必要な言語環境を整え，児童の言語活動を充実すること。

(2) 各教科等の指導に当たっては，体験的な学習や基礎的・基本的な知識及び技能を活用した問題解決的な学習を重視するとともに，児童の興味・関心を生かし，自主的，自発的な学習が促されるよう工夫すること。

(3) 日ごろから学級経営の充実を図り，教師と児童の信頼関係及び児童相互の好ましい人間関係を育てるとともに児童理解を深め，生徒指導の充実を図ること。

(4) 各教科等の指導に当たっては，児童が学習の見通しを立てたり学習したことを振り返ったりする活動を計画的に取り入れるよう工夫すること。

(5) 各教科等の指導に当たっては，児童が学習課題や活動を選択したり，自らの将来について考えたりする機会を設けるなど工夫すること。

# (Reference) Courses of Study: Chapter 1 General Provisions (Excerpt)

Matters to be considered in the preparation of instructional plans, etc.
Each school shall prepare a specific and harmonious teaching plan as a whole, making use of the originality and ingenuity of the school, while giving consideration to the following items.

(1) To make a link between each subject and each grade level, and to provide systematic and developed guidance.
(2) With regard to subjects and foreign language activities for which the objectives and contents for two grades are presented together, effective and step-by-step guidance should be provided throughout the school year, in accordance with the actual conditions of the region, school and children, and taking into consideration the stage of development of the children.
(3) The content of instruction in each subject area at each grade level should be summarized and emphasized in an appropriate manner so that effective instruction can be provided.
(4) In consideration of the actual conditions of the children, promote combined and related instruction in order to increase the effectiveness of instruction.

In addition to the above, the following items should be considered

(1) In teaching each subject, etc., from the viewpoint of nurturing children's ability to think, make judgments, and express themselves, emphasis shall be placed on learning activities to utilize basic and fundamental knowledge and skills, and the language environment necessary to deepen interest in and understanding of language and to develop language-related abilities shall be prepared to enrich children's language activities. (2) To provide guidance in each subject area, etc.
(2) In teaching each subject, emphasis should be placed on experiential learning and problem-solving learning that utilizes basic and fundamental knowledge and skills, and efforts should be made to encourage independent and selfmotivated learning by making the most of children's interests.
(3) To enhance classroom management on a daily basis, to foster trust between teachers and students and good human relations among students, to deepen understanding of students, and to improve student guidance.
(4) In teaching each subject, etc., devise ways to systematically incorporate activities that allow students to formulate a learning outlook and reflect on what they have learned.
(5) In teaching each subject, etc., devise ways to provide opportunities for children to select learning tasks and activities, and to think about their own future.

(6) 各教科等の指導に当たっては，児童が学習内容を確実に身に付けることができるよう，学校や児童の実態に応じ，個別指導やグループ別指導，繰り返し指導，学習内容の習熟の程度に応じた指導，児童の興味・関心等に応じた課題学習，補充的な学習や発展的な学習などの学習活動を取り入れた指導，教師間の協力的な指導など指導方法や指導体制を工夫改善し，個に応じた指導の充実を図ること。

(7) 障害のある児童などについては，特別支援学校等の助言又は援助を活用しつつ，例えば指導についての計画又は家庭や医療，福祉等の業務を行う関係機関と連携した支援のための計画を個別に作成することなどにより，個々の児童の障害の状態等に応じた指導内容や指導方法の工夫を計画的，組織的に行うこと。特に，特別支援学級又は通級による指導については，教師間の連携に努め，効果的な指導を行うこと。

(8) 海外から帰国した児童などについては，学校生活への適応を図るとともに，外国における生活経験を生かすなどの適切な指導を行うこと。

(9) 各教科等の指導に当たっては，児童がコンピュータや情報通信ネットワークなどの情報手段に慣れ親しみ，コンピュータで文字を入力するなどの基本的な操作や情報モラルを身に付け，適切に活用できるようにするための学習活動を充実するとともに，これらの情報手段に加え視聴覚教材や教育機器などの教材・教具の適切な活用を図ること。

(10) 学校図書館を計画的に利用しその機能の活用を図り，児童の主体的，意欲的な学習活動や読書活動を充実すること。

(11) 児童のよい点や進歩の状況などを積極的に評価するとともに，指導の過程や成果を評価し，指導の改善を行い学習意欲の向上に生かすようにすること。

(12) 学校がその目的を達成するため，地域や学校の実態等に応じ，家庭や地域の人々の協力を得るなど家庭や地域社会との連携を深めること。また，小学校間，幼稚園や保育所，中学校及び特別支援学校などとの間の連携や交流を図るとともに，障害のある幼児児童生徒との交流及び共同学習や高齢者などとの交流の機会を設けること。

(6) In teaching each subject, etc., in order to ensure that children acquire the contents of their studies, in accordance with the actual conditions of the school and the children, provide individual instruction, group instruction, repeated instruction, instruction according to the level of proficiency of the contents of study, provide problem-based learning according to the interests of the children, learning activities such as supplementary learning and developmental learning, instruction that incorporates cooperative work between teachers, and instruction that incorporates the learning activities of the children.

(7) With regard to children with disabilities, while utilizing advice and assistance from special-needs schools, etc., devise the contents and methods of instruction in accor dance with the disabilities of each child in a systematic and organized manner by, for example, preparing individual plans for guidance or plans for support in cooperation with related organizations that provide services such as families, medical care and welfare, etc. (2) The school shall systematically and systematically devise the contents and methods of instruction according to the disabilities of each child. In particular, with regard to guidance in special-needs classes or day classes, efforts should be made for cooperation among teachers and effective guidance should be provided.

(8) For children who have returned from abroad, appropriate guidance should be provided to help them adjust to school life and to make use of their life experiences in foreign countries.

(9) In teaching each subject area, etc., the school should enhance learning activities to familiarize children with information means such as computers and information communication networks, and help them acquire basic operations such as typing on computers and information morals so that they can use them appropriately, and in addition to these information means, appropriate use of teaching materials and teaching tools such as audio-visual materials and educational equipment should also be made.

(10) To systematically use the school library and make the most of its functions to enhance the children's independent and motivated learning activities and reading activities.

(11) To actively evaluate the good points and progress of the students, as well as to evaluate the process and results of instruction, in order to improve the instruction and to use it to improve the motivation for learning.

(12) In order for schools to achieve their objectives, they should deepen cooperation with families and local communities, such as by obtaining cooperation from families and local people, in accordance with the actual conditions of the community and school.
In addition, schools should seek cooperation and exchange among elementary schools, kindergartens and nursery schools, junior high schools, and special-needs schools, and provide opportunities for exchange and joint learning with disabled infants and children, and exchange with the elderly, etc.

# 教職英語検定受検ガイド

# 教職英語検定実施要領

## LEVEL

基礎
- リスニング
- 筆記

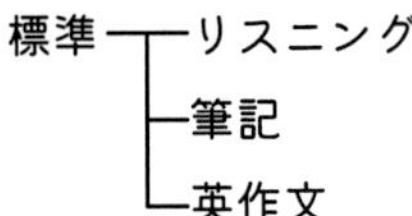

標準
- リスニング
- 筆記
- 英作文

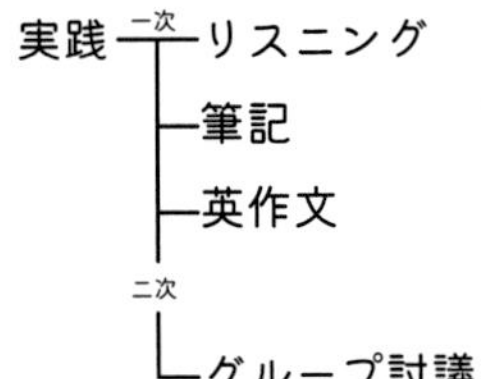

実践
- 一次
  - リスニング
  - 筆記
  - 英作文
- 二次
  - グループ討議

## 検定日程

年２回実施

第１回
- 一次　１月第４日曜日
- 二次　２月第４日曜日
  ※実践レベルのみ

第２回
- 一次　８月第４日曜日
- 二次　９月第４日曜日
  ※実践レベルのみ

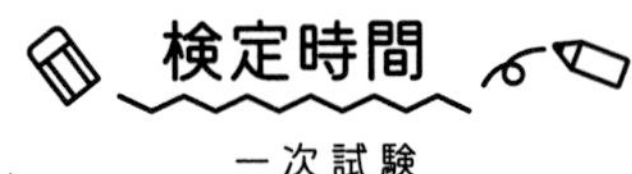

## 検定時間

一次試験

基礎（65分）９時30分～

標準（70分）11時30分～

実践（80分）13時30分～

## 検定方法

各地一般会場

オンライン（個人・団体）

団体指定会場

## 検定料金

※団体受検は検定料から1,000引き

| | |
|---|---|
| 基礎 | ¥5,000 |
| 標準 | ¥7,000 |
| 実践 | ¥9,000 |

## 検定内容

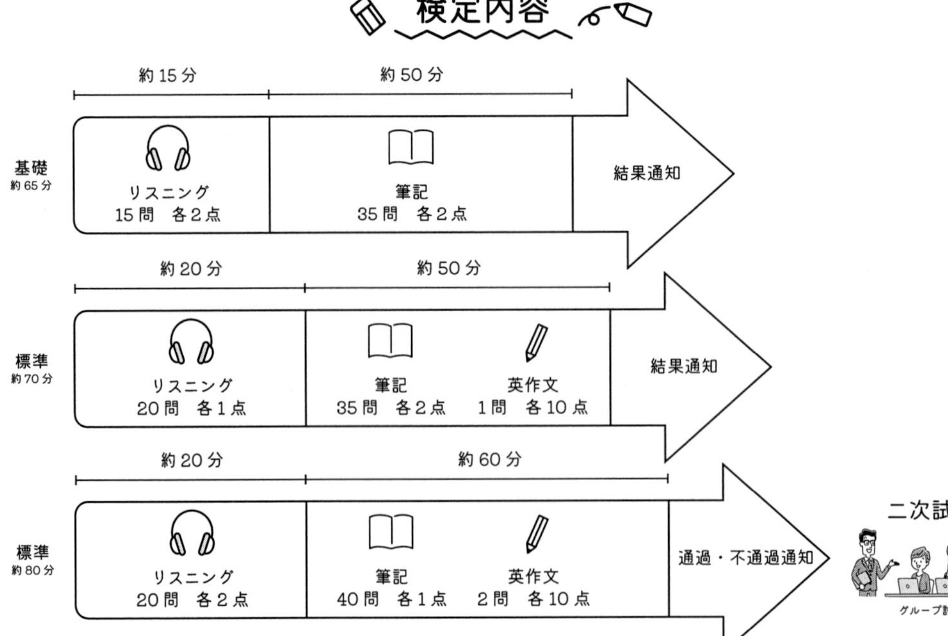

# 教職英語検定実施要領

## 申込方法

### 個人受検

STEP 1　ホームページを確認

STEP 2　受検方法、会場を選択して申込

STEP 3　お支払を各方法で完了する

- カード払い
- 銀行振込
- 郵便局振替
- コンビニ払い
- その他マルチ決済

STEP 4　受検のご案内がメールに届く

STEP 5　各会場またはオンラインで受検

### 団体受検

STEP 1　事務局へご連絡ください

STEP 2　団体番号を発行

STEP 3　団体責任者の団体申込をする

STEP 4　検定料のお支払

方法 1）各受検者が個人受検者と同じ方法で申込・お支払をする
方法 1）団体責任者が全受検者のお支払をまとめて当協会指定口座へ振込をする

STEP 5　団体会場またはオンラインでの実施

## 資格証

教職英語検定合格者へ

特別な資格証を発行しています。

申込・詳細はホームページにてご確認ください。

※記載内容は改訂されることがあります。最新情報はホームページを確認下さい。

www.senseieigo.com

# 教職英語検定小学校担当用テキスト　第1巻

2023年11月1日初版1刷発行

著　者　一般社団法人 教職英語検定協会
〒224-0003　東京都目黒区中目黒3-6-2　F・Sビル5階
TEL　03-5725-0553
Fax　03-6452-4148
Web　https://www.senseieigo.com

発売所　株式会社　ブックフォレ
〒113-0033　神奈川県横浜市都筑区中川中央1-20-15-201
TEL　03-5800-8494
Fax　03-5800-5353
Web　https://bookfore.co.jp/

印刷・製本　冊子印刷社


ISBN：978-4-909846-56-3　C2082



テキストブック読み上げ音源ダウンロードリンク
https://bookfore.co.jp/glh/download/

本書掲載写真・イラストについて
1. イラストライター 千野六久 様 (http://rokuhisachino.tumblr.com)
2. かわいいフリー素材集 いらすとや みふね たかし様 (https://www.irasutoya.com)
等のイラストを掲載しております。
本書掲載させて頂いたイラスト・写真については、使用のご快諾とご協力を頂いております。
上記の方々のホームページには、大変素晴らしいイラストデザイン集が掲載されています。
生徒への指導に当たってのご参考、また、より分かりやすい教材、プリント作成等に
活用できるものが多数ですので、是非、多くの先生方にご覧頂きたい次第です。
多くの方々の著作物を掲載させて頂き、より分かりやすい教材となりました。お礼申し上げます。